YOUR 15-MONT
COMPREHENS
INDIVIDUAL FO

LIBRA

September 23 - October 22

1994 SUPER HOROSCOPE

ARROW BOOKS LIMITED
20 Vauxhall Bridge Road
London SW1V 2SA

CONTENTS

FIRST PUBLISHED IN GREAT BRITAIN BY ARROW BOOKS, 20 VAUXHALL BRIDGE ROAD, LONDON, SW1V 2SA, 1993

THIS EDITION PUBLISHED BY AGREEMENT WITH THE BERKLEY PUBLISHING GROUP

PRINTED IN GREAT BRITAIN BY
THE GUERNSEY PRESS CO. LTD
GUERNSEY, C.I
ISBN 0 09 923201 4

NOTE TO THE CUSP-BORN

First find the year of your birth, and then find the sign under which you were born according to your day of birth. Thus, you can determine if you are a true Libra (or Virgo or Scorpio), according to the variations of the dates of the Zodiac. (See also page 7.)

Are you *really* a Libra? If your birthday falls around the fourth week in September, at the very beginning of Libra, will you still retain the traits of Virgo, the sign of the Zodiac before Libra? And what if you were born later in October—are you more Scorpio than Libra? Many people born at the edge, or cusp, of a sign have great difficulty in determining exactly what sign they are. If you are one of these people, here's how you can figure it out, once and for all.

Consult the following table. It will tell you the precise days on which the Sun entered and left your sign for the year of your birth. If you were born at the beginning or end of Libra, yours is a lifetime reflecting a process of subtle transformation. Your life on Earth will symbolize a significant change in consciousness, for you are either about to enter a whole new way of living or are leaving one behind.

If you were born at the beginning of Libra, you may want to read the horoscope book for Virgo as well as Libra, for Virgo holds the keys to much of the complexity of your spirit, reflects certain hidden weaknesses, uncertainties, and your secret wishes. You are eager to get involved with another person, yet you are pulled back often from total involvement by your sense of propriety or your wish to be pure and unspoiled. You hover between poetic romanticism and stiff mental analyzing. At best, your powers of criticism serve you to develop your potentials and enhance the life of your partner. In that way, you are helpful and loving, considerate and faithful—a pure marriage of mind and body, head and heart.

Cusp-Born

If you were born at the end of Libra you may want to read the horoscope book for Scorpio as well as Libra. Scorpio dominates your finances, money, assets, potentials and your values in general. Although your sexual expectancies can be naive, unrealistic and even adolescent, you are passionate, excitable and highly seductive.

You may vacillate between a desire to please another and a fanatical determination to maintain control and survive on your own. You can love with a fatal obsession, where you will blind your eyes to keep peace in a relationship—then suddenly declare war. Although you could prolong the agony of a situation in order to avoid a confrontation, you are the personification of awakening passion and a spirit that longs for the joys of companionship and the simple harmonies of life.

DATES SUN ENTERS LIBRA (LEAVES VIRGO)

September 23 every year from 1900 to 2000, except for the following:

September 22:				September 24:
1948	1968	1981	1992	1903
52	72	84	93	07
56	76	85	96	
60	77	88	97	
64	80	89		

DATES SUN LEAVES LIBRA (ENTERS SCORPIO)

October 23 every year from 1900 to 2000, except for the following:

October 22:	October 24:			
1992	1902	1911	1923	1943
96	03	14	27	47
	06	15	31	51
	07	18	35	55
	10	19	39	59

HISTORY AND USES OF ASTROLOGY

Does astrology have a place in the fast-moving, ultra-scientific world we live in today? Can it be justified in a sophisticated society whose outriders are already preparing to step off the moon into the deep space of the planets themselves? Or is it just a hangover of ancient superstition, a psychological dummy for neurotics and dreamers of every historical age?

These are the kind of questions that any inquiring person can be expected to ask when they approach a subject like astrology which goes beyond, but never excludes, the materialistic side of life.

The simple, single answer is that astrology works. It works for tens of millions of people in the western world alone. In the United States there are 10 million followers and in Europe, an estimated 25 million. America has more than 4000 practicing astrologers, Europe nearly three times as many. Even down-under Australia has its hundreds of thousands of adherents. The importance of such vast numbers of people from diverse backgrounds and cultures is recognized by the world's biggest newspapers and magazines who probably devote more of their space to this subject in a year than to any other. In the eastern countries, astrology has enormous followings, again, because it has been proved to work. In countries like India, brides and grooms for centuries have been chosen on the basis of astrological compatibility. The low divorce rate there, despite today's heavy westernizing influence, is attributed largely to this practice.

In the western world, astrology today is more vital than ever before; more practicable because it needs a sophisticated society like ours to understand and develop its contribution to the full; more valid because science itself is confirming the precepts of astrological knowledge with every new exciting step. The ordinary person who daily applies astrology intelligently does not have to wonder whether it is true nor believe in it blindly. He can see it working for himself. And, if he can use it—and this book is designed to help the reader to do just that—he can make living a far richer experience, and become a more developed personality and a better person.

Astrology is the science of relationships. It is not just a study of planetary influences on man and his environment. It is the study of man himself.

We are at the center of our personal universe, of all our relationships. And our happiness or sadness depends on how we act, how we relate to the people and things that surround us. The emotions that we generate have a distinct affect—for better or worse—on the world around us. Our friends and our enemies will confirm this. Just look in the mirror the next time you are angry. In other words, each of us is a kind of sun or planet or star and our influence on our personal universe, whether loving, helpful or destructive, varies with our changing moods, expressed through our individual character.

And to an extent that includes the entire galaxy, this is true of the planetary bodies. Their radiations affect each other, including the earth and all the things on it. And in comparatively recent years, giant constellations called "quasars" have been discovered. These exist far beyond the night stars that we can observe, and science says these quasars are emitting radiating influences more powerful and different than ever recorded on earth. Their effect on man from an astrological point of view is under deep study. Compared with these inter-stellar forces, our personal "radiations" are negligible on the planetary scale. But ours are just as potent in the way they affect our moods, and our ability to control them. To this extent they determine much of the happiness and satisfaction in our lives. For instance, if we were bound and gagged and had to hold some strong emotion within us without being able to move, we would soon start to feel very uncomfortable. We are obviously pretty powerful radiators inside, in our own way. But usually, we are able to throw off our emotion in some sort of action—we have a good cry, walk it off, or tell someone our troubles—before it can build up too far and make us physically ill. Astrology helps us to understand the universal forces working on us, and through this understanding, we can become more properly adjusted to our surroundings and find ourselves coping where others may flounder.

Closely related to our emotions is the "other side" of our personal universe, our physical welfare. Our body, of course, is largely influenced by things around us over which we have very little control. The phone rings, we hear it. The train runs late. We snag our stocking or cut our face shaving. Our body is under a constant bombardment of events that influence our lives to varying degrees.

The question that arises from all this is, what makes each of us act so that we have to involve other people and keep the ball of activity and evolution rolling? This is the question that both science and astrology are involved with. The scientists have attacked it from different angles: anthropology, the study of human evolution as body, mind and response to environment; anatomy, the study of bodily structure; psychology, the science of the human mind; and so on. These studies have produced very impressive classifications and valuable information, but because the approach to the problem is fragmented, so is the result. They remain "branches" of science. Science generally studies effects. It keeps turning up wonderful answers but no lasting solutions. Astrology, on the other hand approaches the question from the broader viewpoint. Astrology began its inquiry with the totality of human experience and saw it as an effect. It then looked to find the cause, or at least the prime movers, and during thousands of years of observation of man and his *universal* environment, came up with the extraordinary principle of planetary influence—or astrology, which, from the Greek, means the science of the stars.

Modern science, as we shall see, has confirmed much of astrology's foundations—most of it unintentionally, some of it reluctantly, but still, indisputably.

It is not difficult to imagine that there must be a connection between outer space and the earth. Even today, scientists are not too sure how our earth was created, but it is generally agreed that it is only a tiny part of the universe. And as a part of the universe, people on earth see and feel the influence of heavenly bodies in almost every aspect of our existence. There is no doubt that the sun has the greatest influence on life on this planet. Without it there would be no life, for without it there would be no warmth, no division into day and night, no cycles of time or season at all. This is clear and easy to see. The influence of the moon, on the other hand, is more subtle, though no less definite.

There are many ways in which the influence of the moon manifests itself here on earth, both on human and animal life. It is a well-known fact, for instance, that the large movements of water on our planet—that is the ebb and flow of the tides—are caused by the moon's gravitational pull. Since this is so, it follows that these water movements do not occur only in the oceans, but that all bodies of water are affected, even down to the tiniest puddle.

The human body, too, which consists of about 70 percent water, falls within the scope of this lunar influence. For example the menstrual cycle of most women corresponds to the lunar month; the period of pregnancy in humans is 273 days, or equal to nine lunar months. Similarly, many illnesses reach a crisis at the change of the moon, and statistics in many countries have shown that the crime rate is highest at the time of the full moon. Even human sexual desire has been associated with the phases of the moon. But, it is in the movement of the tides that we get the clearest demonstration of planetary influence, and the irresistible correspondence between the so-called metaphysical and the physical.

Tide tables are prepared years in advance by calculating the future positions of the moon. Science has known for a long time that the moon is the main cause of tidal action. But only in the last few years has it begun to realize the possible extent of this influence on mankind. To begin with, the ocean tides do not rise and fall as we might imagine from our personal observations of them. The moon as it orbits around the earth, sets up a circular wave of attraction which pulls the oceans of the world after it, broadly in an east to west direction. This influence is like a phantom wave crest, a loop of power stretching from pole to pole which passes over and around the earth like an invisible shadow. It travels with equal effect across the land masses and, as scientists were recently amazed to observe, caused oysters placed in the dark in the middle of the United States where there is no sea, to open their shells to receive the non-existent tide. If the land-locked oysters react to this invisible signal, what effect does it have on us who not so long ago in evolutionary time, came out of the sea and still have its salt in our blood and sweat?

Less well known is the fact that the moon is also the primary force behind the circulation of blood in human beings and animals, and the movement of sap in trees and plants. Agriculturists have established that the moon has a distinct influence on crops, which explains why for centuries people have planted according to moon cycles. The habits of many animals, too, are directed by the movement of the moon. Migratory birds, for instance, depart only at or near the time of the full moon. Just as certain fish, eels in particular, move only in accordance with certain phases of the moon.

Know Thyself—Why?

In today's fast-changing world, everyone still longs to know what the future holds. It is the one thing that everyone has in common: rich and poor, famous and infamous, all are deeply concerned about tomorrow.

But the key to the future, as every historian knows, lies in the past. This is as true of individual people as it is of nations. You cannot understand your future without first understanding your past, which is simply another way of saying that you must first of all know yourself.

The motto "know thyself" seems obvious enough nowadays, but it was originally put forward as the foundation of wisdom by the ancient Greek philosophers. It was then adopted by the "mystery religions" of the ancient Middle East, Greece and Rome, and is still used in all genuine schools of mind training or mystical discipline, both in those of the East, based on yoga, and those of the West. So it is universally accepted now, and has been through the ages.

But how do you go about discovering what sort of person you are? The first step is usually classification into some sort of system of types. Astrology did this long before the birth of Christ. Psychology has also done it. So has modern medicine, in its way.

One system classifies men according to the source of the impulses they respond to most readily: the muscles, leading to direct bodily action; the digestive organs, resulting in emotion, or the brain and nerves. Another such system says that character is determined by the endocrine glands, and gives us labels like "pituitary," "thyroid" and "hyperthyroid" types. These different systems are neither contradictory nor mutually exclusive. In fact, they are very often different ways of saying the same thing.

Very popular and useful classifications were devised by Dr. C. G. Jung, the eminent disciple of Freud. Jung observed among the different faculties of the mind, four which have a predominant influence on character. These four faculties exist in all of us without exception, but not in perfect balance. So when we say, for instance, that a man is a "thinking type," it means that in any situation he tries to be rational. It follows that emotion, which some say is the opposite of thinking, will be his weakest function. This type can be sensible and reasonable, or calculating and unsympathetic. The emotional type, on the other hand, can often be recognized by exaggerated language—everything is either marvelous or terrible—and in extreme cases they even invent dramas and quarrels out of nothing just to make life more interesting.

The other two faculties are intuition and physical sensation. The sensation type does not only care for food and drink, nice clothes and furniture; he is also interested in all forms of physical experience. Many scientists are sensation types as are athletes and nature-lovers. Like sensation, intuition is a form of perception and we all possess it. But it works through that part of the mind which is not under conscious control—consequently it sees meanings and connections which are not obvious to thought or emotion. Inventors and original thinkers are always intuitive, but so, too, are superstitious people who see meanings where none exist.

Thus, sensation tells us what is going on in the world, feeling (that is, emotion) tells us how important it is to ourselves, thinking enables us to interpret it and work out what we should do about it, and intuition tells us what it means to ourselves and others. All four faculties are essential, and all are present in every one of us. But some people are guided chiefly by one, others by another.

Besides these four types, Jung observed a division into extrovert and introvert, which cuts across them. By and large, the introvert is one who finds truth inside himself rather than outside. He is not, therefore, ideally suited to a religion or a political party which tells him what to believe. Original thinkers are almost necessarily introverts. The extrovert, on the other hand, finds truth coming to him from outside. He believes in experts and authorities, and wants to think that nature and the laws of nature really exists, that they are what they appear to be and not just generalities made by men.

A disadvantage of all these systems of classification, is that one cannot tell very easily where to place oneself. Some people are reluctant to admit that they act to please their emotions. So they deceive themselves for years by trying to belong to whichever type they think is the "best." Of course, there is no best; each has its faults and each has its good points.

The advantage of the signs of the Zodiac is that they simplify classification. Not only that, but your date of birth is personal—it is unarguably yours. What better way to know yourself than by going back as far as possible to the very moment of your birth? And this is precisely what your horoscope is all about.

What Is a Horoscope?

If you had been able to take a picture of the heavens at the moment of your birth, that photograph would be your horoscope. Lacking such a snapshot, it is still possible to recreate the picture—and this is at the basis of the astrologer's art. In other words, your horoscope is a representation of the skies with the planets in the exact positions they occupied at the time you were born.

This information, of course, is not enough for the astrologer. He has to have a background of significance to put the photograph on. You will get the idea if you imagine two balls—one inside the other. The inner one is transparent. In the center of both is the astrologer, able to look up, down and around in all directions. The outer sphere is the Zodiac which is divided into twelve approximately equal segments, like the segments of an orange. The inner ball is our photograph. It is transparent except for the images of the planets. Looking out from the center, the astrologer sees the planets in various segments of the Zodiac. These twelve segments are known as the signs or houses.

The position of the planets when each of us is born is always different. So the photograph is always different. But the Zodiac and its signs are fixed.

Now, where in all this are you, the subject of the horoscope?

Your character is largely determined by the sign the sun is in. So that is where the astrologer looks first in your horoscope.

There are twelve signs in the Zodiac and the sun spends approximately one month in each. As the sun's motion is almost perfectly regular, the astrologers have been able to fix the dates governing each sign. There are not many people who do not know which sign of the Zodiac they were born under or who have not been amazed at some time or other at the accuracy of the description of their own character. Here are the twelve signs, the ancient zodiacal symbol, and their dates for the year 1994.*

ARIES	Ram	March 20–April 20
TAURUS	Bull	April 20–May 21
GEMINI	Twins	May 21–June 21
CANCER	Crab	June 21–July 22
LEO	Lion	July 22–August 23
VIRGO	Virgin	August 23–September 23
LIBRA	Scales	September 23–October 23
SCORPIO	Scorpion	October 23–November 22
SAGITTARIUS	Archer	November 22–December 21
CAPRICORN	Sea-Goat	December 21–January 20
AQUARIUS	Water-Bearer	January 20–February 18
PISCES	Fish	February 18–March 20

The time of birth—apart from the date—is important in advanced astrology because the planets travel at such great speed that the patterns they form change from minute to minute. For this reason, each person's horoscope is his and his alone. Further on we will see that the practicing astrologer has ways of determining and reading these minute time changes which dictate the finer character differences in us all.

However, it is still possible to draw significant conclusions and make meaningful predictions based simply on the sign of the Zodiac a person is born under. In a horoscope, the signs do not necessarily correspond with the divisions of the houses. It could be that a house begins halfway across a sign. It is the interpretation of such combinations of different influences that distinguishes the professional astrologer from the student and the follower.

However, to gain a workable understanding of astrology, it is not necessary to go into great detail. In fact, the beginner is likely to find himself confused if he attempts to absorb too much too quickly. It should be remembered that this is a science and to become proficient at it, and especially to grasp the tremendous scope of possibilities in man and his affairs and direct them into a worthwhile reading, takes a great deal of study and experience.

*These dates are fluid and change with the motion of the Earth from year to year.

If you do intend to pursue it seriously you will have to learn to figure the exact moment of birth against the degrees of longitude and latitude of the planets at that precise time. This involves adapting local time to Greenwich Mean Time (G.M.T.), reference to tables of houses to establish the Ascendant, as well as making calculations from Ephemeris—the tables of the planets' positions.

After reading this introduction, try drawing up a rough horoscope to get the "feel" of reading some elementary characteristics and natal influences.

Draw a circle with twelve equal segments. Write in counterclockwise the names of the signs—Aries, Taurus, Gemini etc.—one for each segment. Look up an ephemeris for the year of the person's birth and note down the sign each planet was in on the birthday. Do not worry about the number of degrees (although if a planet is on the edge of a sign its position obviously should be considered). Write the name of the planet in the segment/sign on your chart. Write the number 1 in the sign where the sun is. This is the first house. Number the rest of the houses, counterclockwise till you finish at 12. Now you can investigate the probable basic expectation of experience of the person concerned. This is done first of all by seeing what planet or planets is/are in what sign and house. (See also page 72.)

The 12 houses control these functions:

1st.	Individuality, body appearance, general outlook on life	(Personality house)
2nd.	Finance, business	(Money house)
3rd.	Relatives, education, correspondence	(Relatives house)
4th.	Family, neighbors	(Home house)
5th.	Pleasure, children, attempts, entertainment	(Pleasure house)
6th.	Health, employees	(Health house)
7th.	Marriage, partnerships	(Marriage house)
8th.	Death, secret deals, difficulties	(Death house)
9th.	Travel, intellectual affairs	(Travel house)
10th.	Ambition, social standing	(Business and Honor house)
11th.	Friendship, social life, luck	(Friends house)
12th.	Troubles, illness, loss	(Trouble house)

The characteristics of the planets modify the influence of the Sun according to their natures and strengths.

Sun: Source of life. Basic temperament according to sun sign. The will.
Moon: Superficial nature. Moods. Changeable. Adaptive. Mother.
Mercury: Communication. Intellect. Reasoning power. Curiosity. Short travels.
Venus: Love. Delight. Art. Beautiful possessions.
Mars: Energy. Initiative. War. Anger. Destruction. Impulse.
Jupiter: Good. Generous. Expansive. Opportunities. Protection.
Saturn: Jupiter's opposite. Contraction. Servant. Delay. Hardwork. Cold. Privation. Research. Lasting rewards after long struggle.
Uranus: Fashion. Electricity. Revolution. Sudden changes. Modern science.
Neptune: Sensationalism. Mass emotion. Devastation. Delusion.
Pluto: Creates and destroys. Lust for power. Strong obsessions.

Superimpose the characteristics of the planets on the functions of the house in which they appear. Express the result through the character of the birth (sun) sign, and you will get the basic idea of how astrology works.

Of course, many other considerations have been taken into account in producing the carefully worked out predictions in this book: The aspects of the planets to each other; their strength according to position and sign; whether they are in a house of exaltation or decline; whether they are natural enemies or not; whether a planet occupies his own sign; the position of a planet in relation to its own house or sign; whether the planet is male, female or neuter; whether the sign is a fire, earth, water or air sign. These are only a few of the colors on the astrologer's pallet which he must mix with the inspiration of the artist and the accuracy of the mathematician.

The Problem of Love

Love, of course, is never a problem. The problem lies in recognizing the difference between infatuation, emotion, sex and, sometimes, the downright deceit of the other person. Mankind, with its record of broken marriages, despair and disillusionment, is obviously not very good at making these distinctions.

Can astrology help?

Yes. In the same way that advance knowledge can usually help in any human situation. And there is probably no situation as human, as poignant, as pathetic and universal, as the failure of man's love.

Love, of course, is not just between man and woman. It involves love of children, parents, home and so on. But the big problems usually involve the choice of partner.

Astrology has established degrees of compatibility that exist between people born under the various signs of the Zodiac. Because people are individuals, there are numerous variations and modifications and the astrologer, when approached on mate and marriage matters makes allowances for them. But the fact remains that some groups of people are suited for each other and some are not and astrology has expressed this in terms of characteristics which all can study and use as a personal guide.

No matter how much enjoyment and pleasure we find in the different aspects of each other's character, if it is not an overall compatibility, the chances of our finding fulfillment or enduring happiness in each other are pretty hopeless. And astrology can help us to find someone compatible.

History of Astrology

The origins of astrology have been lost far back in history, but we do know that reference is made to it as far back as the first written records of the human race. It is not hard to see why. Even in primitive times, people must have looked for an explanation for the various happenings in their lives. They must have wanted to know why people were different from one to another. And in their search they turned to the regular movements of the sun, moon and stars to see if they could provide an answer.

It is interesting to note that as soon as man learned to use his tools in any type of design, or his mind in any kind of calculation, he turned his attention to the heavens. Ancient cave dwellings reveal dim crescents and circles representative of the sun and moon, rulers of day and night. Mesopotamia and the civilization of Chaldea, in itself the foundation of those of Babylonia and Assyria, show a complete picture of astronomical observation and well-developed astrological interpretation.

Humanity has a natural instinct for order. The study of anthropology reveals that primitive people—even as far back as prehistoric times—were striving to achieve a certain order in their lives. They tried to organize the apparent chaos of the universe. They had the desire to attach meaning to things. This demand for order has persisted throughout the history of man. So that observing the regularity of the heavenly bodies made it logical that primitive peoples should turn heavenwards in their search for an understanding of the world in which they found themselves so random and alone.

And they did find a significance in the movements of the stars. Shepherds tending their flocks, for instance, observed that when the cluster of stars now known as the constellation Aries was in sight, it was the time of fertility and they associated it with the Ram. And they noticed that the growth of plants and plant life corresponded with different phases of the moon, so that certain times were favorable for the planting of crops, and other times were not. In this way, there grew up a tradition of seasons and causes connected with the passage of the sun through the twelve signs of the Zodiac.

Astrology was valued so highly that the king was kept informed of the daily and monthly changes in the heavenly bodies, and the results of astrological studies regarding events of the future. Head astrologers were clearly men of great rank and position, and the office was said to be a hereditary one.

Omens were taken, not only from eclipses and conjunctions of the moon or sun with one of the planets, but also from storms and earthquakes. In the eastern civilizations, particularly, the reverence inspired by astrology appears to have remained unbroken since the very earliest days. In ancient China, astrology, astronomy and religion went hand in hand. The astrologer, who was also an astronomer, was part of the official government service and had his own corner in the Imperial Palace. The duties of the Imperial astrologer, whose office was one of the most important in the land, were clearly defined, as this extract from early records shows:

> "This exalted gentleman must concern himself with the stars in the heavens, keeping a record of the changes and movements of the Planets, the Sun and the Moon, in order to examine the movements of the terrestial world with the object of prognosticating good and bad fortune. He divides the territories of the nine regions of the empire in accordance with their dependence on particular celestial bodies. All the fiefs and principalities are connected with the stars and from this their prosperity or misfortune should be ascertained. He makes prognostications according to the twelve years of the Jupiter cycle of good and evil of the terrestial world. From the colors of the five kinds of clouds, he determines the coming of floods or droughts, abundance or famine. From the twelve winds, he draws conclusions about the state of harmony of heaven and earth, and takes note of good and bad signs that result from their accord or disaccord. In general, he concerns himself with five kinds of phenomena so as to warn the Emperor to come to the aid of the government and to allow for variations in the ceremonies according to their circumstances."

The Chinese were also keen observers of the fixed stars, giving them such unusual names as Ghost Vehicle, Sun of Imperial Concubine, Imperial Prince, Pivot of Heaven, Twinkling Brilliance or Weaving Girl. But, great astrologers though they may have been, the Chinese lacked one aspect of mathematics that the Greeks applied to astrology—deductive geometry. Deductive geometry was the basis of much classical astrology in and after the time of the Greeks, and this explains the different methods of prognostication used in the East and West.

Down through the ages the astrologer's art has depended, not so much on the uncovering of new facts, though this is important, as on the interpretation of the facts already known. This is the essence of his skill. Obviously one cannot always tell how people will react (and this underlines the very important difference between astrology and predestination which will be discussed later on) but one can be prepared, be forewarned, to know what to expect.

But why should the signs of the zodiac have any effect at all on the formation of human character? It is easy to see why people thought they did, and even now we constantly use astrological expressions in our everyday speech. The thoughts of "lucky star," "ill-fated," "star-crossed," "mooning around," are interwoven into the very structure of our language.

In the same way that the earth has been created by influences from outside, there remains an indisputable togetherness in the working of the universe. The world, after all, is a coherent structure, for if it were not, it would be quite without order and we would never know what to expect. A dog could turn into an apple, or an elephant sprout wings and fly at any moment without so much as a by your leave. But nature, as we know, functions according to laws, not whims, and the laws of nature are certainly not subject to capricious exceptions.

This means that no part of the universe is ever arbitrarily cut off from any other part. Everything is therefore to some extent linked with everything else. The moon draws an imperceptible tide on every puddle; tiny and trivial events can be effected by outside forces (such as the fall of a feather by the faintest puff of wind). And so it is fair to think that the local events at any moment reflect to a very small extent the evolution of the world as a whole.

From this principle follows the possibility of divination, and also knowledge of events at a distance, provided one's mind were always as perfectly undisturbed, as ideally smooth, as a mirror or unruffled lake. Provided, in other words, that one did not confuse the picture with hopes, guesses, and expectations. When people try to foretell the future by cards or crystal ball gazing they find it much easier to confuse the picture with expectations than to reflect it clearly.

But the present does contain a good deal of the future to which it leads—not all, but a good deal. The diver halfway between bridge and water is going to make a splash; the train whizzing towards the station will pass through it unless interfered with; the burglar breaking a pane of glass has exposed himself to the possibility of a prison sentence. Yet this is not a doctrine of determinism, as was emphasized earlier. Clearly, there are forces already at work in the present, and any one of them could alter the situation in some way. Equally, a change of decision could alter the whole situation as well. So the future depends, not on an irresistible force, but on a small act of free will.

An individual's age, physique, and position on the earth's surface are remote consequences of his birth. Birth counts as the original cause for all that happens subsequently. The horoscope, in this case, means "this person represents the further evolution of the state of the universe pictured in this chart." Such a chart can apply equally to man or woman, dog, ship or even limited company.

If the evolution of an idea, or of a person, is to be understood as a totality, it must continue to evolve from its own beginnings, which is to say, in the terms in which it began. The brown-eyed person will be faithful to brown eyes all his life; the traitor is being faithful to some complex of ideas which has long been evolving in him; and the person born at sunset will always express, as he evolves, the psychological implications or analogies of the moment when the sun sinks out of sight.

This is the doctrine that an idea must continue to evolve in terms of its origin. It is a completely non-materialist doctrine, though it never fails to apply to material objects. And it implies, too, that the individual will continue to evolve in terms of his moment of origin, and therefore possibly of the sign of the Zodiac rising on the eastern horizon at his birth. It also implies that the signs of the Zodiac themselves will evolve in the collective mind of the human race in the same terms that they were first devised and not in the terms in which modern astrologers consciously think they ought to work.

For the human race, like every other kind of animal, has a collective mind, as Professor Jung discovered in his investigation of dreams. If no such collective mind existed, no infant could ever learn anything, for communication would be impossible. Furthermore, it is absurd to suggest that the conscious mind could be older than the "unconscious," for an infant's nervous system functions correctly before it has discovered the difference between "myself" and "something else" or discovered what eyes and hands are for. Indeed, the involuntary muscles function correctly even before birth, and will never be under conscious control. They are part of what we call the "unconscious" which is not really "unconscious" at all. To the contrary, it is totally aware of itself and everything else; it is merely that part of the mind that cannot be controlled by conscious effort.

And human experience, though it varies in detail with every individual, is basically the same for each one of us, consisting of sky and earth, day and night, waking and sleeping, man and woman, birth and death. So there is bound to be in the mind of the human race a very large number of inescapable ideas, which are called our natural archetypes.

There are also, however, artificial or cultural archetypes which are not universal or applicable to everyone, but are nevertheless inescapable within the limits of a given culture. Examples of these are the cross in Christianity, and the notion of "escape from the wheel of rebirth" in India. There was a time when these ideas did not exist. And there was a time, too, when the scheme of the Zodiac did not exist. One would not expect the Zodiac to have any influence on remote and primitive peoples, for example, who have never heard of it. If the Zodiac is only an archetype, their horoscopes probably would not work and it would not matter which sign they were born under.

But where the Zodiac is known, and the idea of it has become worked into the collective mind, then there it could well appear to have an influence, even if it has no physical existence. For ideas do not have a physical existence, anyway. No physical basis has yet been discovered for the telepathy that controls an anthill; young swallows migrate before, not after, their parents; and the weaver-bird builds its intricate nest without being taught. Materialists suppose, but cannot prove, that "instinct" (as it is called, for no one knows how it works) is controlled by nucleic acid in the chromosomes. This is not a genuine explanation, though, for it only pushes the mystery one stage further back.

Does this mean, then, that the human race, in whose civilization the idea of the twelve signs of the Zodiac has long been embedded, is divided into only twelve types? Can we honestly believe that it is really as simple as that? If so, there must be pretty wide ranges of variation within each type. And if, to explain the variation, we call in heredity and environment, experiences in early childhood, the thyroid and other glands, and also the four functions of the mind mentioned at the beginning of this introduction, and extroversion and introversion, then one begins to wonder if the original classification was worth making at all. No sensible person believes that his favorite system explains everything. But even so, he will not find it much use at all if it does not even save him the trouble of bothering with the others.

Under the Jungian system, everyone has not only a dominant or principal function, but also a secondary or subsidiary one, so that the four can be arranged in order of potency. In the intuitive type, sensation is always the most inefficient function, but the second most inefficient function can be either thinking (which tends to make original thinkers such as Jung himself) or else feeling (which tends to make artistic people). Therefore, allowing for introversion and extroversion, there are at least four kinds of intuitive types, and sixteen types in all. Furthermore, one can see how the sixteen types merge into each other, so that there are no unrealistic or unconvincingly rigid divisions.

In the same way, if we were to put every person under only one sign of the Zodiac, the system becomes too rigid and unlike life. Besides, it was never intended to be used like that. It may be convenient to have only twelve types, but we know that in practice there is every possible gradation between aggressiveness and timidity, or between conscientiousness and laziness. How, then, do we account for this?

The Tyrant and the Saint

Just as the thinking type of man is also influenced to some extent by sensation and intuition, but not very much by emotion, so a person born under Leo can be influenced to some extent by one or two (but not more) of the other signs. For instance, famous persons born under the sign of Gemini include Henry VIII, whom nothing and no-one could have induced to abdicate, and Edward VIII, who did just that. Obviously, then, the sign Gemini does not fully explain the complete character of either of them.

Again, under the opposite sign, Sagittarius, were both Stalin, who was totally consumed with the notion of power, and Charles V, who freely gave up an empire because he preferred to go into a monastery. And we find under Scorpio, many uncompromising characters such as Luther, de Gaulle, Indira Gandhi and Montgomery, but also Petain, a successful commander whose name later became synonymous with collaboration.

A single sign is therefore obviously inadequate to explain the differences between people; it can only explain resemblances, such as the combativeness of the Scorpio group, or the far-reaching devotion of Charles V and Stalin to their respective ideals—the Christian heaven and the Communist utopia.

But very few people are born under one sign only. As well as the month of birth, as was mentioned earlier, the day matters, and, even more, the hour, which ought, if possible, to be noted to the nearest minute. Without this, it is impossible to have an actual horoscope, for the word horoscope means literally, "a consideration of the hour."

The month of birth tells you only which sign of the Zodiac was occupied by the sun. The day and hour tell you what sign was occupied by the moon. And the minute tells you which sign was rising on the eastern horizon. This is called the Ascendant, and it is supposed to be the most important thing in the whole horoscope.

If you were born at midnight, the sun is then in an important position, although invisible. But at one o'clock in the morning the sun is not important, so the moment of birth will not matter much. The important thing then will be the Ascendant, and possibly one or two of the planets. At a given day and hour, say, dawn on January 1st, or 9:00 p.m. on the longest day, the Ascendant will always be the same at any given place. But the moon and planets alter from day to day, at different speeds and have to be looked up in an astronomical table.

The sun is said to signify one's heart, that is to say, one's deepest desires and inmost nature. This is quite different from the moon, which, as we have seen, signifies one's superficial way of behaving. When the ancient Romans referred to the Emperor Augustus as a Capricornian, they meant that he had the moon in Capricorn; they did not pay much attention to the sun, although he was born at sunrise. Or, to take another example, a modern astrologer would call Disraeli a Scorpion because he had Scorpio rising, but most people would call him Sagittarian because he had the sun there. The Romans would have called him Leo because his moon was in Leo.

The sun, as has already been pointed out, is important if one is born near sunrise, sunset, noon or midnight, but is otherwise not reckoned as the principal influence. So if one does not seem to fit one's birth month, it is always worthwhile reading the other signs, for one may have been born at a time when any of them were rising or occupied by the moon. It also seems to be the case that the influence of the sun develops as life goes on, so that the month of birth is easier to guess in people over the age of forty. The young are supposed to be influenced mainly by their Ascendant which characterizes the body and physical personality as a whole.

It should be clearly understood that it is nonsense to assume that all people born at a certain time will exhibit the same characteristics, or that they will even behave in the same manner. It is quite obvious that, from the very moment of its birth, a child is subject to the effects of its environment, and that this in turn will influence its character and heritage to a decisive extent. Also to be taken into account are education and economic conditions, which play a very important part in the formation of one's character as well.

However, it is clearly established that people born under one sign of the Zodiac do have certain basic traits in their character which are different from those born under other signs. It is obvious to every thinking person that certain events produce different reactions in various people. For instance, if a man slips on a banana skin and falls heavily on the pavement, one passer-by may laugh and find this extremely amusing, while another may just walk on, thinking: "What a fool falling down like that. He should look where he is going." A third might also walk away saying to himself: "It's none of my business—I'm glad it wasn't me." A fourth might walk past and think: "I'm sorry for that man, but I haven't the time to be bothered with helping him." And a fifth might stop to help the fallen man to his feet, comfort him and take him home. Here is just one event which could produce entirely different reactions in different people. And, obviously, there are many more. One that comes to mind immediately is the violently opposed views to events such as wars, industrial strikes, and so on. The fact that people have different attitudes to the same event is simply another way of saying that they have different characters. And this is not something that can be put down to background, for people of the same race, religion, or class, very often express quite different reactions to happenings or events. Similarly, it is often the case that members of the same family, where there is clearly uniform background of economic and social standing, education, race and religion, often argue bitterly among themselves over political and social issues.

People have, in general, certain character traits and qualities which, according to their environment, develop in either a positive or a negative manner. Therefore, selfishness (inherent selfishness, that is) might emerge as unselfishness; kindness and consideration as cruelty and lack of consideration towards others. In the same way, a naturally constructive person, may, through frustration, become destructive, and so on. The latent characteristics with which people are born can, therefore, through environment and good or bad training, become something that would appear to be its opposite, and so give the lie to the astrologer's description of their character. But this is not the case. The true character is still there, but it is buried deep beneath these external superficialities.

Careful study of the character traits of different signs can be immeasurable help, and can render beneficial service to the intelligent person. Undoubtedly, the reader will already have discovered that, while he is able to get on very well with some people, he just "cannot stand" others. The causes sometimes seem inexplicable. At times there is intense dislike, at other times immediate sympathy. And there is, too, the phenomenon of love at first sight, which is also apparently inexplicable. People appear to be either sympathetic or unsympathetic towards each other for no apparent reason.

Now if we look at this in the light of the Zodiac, we find that people born under different signs are either compatible or incompatible with each other. In other words, there are good and bad interrelating factors among the various signs. This does not, of course, mean that humanity can be divided into groups of hostile camps. It would be quite wrong to be hostile or indifferent toward people who happen to be born under an incompatible sign. There is no reason why everybody should not, or cannot, learn to control and adjust their feelings and actions, especially after they are aware of the positive qualities of other people by studying their character analyses, among other things.

Every person born under a certain sign has both positive and negative qualities, which are developed more or less according to his free will. Nobody is entirely good or entirely bad, and it is up to each one of us to learn to control himself on the one hand, and at the same time to endeavor to learn about himself and others.

It cannot be repeated often enough that, though the intrinsic nature of man and his basic character traits are born in him, nevertheless it is his own free will that determines whether he will make really good use of his talents and abilities—whether, in other words, he will overcome his vices or allow them to rule him. Most of us are born with at least a streak of laziness, irritability, or some other fault in our nature, and it is up to each one of us to see that we exert sufficient willpower to control our failings so that they do not harm ourselves or others.

Astrology can reveal our inclinations and tendencies. Our weaknesses should not be viewed as shortcomings that are impossible to change. The horoscope of a man may show him to have criminal leanings, for instance, but this does not mean he will definitely become a criminal.

The ordinary man usually finds it difficult to know himself. He is often bewildered. Astrology can frequently tell him more about himself than the different schools of psychology are able to do. Knowing his failings and shortcomings, he will do his best to overcome them, and make himself a better and more useful member of society and a helpmate to his family and friends. It can also save him a great deal of unhappiness and remorse.

And yet it may seem absurd that an ancient philosophy, something that is known as a "pseudo-science," could be a prop to the men and women of the twentieth century. But below the materialistic surface of modern life, there are hidden streams of feeling and thought. Symbology is reappearing as a study worthy of the scholar; the psychosomatic factor in illness has passed from the writings of the crank to those of the specialist; spiritual healing in all its forms is no longer a pious hope but an accepted phenomenon. And it is into this context that we consider astrology, in the sense that it is an analysis of human types.

Astrology and medicine had a long journey together, and only parted company a couple of centuries ago. There still remain in medical language such astrological terms as "saturnine," "choleric," and "mercurial," used in the diagnosis of physical tendencies. The herbalist, for long the handyman of the medical profession, has been dominated by astrology since the days of the Greeks. Certain herbs traditionally respond to certain planetary influences, and diseases must therefore be treated to ensure harmony between the medicine and the disease.

No one expects the most eccentric of modern doctors to go back to the practices of his predecessors. We have come a long way since the time when phases of the moon were studied in illness. Those days were a medical nightmare, with epidemics that were beyond control, and an explanation of the Black Death sought in conjunction with the planets. Nowadays, astrological diagnosis of disease has literally no parallel in modern life. And yet, age-old symbols of types and of the vulnerability of, say, the Saturnian to chronic diseases or the choleric to apoplexy and blood pressure and so on, are still applicable.

But the stars are expected to foretell and not only to diagnose. The astrological forecaster has a counterpart on a highly conventional level in the shape of the weather prophet, racing tipster and stock market forecaster, to name just three examples. All in their own way are aiming at the same result. They attempt to look a little further into the pattern of life and also try to determine future patterns accurately.

Astrological forecasting has been remarkably accurate, but often it is wide of the mark. The brave man who cares to predict world events takes dangerous chances. Individual forecasting is less clear cut; it can be a help or a disillusionment. Then welcome to the nagging question: if it is possible to foreknow, is it right to foretell? A complex point of ethics on which it is hard to pronounce judgment. The doctor faces the same dilemma if he finds that symptoms of a mortal disease are present in his patient and that he can only prognosticate a steady decline. How much to tell an individual in a crisis is a problem that has perplexed many distinguished scholars. Honest and conscientious astrologers in this modern world, where so many people are seeking guidance, face the same problem.

The ancient cults, the symbols of old religions, are eclipsed for the moment. They may return with their old force within a decade or two. But at present the outlook is dark. Human beings badly need assurance, as they did in the past, that all is not chaos. Somewhere, somehow, there is a pattern that must be worked out. As to the why and wherefore, the astrologer is not expected to give judgment. He is just someone who, by dint of talent and training, can gaze into the future.

Five hundred years ago it was customary to call in a learned man who was an astrologer who was probably also a doctor and a philosopher. By his knowledge of astrology, his study of planetary influences, he felt himself qualified to guide those in distress. The world has moved forward at a fantastic rate since then, and in this twentieth century speed has been the keyword everywhere. Tensions have increased, the spur of ambition has been applied indiscriminately. People are uncertain of themselves. At first sight it seems fantastic in the light of modern thinking that they turn to the most ancient of all studies, and get someone to calculate a horoscope for them. But is it *really* so fantastic if you take a second look? For astrology is concerned with tomorrow, with survival. And in a world such as ours, those two things are the keywords of the time in which we live.

HOW TO USE THESE PREDICTIONS

A person reading the predictions in this book should understand that they are produced from the daily position of the planets for a group of people and are not, of course, individually specialized. To get the full benefit of them he should relate the predictions to his own character and circumstances, co-ordinate them, and draw his own conclusions from them.

If he is a serious observer of his own life he should find a definite pattern emerge that will be a helpful and reliable guide.

The point is that we always retain our free will. The stars indicate certain directional tendencies but we are not compelled to follow. We can do or not do, and wisdom must make the choice.

We all have our good and bad days. Sometimes they extend into cycles of weeks. It is therefore advisable to study daily predictions in a span ranging from the day before to several days ahead; also to re-read the monthly predictions for similar cycles.

Daily predictions should be taken very generally. The word "difficult" does not necessarily indicate a whole day of obstruction or inconvenience. It is a warning to you to be cautious. Your caution will often see you around the difficulty before you are involved. This is the correct use of astrology.

In another section, detailed information is given about the influence of the moon as it passes through the various signs of the Zodiac. It includes instructions on how to use the Moon Tables. This information should be used in conjunction with the daily forecasts to give a fuller picture of the astrological trends.

THE MOON

Moon is the nearest planet to the earth. It exerts more observable influence on us from day to day than any other planet. The effect is very personal, very intimate, and if we are not aware of how it works it can make us quite unstable in our ideas. And the annoying thing is that at these times we often see our own instability but can do nothing about it. A knowledge of what can be expected may help considerably. We can then be prepared to stand strong against the moon's negative influences and use its positive ones to help us to get ahead. Who has not heard of going with the tide?

Moon reflects, has no light of its own. It reflects the sun—the life giver—in the form of vital movement. Moon controls the tides, the blood rhythm, the movement of sap in trees and plants. Its nature is inconstancy and change so it signifies our moods, our superficial behavior—walking, talking and especially thinking. Being a true reflector of other forces, moon is cold, watery like the surface of a still lake, brilliant and scintillating at times, but easily ruffled and disturbed by the winds of change.

The moon takes 28½ days to circle the earth and the Zodiac. It spends just over 2¼ days in each sign. During that time it reflects the qualities, energies and characteristics of the sign and, to a degree, the planet which rules the sign. While the moon in its transit occupies a sign incompatible with our own birth sign, we can expect to feel a vague uneasiness, perhaps a touch of irritableness. We should not be discouraged nor let the feeling get us down, or, worse still, allow ourselves to take the discomfort out on others. Try to remember that the moon has to change signs within 55 hours and, provided you are not physically ill, your mood will probably change with it. It is amazing how frequently depression lifts with the shift in the moon's position. And, of course, when the moon is transiting a sign compatible or sympathetic to yours you will probably feel some sort of stimulation or just plain happy to be alive.

In the horoscope, the moon is such a powerful indicator that competent astrologers often use the sign it occupied at birth as the birth sign of the person. This is done particularly when the sun is on the cusp, or edge, of two signs. Most experienced astrologers, however, coordinate both sun and moon signs by reading and confirming from one to the other and secure a far more accurate and personalized analysis.

For these reasons, the moon tables which follow this section (see pages 28–35) are of great importance to the individual. They show the days and the exact times the moon will enter each sign of the Zodiac for the year. Remember, you have to adjust the indicated times to local time. The corrections, already calculated for most of the main cities, are at the beginning of the tables. What follows now is a guide to the influences that will be reflected to the earth by the moon while it transits each of the twelve signs. The influence is at its peak about 26 hours after the moon enters a sign.

MOON IN ARIES

This is a time for action, for reaching out beyond the usual self-imposed limitations and faint-hearted cautions. If you have plans in your head or on your desk, put them into practice. New ventures, applications, new jobs, new starts of any kind—all have a good chance of success. This is the period when original and dynamic impulses are being reflected onto the earth. The energies are extremely vital and favor the pursuit of pleasure and adventure in practically every form. Sick people should feel an improvement. Those who are well will probably find themselves exuding confidence and optimism. People fond of physical exercise should find their bodies growing with tone and well-being. Boldness, strength, determination should characterize most of your activities with a readiness to face up to old challenges. Yesterday's problems may seem petty and exaggerated—so deal with them. Strike out alone. Self-reliance will attract others to you. This is a good time for making friends. Business and marriage partners are more likely to be impressed with the man and woman of action. Opposition will be overcome or thrown aside with much less effort than usual. CAUTION: Be dominant but not domineering.

MOON IN TAURUS

The spontaneous, action-packed person of yesterday gives way to the cautious, diligent, hardworking "thinker." In this period ideas will probably be concentrated on ways of improving finances. A great deal of time may be spent figuring out and going over schemes and plans. It is the right time to be careful with detail. People will find themselves working longer than usual at their desks. Or devoting more time to serious thought about the future. A strong desire to put order into business and financial arrangements may cause extra work. Loved ones may complain of being neglected and may fail to appreciate that your efforts are for their ultimate benefit. Your desire for system may extend to criticism of arrangements in the home and lead to minor upsets. Health may be affected through overwork. Try to secure a reasonable amount of rest and relaxation, although the tendency will be to "keep going" despite good advice. Work done conscientiously in this period should result in a solid contribution to your future security. CAUTION: Try not to be as serious with people as the work you are engaged in.

MOON IN GEMINI

The humdrum of routine and too much work should suddenly end. You are likely to find yourself in an expansive, quicksilver world of change and self-expression. Urges to write, to paint, to experience the freedom of some sort of artistic outpouring, may be very strong. Take full advantage of them. You may find yourself finishing something you began and put aside long ago. Or embarking on something new which could easily be prompted by a chance meeting, a new acquaintance, or even an advertisement. There may be a yearning for a change of scenery, the feeling to visit another country (not too far away), or at least to get away for a few days. This may result in short, quick journeys. Or, if you are planning a single visit, there may be some unexpected changes or detours on the way. Familiar activities will seem to give little satisfaction unless they contain a fresh element of excitement or expectation. The inclination will be towards untried pursuits, particularly those that allow you to express your inner nature. The accent is on new faces, new places. CAUTION: Do not be too quick to commit yourself emotionally.

MOON IN CANCER

Feelings of uncertainty and vague insecurity are likely to cause problems while the moon is in Cancer. Thoughts may turn frequently to the warmth of the home and the comfort of loved ones. Nostalgic impulses could cause you to bring out old photographs and letters and reflect on the days when your life seemed to be much more rewarding and less demanding. The love and understanding of parents and family may be important, and, if it is not forthcoming you may have to fight against a bit of self-pity. The cordiality of friends and the thought of good times with them that are sure to be repeated will help to restore you to a happier frame of mind. The feeling to be alone may follow minor setbacks or rebuffs at this time, but solitude is unlikely to help. Better to get on the telephone or visit someone. This period often causes peculiar dreams and upsurges of imaginative thinking which can be very helpful to authors of occult and mystical works. Preoccupation with the more personal world of simple human needs should overshadow any material strivings. CAUTION: Do not spend too much time thinking—seek the company of loved ones or close friends.

MOON IN LEO

New horizons of exciting and rather extravagant activity open up. This is the time for exhilarating entertainment, glamorous and lavish parties, and expensive shopping sprees. Any merrymaking that relies upon your generosity as a host has every chance of being a spectacular success. You should find yourself right in the center of the fun, either as the life of the party or simply as a person whom happy people like to be with. Romance thrives in this heady atmosphere and friendships are likely to explode unexpectedly into serious attachments. Children and younger people should be attracted to you and you may find yourself organizing a picnic or a visit to a fun-fair, the cinema or the seaside. The sunny company and vitality of youthful companions should help you to find some unsuspected energy. In career, you could find an opening for promotion or advancement. This should be the time to make a direct approach. The period favors those engaged in original research. CAUTION: Bask in popularity but not in flattery.

MOON IN VIRGO

Off comes the party cap and out steps the busy, practical worker. He wants to get his personal affairs straight, to rearrange them, if necessary, for more efficiency, so he will have more time for more work. He clears up his correspondence, pays outstanding bills, makes numerous phone calls. He is likely to make inquiries, or sign up for some new insurance and put money into gilt-edged investment. Thoughts probably revolve around the need for future security—to tie up loose ends and clear the decks. There may be a tendency to be "finicky," to interfere in the routine of others, particularly friends and family members. The motive may be a genuine desire to help with suggestions for updating or streamlining their affairs, but these will probably not be welcomed. Sympathy may be felt for less fortunate sections of the community and a flurry of some sort of voluntary service is likely. This may be accompanied by strong feelings of responsibility on several fronts and health may suffer from extra efforts made. CAUTION: Everyone may not want your help or advice.

MOON IN LIBRA

These are days of harmony and agreement and you should find yourself at peace with most others. Relationships tend to be smooth and sweet-flowing. Friends may become closer and bonds deepen in mutual understanding. Hopes will be shared. Progress by cooperation could be the secret of success in every sphere. In business, established partnerships may flourish and new ones get off to a good start. Acquaintances could discover similar interests that lead to congenial discussions and rewarding exchanges of some sort. Love, as a unifying force, reaches its optimum. Marriage partners should find accord. Those who wed at this time face the prospect of a happy union. Cooperation and tolerance are felt to be stronger than dissension and impatience. The argumentative are not quite so loud in their bellowings, nor as inflexible in their attitudes. In the home, there should be a greater recognition of the other point of view and a readiness to put the wishes of the group before selfish insistence. This is a favorable time to join an art group. CAUTION: Do not be too independent—let others help you if they want to.

MOON IN SCORPIO

Driving impulses to make money and to economize are likely to cause upsets all round. No area of expenditure is likely to be spared the axe, including the household budget. This is a time when the desire to cut down on extravagance can become near fanatical. Care must be exercised to try to keep the aim in reasonable perspective. Others may not feel the same urgent need to save and may retaliate. There is a danger that possessions of sentimental value will be sold to realize cash for investment. Buying and selling of stock for quick profit is also likely. The attention may turn to having a good clean up round the home and at the office. Neglected jobs could suddenly be done with great bursts of energy. The desire for solitude may intervene. Self-searching thoughts could disturb. The sense of invisible and mysterious energies at work could cause some excitability. The reassurance of loves ones may help. CAUTION: Be kind to the people you love.

MOON IN SAGITTARIUS

These are days when you are likely to be stirred and elevated by discussions and reflections of a religious and philosophical nature. Ideas of far-away places may cause unusual response and excitement. A decision may be made to visit someone overseas, perhaps a person whose influence was important to your earlier character development. There could be a strong resolution to get away from present intellectual patterns, to learn new subjects and to meet more interesting people. The superficial may be rejected in all its forms. An impatience with old ideas and unimaginative contacts could lead to a change of companions and interests. There may be an upsurge of religious feeling and metaphysical inquiry. Even a new insight into the significance of astrology and other occult studies is likely under the curious stimulus of the moon in Sagittarius. Physically, you may express this need for fundamental change by spending more time outdoors: sports, gardening or going for long walks. CAUTION: Try to channel any restlessness into worthwhile study.

MOON IN CAPRICORN

Life in these hours may seem to pivot around the importance of gaining prestige and honor in the career, as well as maintaining a spotless reputation. Ambitious urges may be excessive and could be accompanied by quite acquisitive drives for money. Effort should be directed along strictly ethical lines where there is no possibility of reproach or scandal. All endeavors are likely to be characterized by great earnestness, and an air of authority and purpose which should impress those who are looking for leadership or reliability. The desire to conform to accepted standards may extend to sharp criticism of family members. Frivolity and unconventional actions are unlikely to amuse while the moon is in Capricorn. Moderation and seriousness are the orders of the day. Achievement and recognition in this period could come through community work or organizing for the benefit of some amateur group. CAUTION: Dignity and esteem are not always self-awarded.

MOON IN AQUARIUS

Moon in Aquarius is in the second last sign of the Zodiac where ideas can become disturbingly fine and subtle. The result is often a mental "no-man's land" where imagination cannot be trusted with the same certitude as other times. The dangers for the individual are the extremes of optimism and pessimism. Unless the imgination is held in check, situations are likely to be misread, and rosy conclusions drawn where they do not exist. Consequences for the unwary can be costly in career and business. Best to think twice and not speak or act until you think again. Pessimism can be a cruel self-inflicted penalty for delusion at this time. Between the two extremes are strange areas of self-deception which, for example, can make the selfish person think he is actually being generous. Eerie dreams which resemble the reality and even seem to continue into the waking state are also possible. CAUTION: Look for the fact and not just for the image in your mind.

MOON IN PISCES

Everything seems to come to the surface now. Memory may be crystal clear, throwing up long-forgotten information which could be valuable in the career or business. Flashes of clairvoyance and intuition are possible along with sudden realizations of one's own nature, which may be used for self-improvement. A talent, never before suspected, may be discovered. Qualities not evident before in friends and marriage partners are likely to be noticed. As this is a period in which the truth seems to emerge, the discovery of false characteristics is likely to lead to disenchantment or a shift in attachments. However, where qualities are realized it should lead to happiness and deeper feeling. Surprise solutions could bob up for old problems. There may be a public announcement of the solving of a crime or mystery. People with secrets may find someone has "guessed" correctly. The secrets of the soul or the inner self also tend to reveal themselves. Religious and philosophical groups may make some interesting discoveries. CAUTION: Not a time for activities that depend on secrecy.

MOON TABLES

TIME CORRECTIONS FOR GREENWICH MOON TABLES

London, Glasgow, Dublin, Dakar	Same time
Vienna, Prague, Rome, Kinshasa, Frankfurt, Stockholm, Brussels, Amsterdam, Warsaw, Zurich	Add 1 hour
Bucharest, Istanbul, Beirut, Cairo, Johannesburg, Athens, Cape Town, Helsinki, Tel Aviv	Add 2 hours
Dhahran, Baghdad, Moscow, Leningrad, Nairobi, Addis Ababa, Zanzibar	Add 3 hours
Delhi, Calcutta, Bombay, Colombo	Add 5½ hours
Rangoon	Add 6½ hours
Saigon, Bangkok, Chungking	Add 7 hours
Canton, Manila, Hong Kong, Shanghai, Peking	Add 8 hours
Tokyo, Pusan, Seoul, Vladivostok, Yokohama	Add 9 hours
Sydney, Melbourne, Guam, Port Moresby	Add 10 hours
Azores, Reykjavik	Deduct 1 hour
Rio de Janeiro, Montevideo, Buenos Aires, Sao Paulo, Recife	Deduct 3 hours
LaPaz, San Juan, Santiago, Bermuda, Caracas, Halifax	Deduct 4 hours
New York, Washington, Boston, Detroit, Lima, Havana, Miami, Bogota	Deduct 5 hours
Mexico, Chicago, New Orleans, Houston	Deduct 6 hours
San Francisco, Seattle, Los Angeles, Hollywood, Ketchikan, Juneau	Deduct 8 hours
Honolulu, Fairbanks, Anchorage, Papeete	Deduct 10 hours

1994 MOON TABLES—GREENWICH TIME

JANUARY		FEBRUARY		MARCH	
Day Moon Enters		**Day Moon Enters**		**Day Moon Enters**	
1. Virgo	8:16 pm	1. Libra		1. Scorpio	2:44 pm
2. Virgo		2. Scorpio	7:50 am	2. Scorpio	
3. Libra	11:32 pm	3. Scorpio		3. Sagitt.	4:55 pm
4. Libra		4. Sagitt.	11:15 am	4. Sagitt.	
5. Libra		5. Sagitt.		5. Capric.	9:25 pm
6. Scorpio	2:30 am	6. Capric.	4:03 pm	6. Capric.	
7. Scorpio		7. Capric.		7. Capric.	
8. Sagitt.	5:35 am	8. Aquar.	10:17 pm	8. Aquar.	4:16 am
9. Sagitt.		9. Aquar.		9. Aquar.	
10. Capric.	9:17 am	10. Aquar.		10. Pisces	1:10 pm
11. Capric.		11. Pisces	6:24 am	11. Pisces	
12. Aquar.	2:26 pm	12. Pisces		12. Aries	12:00 pm
13. Aquar.		13. Aries	4:50 am	13. Aries	
14. Pisces	10:05 pm	14. Aries		14. Aries	
15. Pisces		15. Aries		15. Taurus	12:28 pm
16. Pisces		16. Taurus	5:21 am	16. Taurus	
17. Aries	8:43 am	17. Taurus		17. Taurus	
18. Aries		18. Gemini	6:06 pm	18. Gemini	1:30 am
19. Taurus	9:23 pm	19. Gemini		19. Gemini	
20. Taurus		20. Gemini		20. Cancer	12:55 pm
21. Taurus		21. Cancer	4:28 am	21. Cancer	
22. Gemini	9:35 am	22. Cancer		22. Leo	8:40 pm
23. Gemini		23. Leo	10:48 am	23. Leo	
24. Cancer	6:56 pm	24. Leo		24. Leo	
25. Cancer		25. Virgo	1:28 pm	25. Virgo	0:15 am
26. Cancer		26. Virgo		26. Virgo	
27. Leo	0:39 am	27. Libra	2:07 pm	27. Libra	0:47 am
28. Leo		28. Libra		28. Libra	
29. Virgo	3:40 am			29. Scorpio	0:16 am
30. Virgo				30. Scorpio	
31. Libra	5:35 am			31. Sagitt.	0:42 am

Summer time to be considered where applicable.

1994 MOON TABLES—GREENWICH TIME

APRIL			MAY			JUNE	
Day	**Moon Enters**		**Day**	**Moon Enters**		**Day**	**Moon Enters**	

APRIL Day Moon Enters		MAY Day Moon Enters		JUNE Day Moon Enters	
1. Sagitt.		1. Aquar.	4:35 pm	1. Pisces	
2. Capric.	3:38 am	2. Aquar.		2. Aries	6:32 pm
3. Capric.		3. Aquar.		3. Aries	
4. Aquar.	9:46 am	4. Pisces	0:48 am	4. Aries	
5. Aquar.		5. Pisces		5. Taurus	8:15 am
6. Pisces	6:52 pm	6. Aries	12:02 pm	6. Taurus	
7. Pisces		7. Aries		7. Gemini	8:04 pm
8. Pisces		8. Aries		8. Gemini	
9. Aries	6:10 am	9. Taurus	0:51 am	9. Gemini	
10. Aries		10. Taurus		10. Cancer	7:23 am
11. Taurus	6:49 pm	11. Gemini	1:44 pm	11. Cancer	
12. Taurus		12. Gemini		12. Leo	4:30 pm
13. Taurus		13. Gemini		13. Leo	
14. Gemini	7:49 am	14. Cancer	1:28 am	14. Virgo	11:17 pm
15. Gemini		15. Cancer		15. Virgo	
16. Cancer	7:42 pm	16. Leo	10:59 am	16. Virgo	
17. Cancer		17. Leo		17. Libra	3:49 am
18. Cancer		18. Virgo	5:32 pm	18. Libra	
19. Leo	4:46 am	19. Virgo		19. Scorpio	6:21 am
20. Leo		20. Libra	8:55 pm	20. Scorpio	
21. Virgo	9:59 am	21. Libra		21. Sagitt.	7:33 am
22. Virgo		22. Scorpio	9:52 pm	22. Sagitt.	
23. Libra	11:41 am	23. Scorpio		23. Capric.	8:38 am
24. Libra		24. Sagitt.	9:44 pm	24. Capric.	
25. Scorpio	11:19 am	25. Sagitt.		25. Aquar.	11:11 am
26. Scorpio		26. Capric.	10:18 pm	26. Aquar.	
27. Sagitt.	10:49 am	27. Capric.		27. Pisces	4:45 pm
28. Sagitt.		28. Capric.		28. Pisces	
29. Capric.	12:06 pm	29. Aquar.	1:20 am	29. Pisces	
30. Capric.		30. Aquar.		30. Aries	2:08 am
		31. Pisces	8:04 am		

Summer time to be considered where applicable.

1994 MOON TABLES—GREENWICH TIME

JULY		AUGUST		SEPTEMBER	
Day Moon Enters		**Day Moon Enters**		**Day Moon Enters**	
1. Aries		1. Gemini	11:06 am	1. Cancer	
2. Taurus	2:24 pm	2. Gemini		2. Leo	3:38 pm
3. Taurus		3. Cancer	10:23 pm	3. Leo	
4. Taurus		4. Cancer		4. Virgo	8:34 pm
5. Gemini	3:13 am	5. Cancer		5. Virgo	
6. Gemini		6. Leo	6:32 am	6. Libra	10:58 pm
7. Cancer	2:18 pm	7. Leo		7. Libra	
8. Cancer		8. Virgo	11:43 am	8. Libra	
9. Leo	10:44 pm	9. Virgo		9. Scorpio	0:27 am
10. Leo		10. Libra	3:08 pm	10. Scorpio	
11. Leo		11. Libra		11. Sagitt.	2:26 am
12. Virgo	4:49 am	12. Scorpio	5:57 pm	12. Sagitt.	
13. Virgo		13. Scorpio		13. Capric.	5:45 am
14. Libra	9:16 am	14. Sagitt.	8:54 pm	14. Capric.	
15. Libra		15. Sagitt.		15. Aquar.	10:43 am
16. Scorpio	12:36 pm	16. Sagitt.		16. Aquar.	
17. Scorpio		17. Capric.	0:19 am	17. Pisces	5:32 pm
18. Sagitt.	3:10 pm	18. Capric.		18. Pisces	
19. Sagitt.		19. Aquar.	4:35 am	19. Pisces	
20. Capric.	5:31 pm	20. Aquar.		20. Aries	2:31 am
21. Capric.		21. Pisces	10:28 am	21. Aries	
22. Aquar.	8:39 pm	22. Pisces		22. Taurus	1:48 pm
23. Aquar.		23. Aries	6:56 pm	23. Taurus	
24. Aquar.		24. Aries		24. Taurus	
25. Pisces	1:57 am	25. Aries		25. Gemini	2:42 am
26. Pisces		26. Taurus	6:14 am	26. Gemini	
27. Aries	10:32 am	27. Taurus		27. Gemini	
28. Aries		28. Gemini	7:08 pm	28. Cancer	3:13 am
29. Taurus	10:14 pm	29. Gemini		29. Cancer	
30. Taurus		30. Gemini		30. Leo	0:56 am
31. Taurus		31. Cancer	7:01 am		

Summer time to be considered where applicable.

1994 MOON TABLES—GREENWICH TIME

OCTOBER		NOVEMBER		DECEMBER	
Day Moon Enters		**Day Moon Enters**		**Day Moon Enters**	
1. Leo		1. Libra		1. Scorpio	
2. Virgo	6:40 am	2. Scorpio	8:20 pm	2. Sagitt.	7:14 am
3. Virgo		3. Scorpio		3. Sagitt.	
4. Libra	8:57 am	4. Sagitt.	7:47 pm	4. Capric.	6:43 am
5. Libra		5. Sagitt.		5. Capric.	
6. Scorpio	9:23 am	6. Capric.	8:03 pm	6. Aquar.	7:53 am
7. Scorpio		7. Capric.		7. Aquar.	
8. Sagitt.	9:48 am	8. Aquar.	10:49 pm	8. Pisces	12:25 pm
9. Sagitt.		9. Aquar.		9. Pisces	
10. Capric.	11:45 am	10. Aquar.		10. Aries	9:04 pm
11. Capric.		11. Pisces	5:05 am	11. Aries	
12. Aquar.	4:10 pm	12. Pisces		12. Aries	
13. Aquar.		13. Aries	2:45 pm	13. Taurus	8:57 am
14. Pisces	11:19 pm	14. Aries		14. Taurus	
15. Pisces		15. Aries		15. Gemini	10:01 pm
16. Pisces		16. Taurus	2:45 am	16. Gemini	
17. Aries	8:57 am	17. Taurus		17. Gemini	
18. Aries		18. Gemini	3:42 pm	18. Cancer	10:26 am
19. Taurus	8:35 pm	19. Gemini		19. Cancer	
20. Taurus		20. Gemini		20. Leo	9:14 pm
21. Taurus		21. Cancer	4:22 am	21. Leo	
22. Gemini	9:29 am	22. Cancer		22. Leo	
23. Gemini		23. Leo	3:34 pm	23. Virgo	6:02 am
24. Cancer	10:16 pm	24. Leo		24. Virgo	
25. Cancer		25. Leo		25. Libra	12:28 pm
26. Cancer		26. Virgo	0:10 am	26. Libra	
27. Leo	9:05 am	27. Virgo		27. Scorpio	4:18 pm
28. Leo		28. Libra	5:23 am	28. Scorpio	
29. Virgo	4:22 pm	29. Libra		29. Sagitt.	6:46 pm
30. Virgo		30. Scorpio	7:22 am	30. Sagitt.	
31. Libra	7:47 pm			31. Capric.	6:58 pm

Summer time to be considered where applicable.

1994 PHASES OF THE MOON—GREENWICH TIME

New Moon	First Quarter	Full Moon	Last Quarter
			Jan. 3
Jan. 11	Jan. 18	Jan. 27	Feb. 3
Feb. 10	Feb. 18	Feb. 26	Mar. 4
Mar. 12	Mar. 19	Mar. 27	Apr. 3
Apr. 11	Apr. 18	Apr. 25	May 3
May 10	May 17	May 25	June 2
June 9	June 16	June 23	June 30
July 8	July 15	July 22	July 30
Aug. 7	Aug. 14	Aug. 21	Aug. 29
Sep. 5	Sep. 12	Sep. 19	Sep. 27
Oct. 5	Oct. 12	Oct. 19	Oct. 27
Nov. 3	Nov. 10	Nov. 18	Nov. 25
Dec. 3	Dec. 10	Dec. 18	Dec. 25

1994 PLANTING GUIDE

	Aboveground Crops	Root Crops	Pruning	Weeds Pests
January	2-6-15-25-29	4-11-20-25	9-18-20	13-18-23-27
February	3-12-14-21-26	7-19-24-28	5-14-15	9-14-19-24
March	4-6-21-25-29	2-6-18-29	4-13-14	8-18-23
April	7-17-22-26	2-12-24	9-10-28	5-15-20
May	4-14-19-23-31	9-10-21-27	6-7-25	2-12-17-29
June	1-11-15-20-28	6-17-20-24	3-4-21-22	8-13-26
July	8-12-17-25	3-15-21-30	1-19-27-28	5-10-23
August	4-9-13-22	11-17-27	15-16-24-25	2-19-30
September	1-5-9-18-28	7-14-23	11-12-20-21	3-16-25-30
October	3-7-15-25-30	4-5-11-20	9-18-19	1-13-23-28
November	3-12-21-26	1-7-16-29	5-14-15	9-19-24
December	1-9-19-24-28	5-14-26	3-11-12-30	7-16-21

1994 FISHING GUIDE

	Good	Best
January	4-5-9-13-20-23	6-15-25
February	2-11-16-17-21-22	3-12-19-28
March	2-3-11-12-21-22	4-13-19-20-27
April	5-7-8-9-17-23	4-15-24-28
May	4-9-14-15-21-23-24	2-5-12-21
June	1-10-19-21-26-27-28	3-11-17-20-22
July	8-9-16-23-25-26	7-15-17-21
August	5-10-11-14-22-23	4-13-19-27
September	1-8-9-10-19-28-29	7-9-16-18-20
October	8-16-18-20-22-27	6-15-19-24-26
November	2-3-13-18-23-30	4-12-15-18-21
December	3-12-13-14-18-30	5-9-19-28

MOON'S INFLUENCE OVER DAILY AFFAIRS

The Moon makes a complete transit of the Zodiac every 27 days 7 hours and 43 minutes. In making this transit the Moon forms different aspects with the planets and consequently has favorable or unfavorable bearings on affairs and events for persons according to the sign of the Zodiac under which they were born. Whereas the Sun exclusively represents fire, the Moon rules water. The action of the Moon may be described as fluctuating, variable, absorbent and receptive.

When the Moon is in conjunction with the Sun it is called a New Moon; when the Moon and Sun are in opposition it is called a Full Moon. From New Moon to Full Moon, first and second quarter—which takes about two weeks—the Moon is increasing or waxing. From Full Moon to New Moon, third and fourth quarter, the Moon is decreasing or waning. The Moon Table indicates the New Moon and Full Moon and the quarters.

ACTIVITY	MOON IN
Business:	
buying and selling	Sagittarius, Aries, Gemini, Virgo
new, requiring public support	1st and 2nd quarter
meant to be kept quiet	3rd and 4th quarter
Investigation	3rd and 4th quarter
Signing documents	1st & 2nd quarter, Cancer, Scorpio, Pisces
Advertising	2nd quarter, Sagittarius
Journeys and trips	1st & 2nd quarter, Gemini, Virgo
Renting offices, etc.	Taurus, Leo, Scorpio, Aquarius
Painting of house/apartment	3rd & 4th quarter, Taurus, Scorpio, Aquarius
Decorating	Gemini, Libra, Aquarius
Buying clothes and accessories	Taurus, Virgo
Beauty salon or barber shop visit	1st & 2nd quarter, Taurus, Leo, Libra, Scorpio, Aquarius
Weddings	1st & 2nd quarter

MOON'S INFLUENCE OVER YOUR HEALTH

ARIES	Head, brain, face, upper jaw
TAURUS	Throat, neck, lower jaw
GEMINI	Hands, arms, lungs, shoulders, nervous system
CANCER	Esophagus, stomach, breasts, womb, liver
LEO	Heart, spine
VIRGO	Intestines, liver
LIBRA	Kidneys, lower back
SCORPIO	Sex and eliminative organs
SAGITTARIUS	Hips, thighs, liver
CAPRICORN	Skin, bones, teeth, knees
AQUARIUS	Circulatory system, lower legs
PISCES	Feet, tone of being

Try to avoid work being done on that part of the body when the Moon is in the sign governing that part.

MOON'S INFLUENCE OVER PLANTS

Centuries ago it was established that seeds planted when the Moon is in certain signs and phases called Fruitful will produce more growth than seeds planted when the Moon is in a Barren sign.

FRUITFUL SIGNS	BARREN SIGNS	DRY SIGNS
Taurus	Aries	Aries
Cancer	Gemini	Gemini
Libra	Leo	Sagittarius
Scorpio	Virgo	Aquarius
Capricorn	Sagittarius	
Pisces	Aquarius	

ACTIVITY	MOON IN
Mow lawn, trim plants	**Fruitful sign:** 1st & 2nd quarter
Plant flowers	**Fruitful sign:** 2nd quarter; best in Cancer and Libra
Prune	**Fruitful sign:** 3rd & 4th quarter
Destroy pests; spray	**Barren sign:** 4th quarter
Harvest potatoes, root crops	**Dry sign:** 3rd & 4th quarter; Taurus, Leo, and Aquarius

THE SIGNS: DOMINANT CHARACTERISTICS

March 21–April 20

The Positive Side of Aries

The Arien has many positive points to his character. People born under this first sign of the Zodiac are often quite strong and enthusiastic. On the whole, they are forward-looking people who are not easily discouraged by temporary setbacks. They know what they want out of life and they go out after it. Their personalities are strong. Others are usually quite impressed by the Arien's way of doing things. Quite often they are sources of inspiration for others traveling the same route. Aries men and women have a special zest for life that is often contagious; for others, they are often the example of how life should be lived.

The Aries person usually has a quick and active mind. He is imaginative and inventive. He enjoys keeping busy and active. He generally gets along well with all kinds of people. He is interested in mankind, as a whole. He likes to be challenged. Some would say he thrives on opposition, for it is when he is set against that he often does his best. Getting over or around obstacles is a challenge he generally enjoys. All in all, the Arien is quite positive and young-thinking. He likes to keep abreast of new things that are happening in the world. Ariens are often fond of speed. They like things to be done quickly and this sometimes aggravates their slower colleagues and associates.

The Aries man or woman always seems to remain young. Their whole approach to life is youthful and optimistic. They never say die, no matter what the odds. They may have an occasional setback, but it is not long before they are back on their feet again.

The Negative Side of Aries

Everybody has his less positive qualities—and Aries is no exception. Sometimes the Aries man or woman is not very tactful in communicating with others; in his hurry to get things done he is apt to

be a little callous or inconsiderate. Sensitive people are likely to find him somewhat sharp-tongued in some situations. Often in his eagerness to achieve his aims, he misses the mark altogether. At times the Arien is too impulsive. He can occasionally be stubborn and refuse to listen to reason. If things do not move quickly enough to suit the Aries man or woman, he or she is apt to become rather nervous or irritable. The uncultivated Arien is not unfamiliar with moments of doubt and fear. He is capable of being destructive if he does not get his way. He can overcome some of his emotional problems by steadily trying to express himself as he really is, but this requires effort.

April 21–May 20

The Positive Side of Taurus

The Taurus person is known for his ability to concentrate and for his tenacity. These are perhaps his strongest qualities. The Taurus man or woman generally has very little trouble in getting along with others; it's his nature to be helpful toward people in need. He can always be depended on by his friends, especially those in trouble.

The Taurean generally achieves what he wants through his ability to persevere. He never leaves anything unfinished but works on something until it has been completed. People can usually take him at his word; he is honest and forthright in most of his dealings. The Taurus person has a good chance to make a success of his life because of his many positive qualities. The Taurean who aims high seldom falls short of his mark. He learns well by experience. He is thorough and does not believe in short-cuts of any kind. The Taurean's thoroughness pays off in the end, for through his deliberateness he learns how to rely on himself and what he has learned. The Taurus person tries to get along with others, as a rule. He is not overly critical and likes people to be themselves. He is a tolerant person and enjoys peace and harmony—especially in his home life.

The Taurean is usually cautious in all that he does. He is not a person who believes in taking unnecessary risks. Before adopting any one line of action, he will weigh all of the pros and cons. The

Taurus person is steadfast. Once his mind is made up it seldom changes. The person born under this sign usually is a good family person—reliable and loving.

The Negative Side of Taurus

Sometimes the Taurus man or woman is a bit too stubborn. He won't listen to other points of view if his mind is set on something. To others, this can be quite annoying. The Taurean also does not like to be told what to do. He becomes rather angry if others think him not too bright. He does not like to be told he is wrong, even when he is. He dislikes being contradicted.

Some people who are born under this sign are very suspicious of others—even of those persons close to them. They find it difficult to trust people fully. They are often afraid of being deceived or taken advantage of. The Taurean often finds it difficult to forget or forgive. His love of material things sometimes makes him rather avaricious and petty.

May 21–June 20

The Positive Side of Gemini

The person born under this sign of the Heavenly Twins is usually quite bright and quick-witted. Some of them are capable of doing many different things. The Gemini person very often has many different interests. He keeps an open mind and is always anxious to learn new things.

The Geminian is often an analytical person. He is a person who enjoys making use of his intellect. He is governed more by his mind than by his emotions. He is a person who is not confined to one view; he can often understand both sides to a problem or question. He knows how to reason; how to make rapid decisions if need be.

He is an adaptable person and can make himself at home almost anywhere. There are all kinds of situations he can adapt to. He is a person who seldom doubts himself; he is sure of his talents and his

ability to think and reason. The Geminian is generally most satisfied when he is in a situation where he can make use of his intellect. Never short of imagination, he often has strong talents for invention. He is rather a modern person when it comes to life; the Geminian almost always moves along with the times—perhaps that is why he remains so youthful throughout most of his life.

Literature and art appeal to the person born under this sign. Creativity in almost any form will interest and intrigue the Gemini man or woman.

The Geminian is often quite charming. A good talker, he often is the center of attraction at any gathering. People find it easy to like a person born under this sign because he can appear easygoing and usually has a good sense of humor.

The Negative Side of Gemini

Sometimes the Gemini person tries to do too many things at one time—and as a result, winds up finishing nothing. Some Geminians are easily distracted and find it rather difficult to concentrate on one thing for too long a time. Sometimes they give in to trifling fancies and find it rather boring to become too serious about any one thing. Some of them are never dependable, no matter what they promise.

Although the Gemini man or woman often appears to be well-versed on many subjects, this is sometimes just a veneer. His knowledge may be only superficial, but because he speaks so well he gives people the impression of erudition. Some Geminians are sharp-tongued and inconsiderate; they think only of themselves and their own pleasure.

June 21–July 20

The Positive Side of Cancer

The Cancerians's most positive point is his understanding nature. On the whole, he is a loving and sympathetic person. He would never go out of his way to hurt anyone. The Cancer man or woman

is often very kind and tender; they give what they can to others. They hate to see others suffering and will do what they can to help someone in less fortunate circumstances than themselves. They are often very concerned about the world. Their interest in people generally goes beyond that of just their own families and close friends; they have a deep sense of brotherhood and respect humanitarian values. The Cancerian means what he says, as a rule; he is honest about his feelings.

The Cancer man or woman is a person who knows the art of patience. When something seems difficult, he is willing to wait until the situation becomes manageable again. He is a person who knows how to bide his time. The Cancerian knows how to concentrate on one thing at a time. When he has made his mind up he generally sticks with what he does, seeing it through to the end.

The Cancerian is a person who loves his home. He enjoys being surrounded by familiar things and the people he loves. Of all the signs, Cancer is the most maternal. Even the men born under this sign often have a motherly or protective quality about them. They like to take care of people in their family—to see that they are well loved and well provided for. They are usually loyal and faithful. Family ties mean a lot to the Cancer man or woman. Parents and in-laws are respected and loved. The Cancerian has a strong sense of tradition. He is very sensitive to the moods of others.

The Negative Side of Cancer

Sometimes the Cancerian finds it rather hard to face life. It becomes too much for him. He can be a little timid and retiring, when things don't go too well. When unfortunate things happen, he is apt to just shrug and say, "Whatever will be will be." He can be fatalistic to a fault. The uncultivated Cancerian is a bit lazy. He doesn't have very much ambition. Anything that seems a bit difficult he'll gladly leave to others. He may be lacking in initiative. Too sensitive, when he feels he's been injured, he'll crawl back into his shell and nurse his imaginary wounds. The Cancer woman often is given to crying when the smallest thing goes wrong.

Some Cancerians find it difficult to enjoy themselves in environments outside their homes. They make heavy demands on others, and need to be constantly reassured that they are loved.

July 21–August 21

The Positive Side of Leo

Often Leos make good leaders. They seem to be good organizers and administrators. Usually they are quite popular with others. Whatever group it is that he belongs to, the Leo man is almost sure to be or become the leader.

The Leo person is generous most of the time. It is his best characteristic. He or she likes to give gifts and presents. In making others happy, the Leo person becomes happy himself. He likes to splurge when spending money on others. In some instances it may seem that the Leo's generosity knows no boundaries. A hospitable person, the Leo man or woman is very fond of welcoming people to his house and entertaining them. He is never short of company.

The Leo person has plenty of energy and drive. He enjoys working toward some specific goal. When he applies himself correctly, he gets what he wants most often. The Leo person is almost never unsure of himself. He has plenty of confidence and aplomb. He is a person who is direct in almost everything he does. He has a quick mind and can make a decision in a very short time.

He usually sets a good example for others because of his ambitious manner and positive ways. He knows how to stick to something once he's started. Although the Leo person may be good at making a joke, he is not superficial or glib. He is a loving person, kind and thoughtful.

There is generally nothing small or petty about the Leo man or woman. He does what he can for those who are deserving. He is a person others can rely upon at all times. He means what he says. An honest person, generally speaking, he is a friend that others value.

The Negative Side of Leo

Leo, however, does have his faults. At times, he can be just a bit too arrogant. He thinks that no one deserves a leadership position except him. Only he is capable of doing things well. His opinion of himself is often much too high. Because of his conceit, he is sometimes rather unpopular with a good many people. Some Leos are too materialistic; they can only think in terms of money and profit.

Some Leos enjoy lording it over others—at home or at their place of business. What is more, they feel they have the right to. Egocentric to an impossible degree, this sort of Leo cares little about how others think or feel. He can be rude and cutting.

August 22–September 22

The Positive Side of Virgo

The person born under the sign of Virgo is generally a busy person. He knows how to arrange and organize things. He is a good planner. Above all, he is practical and is not afraid of hard work.

The person born under this sign, Virgo, knows how to attain what he desires. He sticks with something until it is finished. He never shirks his duties, and can always be depended upon. The Virgo person can be thoroughly trusted at all times.

The man or woman born under this sign tries to do everything to perfection. He doesn't believe in doing anything half-way. He always aims for the top. He is the sort of a person who is constantly striving to better himself—not because he wants more money or glory, but because it gives him a feeling of accomplishment.

The Virgo man or woman is a very observant person. He is sensitive to how others feel, and can see things below the surface of a situation. He usually puts this talent to constructive use.

It is not difficult for the Virgoan to be open and earnest. He believes in putting his cards on the table. He is never secretive or under-handed. He's as good as his word. The Virgo person is generally plain-spoken and down-to-earth. He has no trouble in expressing himself.

The Virgo person likes to keep up to date on new developments in his particular field. Well-informed, generally, he sometimes has a keen interest in the arts or literature. What he knows, he knows well. His ability to use his critical faculties is well-developed and sometimes startles others because of its accuracy.

The Virgoan adheres to a moderate way of life; he avoids excesses. He is a responsible person and enjoys being of service.

The Negative Side of Virgo

Sometimes a Virgo person is too critical. He thinks that only he can do something the way it should be done. Whatever anyone else does is inferior. He can be rather annoying in the way he quibbles over insignificant details. In telling others how things should be done, he can be rather tactless and mean.

Some Virgos seem rather emotionless and cool. They feel emo-

tional involvement is beneath them. They are sometimes too tidy, too neat. With money they can be rather miserly. Some try to force their opinions and ideas on others.

September 23–October 22

The Positive Side of Libra

Librans love harmony. It is one of their most outstanding character traits. They are interested in achieving balance; they admire beauty and grace in things as well as in people. Generally speaking, they are kind and considerate people. Librans are usually very sympathetic. They go out of their way not to hurt another person's feelings. They are outgoing and do what they can to help those in need.

People born under the sign of Libra almost always make good friends. They are loyal and amiable. They enjoy the company of others. Many of them are rather moderate in their views; they believe in keeping an open mind, however, and weighing both sides of an issue fairly before making a decision.

Alert and often intelligent, the Libran, always fair-minded, tries to put himself in the position of the other person. They are against injustice; quite often they take up for the underdog. In most of their social dealings, they try to be tactful and kind. They dislike discord and bickering, and most Libras strive for peace and harmony in all their relationships.

The Libra man or woman has a keen sense of beauty. They appreciate handsome furnishings and clothes. Many of them are artistically inclined. Their taste is usually impeccable. They know how to use color. Their homes are almost always attractively arranged and inviting. They enjoy entertaining people and see to it that their guests always feel at home and welcome.

The Libran gets along with almost everyone. He is well-liked and socially much in demand.

The Negative Side of Libra

Some people born under this sign tend to be rather insincere. So eager are they to achieve harmony in all relationships that they will even go so far as to lie. Many of them are escapists. They find facing

the truth an ordeal and prefer living in a world of make-believe.

In a serious argument, some Librans give in rather easily even when they know they are right. Arguing, even about something they believe in, is too unsettling for some of them.

Librans sometimes care too much for material things. They enjoy possessions and luxuries. Some are vain and tend to be jealous.

October 23–November 22

The Positive Side of Scorpio

The Scorpio man or woman generally knows what he or she wants out of life. He is a determined person. He sees something through to the end. The Scorpion is quite sincere, and seldom says anything he doesn't mean. When he sets a goal for himself he tries to go about achieving it in a very direct way.

The Scorpion is brave and courageous. They are not afraid of hard work. Obstacles do not frighten them. They forge ahead until they achieve what they set out for. The Scorpio man or woman has a strong will.

Although the Scorpion may seem rather fixed and determined, inside he is often quite tender and loving. He can care very much for others. He believes in sincerity in all relationships. His feelings about someone tend to last; they are profound and not superficial.

The Scorpio person is someone who adheres to his principles no matter what happens. He will not be deterred from a path he believes to be right.

Because of his many positive strengths, the Scorpion can often achieve happiness for himself and for those that he loves.

He is a constructive person by nature. He often has a deep understanding of people and of life, in general. He is perceptive and unafraid. Obstacles often seem to spur him on. He is a positive person who enjoys winning. He has many strengths and resources; challenge of any sort often brings out the best in him.

The Negative Side of Scorpio

The Scorpio person is sometimes hypersensitive. Often he imagines injury when there is none. He feels that others do not bother to

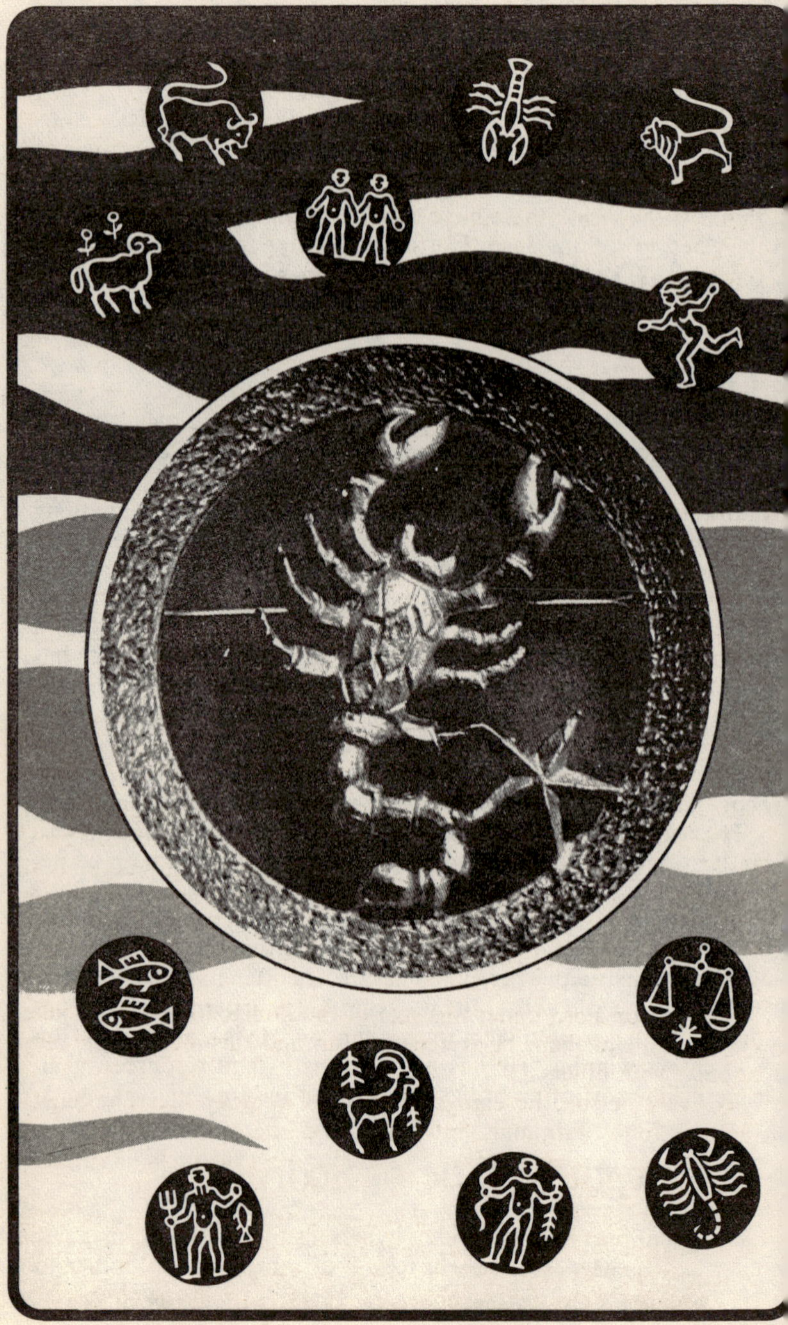

recognize him for his true worth. Sometimes he is given to excessive boasting in order to compensate for what he feels is neglect

The Scorpio person can be rather proud and arrogant. They can be rather sly when they put their minds to it and they enjoy outwitting persons or institutions noted for their cleverness.

Their tactics for getting what they want are sometimes devious and ruthless. They don't care too much about what others may think. If they feel others have done them an injustice, they will do their best to seek revenge. The Scorpion often has a sudden, violent temper; and this person's interest in sex is sometimes quite unbalanced or excessive.

November 23–December 20

The Positive Side of Sagittarius

People born under this sign are often honest and forthright. Their approach to life is earnest and open. The Sagittarian is often quite adult in his way of seeing things. They are broadminded and tolerant people. When dealing with others the person born under the sign of Sagittarius is almost always open and forthright. He doesn't believe in deceit or pretension. His standards are high. People who associate with the Sagittarian, generally admire and respect him.

The Sagittarian trusts others easily and expects them to trust him. He is never suspicious or envious and almost always thinks well of others. People always enjoy his company because he is so friendly and easy-going. The Sagittarius man or woman is often good-humored. He can always be depended upon by his friends, family, and co-workers.

The person born under this sign of the Zodiac likes a good joke every now and then; he is keen on fun and this makes him very popular with others.

A lively person, he enjoys sports and outdoor life. The Sagittarian is fond of animals. Intelligent and interesting, he can begin an animated conversation with ease. He likes exchanging ideas and discussing various views.

He is not selfish or proud. If someone proposes an idea or plan that is better than his, he will immediately adopt it. Imaginative yet practical, he knows how to put ideas into practice.

He enjoys sport and game, and it doesn't matter if he wins or loses. He is a forgiving person, and never sulks over something that has not worked out in his favor.

He is seldom critical, and is almost always generous.

The Negative Side of Sagittarius

Some Sagittarians are restless. They take foolish risks and seldom learn from the mistakes they make. They don't have heads for money and are often mismanaging their finances. Some of them devote much of their time to gambling.

Some are too outspoken and tactless, always putting their feet in their mouths. They hurt others carelessly by being honest at the wrong time. Sometimes they make promises which they don't keep. They don't stick close enough to their plans and go from one failure to another. They are undisciplined and waste a lot of energy.

December 21–January 19

The Positive Side of Capricorn

The person born under the sign of Capricorn is usually very stable and patient. He sticks to whatever tasks he has and sees them through. He can always be relied upon and he is not averse to work.

An honest person, the Capricornian is generally serious about whatever he does. He does not take his duties lightly. He is a practical person and believes in keeping his feet on the ground.

Quite often the person born under this sign is ambitious and knows how to get what he wants out of life. He forges ahead and never gives up his goal. When he is determined about something, he almost always wins. He is a good worker—a hard worker. Although things may not come easy to him, he will not complain, but continue working until his chores are finished.

He is usually good at business matters and knows the value of money. He is not a spendthrift and knows how to put something away for a rainy day; he dislikes waste and unnecessary loss.

The Capricornian knows how to make use of his self-control. He

can apply himself to almost anything once he puts his mind to it. His ability to concentrate sometimes astounds others. He is diligent and does well when involved in detail work.

The Capricorn man or woman is charitable, generally speaking, and will do what is possible to help others less fortunate. As a friend, he is loyal and trustworthy. He never shirks his duties or responsibilities. He is self-reliant and never expects too much of the other fellow. He does what he can on his own. If someone does him a good turn, then he will do his best to return the favor.

The Negative Side of Capricorn

Like everyone, the Capricornian, too, has his faults. At times, he can be over-critical of others. He expects others to live up to his own high standards. He thinks highly of himself and tends to look down on others.

His interest in material things may be exaggerated. The Capricorn man or woman thinks too much about getting on in the world and having something to show for it. He may even be a little greedy.

He sometimes thinks he knows what's best for everyone. He is too bossy. He is always trying to organize and correct others. He may be a little narrow in his tninking.

January 20–February 18

The Positive Side of Aquarius

The Aquarius man or woman is usually very honest and forthright. These are his two greatest qualities. His standards for himself are generally very high. He can always be relied upon by others. His word is his bond.

The Aquarian is perhaps the most tolerant of all the Zodiac personalities. He respects other people's beliefs and feels that everyone is entitled to his own approach to life.

He would never do anything to injure another's feelings. He is never unkind or cruel. Always considerate of others, the Aquarian is always willing to help a person in need. He feels a very strong tie between himself and all the other members of mankind.

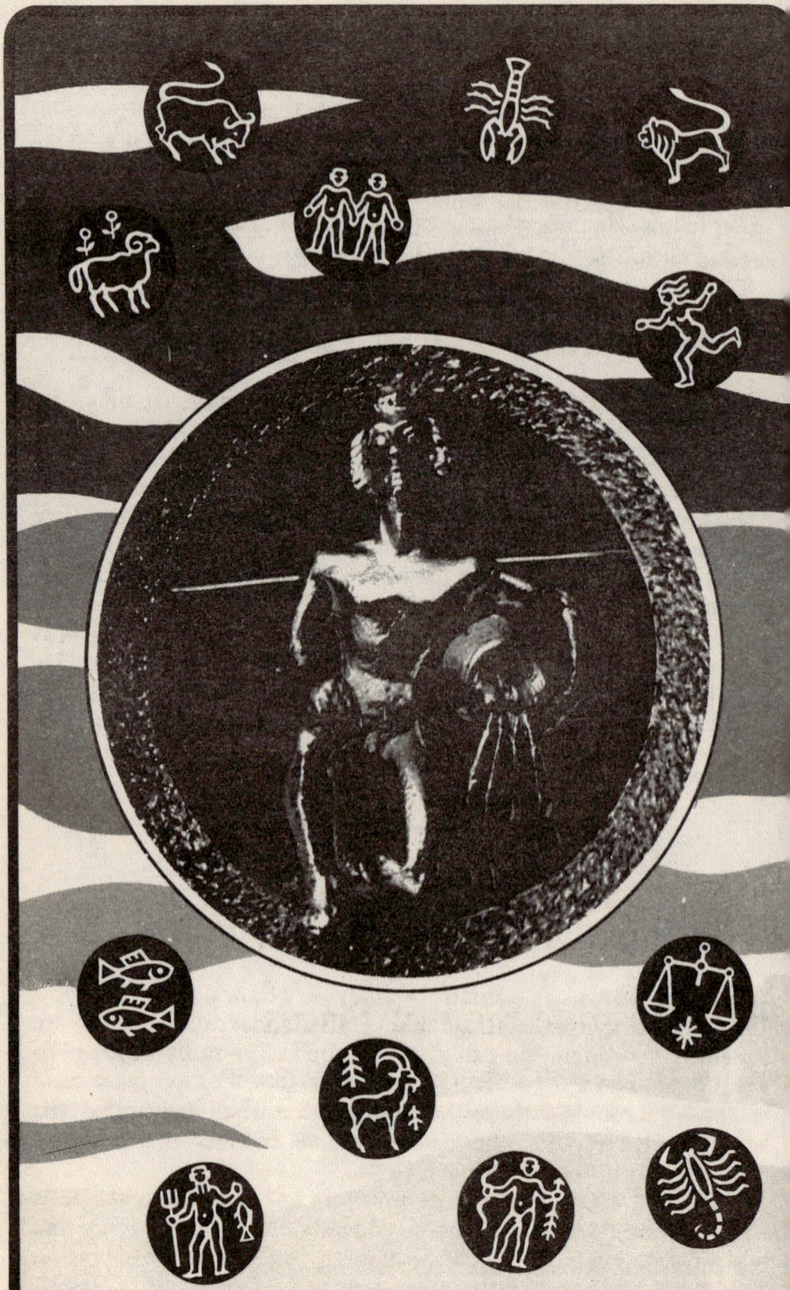

The person born under this sign is almost always an individualist. He does not believe in teaming up with the masses, but prefers going his own way. His ideas about life and mankind are often quite advanced. There is a saying to the effect that the average Aquarian is fifty years ahead of his time.

He is broadminded. The problems of the world concern him greatly. He is interested in helping others no matter what part of the globe they live in. He is truly a humanitarian sort. He likes to be of service to others.

Giving, considerate, and without prejudice, Aquarians have no trouble getting along with others.

The Negative Side of Aquarius

The Aquarian may be too much of a dreamer. He makes plans but seldom carries them out. He is rather unrealistic. His imagination has a tendency to run away with him. Because many of his plans are impractical, he is always in some sort of a dither.

Others may not approve of him at all times because of his unconventional behavior. He may be a bit eccentric. Sometimes he is so busy with his own thoughts, that he loses touch with the realities of existence.

Some Aquarians feel they are more clever and intelligent than others. They seldom admit to their own faults, even when they are quite apparent. Some become rather fanatic in their views. Their criticism of others is sometimes destructive and negative.

February 19–March 20

The Positive Side of Pisces

The Piscean can often understand the problems of others quite easily. He has a sympathetic nature. Kindly, he is often dedicated in the way he goes about helping others. The sick and the troubled often turn to him for advice and assistance.

He is very broadminded and does not criticize others for their faults. He knows how to accept people for what they are. On the whole, he is a trustworthy and earnest person. He is loyal to his

friends and will do what he can to help them in time of need. Generous and good-natured, he is a lover of peace; he is often willing to help others solve their differences. People who have taken a wrong turn in life often interest him and he will do what he can to persuade them to rehabilitate themselves.

He has a strong intuitive sense and most of the time he knows how to make it work for him; the Piscean is unusually perceptive and often knows what is bothering someone before that person, himself, is aware of it. The Pisces man or woman is an idealistic person, basically, and is interested in making the world a better place in which to live. The Piscean believes that everyone should help each other. He is willing to do more than his share in order to achieve cooperation with others.

The person born under this sign often is talented in music or art. He is a receptive person; he is able to take the ups and downs of life with philosophic calm.

The Negative Side of Pisces

Some Pisceans are often depressed; their outlook on life is rather glum. They may feel that they have been given a bad deal in life and that others are always taking unfair advantage of them. The Piscean sometimes feel that the world is a cold and cruel place. He is easily discouraged. He may even withdraw from the harshness of reality into a secret shell of his own where he dreams and idles away a good deal of his time.

The Piscean can be rather lazy. He lets things happen without giving the least bit of resistance. He drifts along, whether on the high road or on the low. He is rather short on willpower.

Some Pisces people seek escape through drugs or alcohol. When temptation comes along they find it hard to resist. In matters of sex, they can be rather permissive.

THE SIGNS AND THEIR KEY WORDS

		POSITIVE	NEGATIVE
ARIES	self	courage, initiative, pioneer instinct	brash rudeness, selfish impetuosity
TAURUS	money	endurance, loyalty, wealth	obstinacy, gluttony
GEMINI	mind	versatility	capriciousness, unreliability
CANCER	family	sympathy, homing instinct	clannishness, childishness
LEO	children	love, authority, integrity	egotism, force
VIRGO	work	purity, industry, analysis	fault-finding, cynicism
LIBRA	marriage	harmony, justice	vacillation, superficiality
SCORPIO	sex	survival, regeneration	vengeance, discord
SAGITTARIUS	travel	optimism, higher learning	lawlessness
CAPRICORN	career	depth	narrowness, gloom
AQUARIUS	friends	human fellowship, genius	perverse unpredictability
PISCES	confinement	spiritual love, universality	diffusion, escapism

THE ELEMENTS AND QUALITIES OF THE SIGNS

ELEMENT	SIGN	QUALITY	SIGN
FIRE	ARIES LEO SAGITTARIUS	CARDINAL	ARIES LIBRA CANCER CAPRICORN
EARTH	TAURUS VIRGO CAPRICORN	FIXED	TAURUS LEO SCORPIO AQUARIUS
AIR	GEMINI LIBRA AQUARIUS	MUTABLE	GEMINI VIRGO SAGITTARIUS PISCES
WATER	CANCER SCORPIO PISCES		

Every sign has both an element and a quality associated with it. The element indicates the basic makeup of the sign, and the quality describes the kind of activity associated with each.

Signs can be grouped together according to their *element* and *quality*. Signs of the same element share many basic traits in common. They tend to form stable configurations and ultimately harmonious relationships. Signs of the same quality are often less harmonious, but they share many dynamic potentials for growth as well as profound fulfillment.

THE FIRE SIGNS

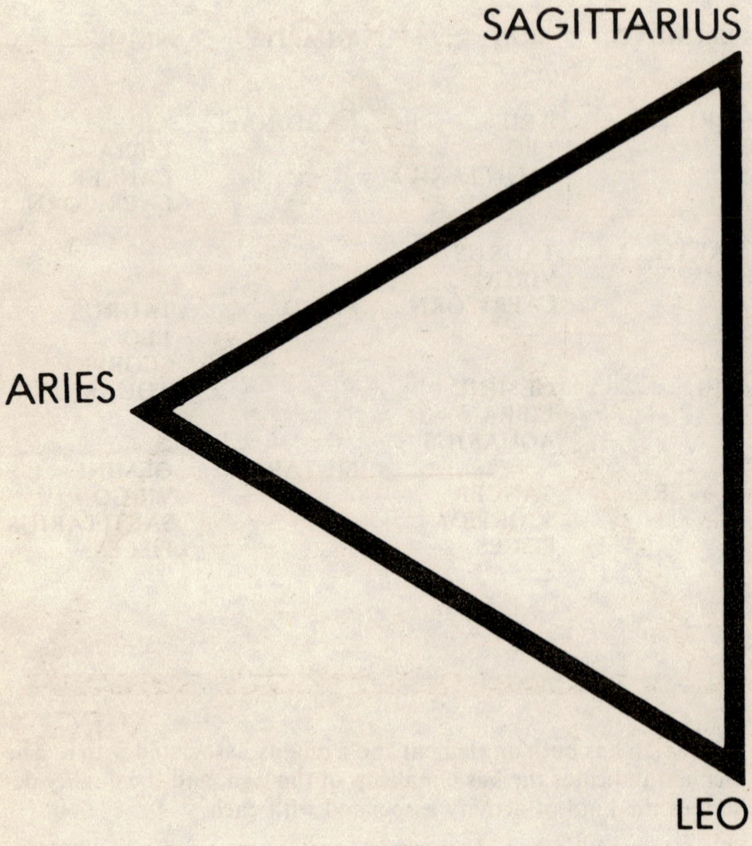

This is the fire group. On the whole these are emotional, volatile types, quick to anger, quick to forgive. They are adventurous, powerful people and act as a source of inspiration for everyone. They spark into action with immediate exuberant impulses. They are intelligent, self-involved, creative and idealistic. They all share a certain vibrancy and glow that outwardly reflects an inner flame and passion for living.

THE EARTH SIGNS

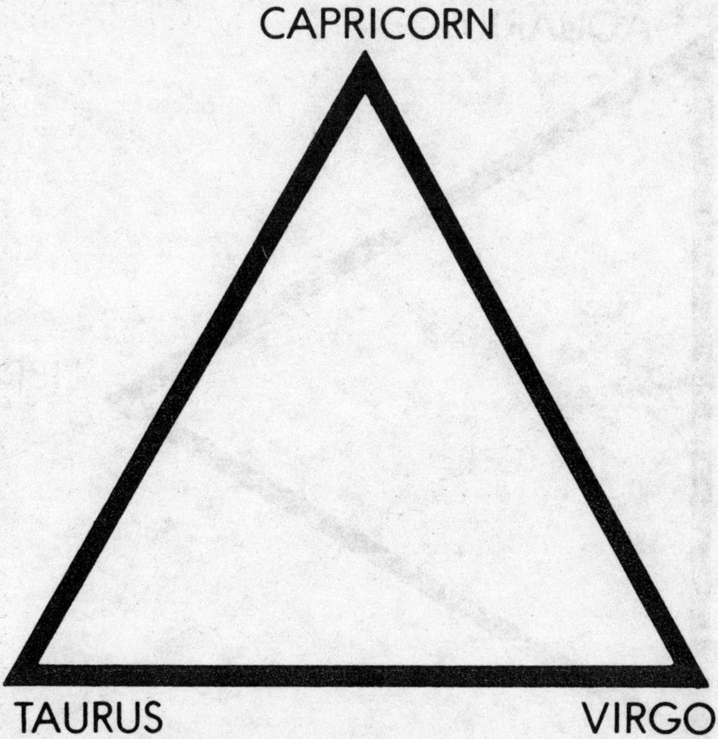

This is the earth group. They are in constant touch with the material world and tend to be conservative. Although they are all capable of spartan self-discipline, they are earthy, sensual people who are stimulated by the tangible, elegant and luxurious. The thread of their lives is always practical, but they do fantasize and are often attracted to dark, mysterious, emotional people. They are like great cliffs overhanging the sea, forever married to the ocean but always resisting erosion from the dark, emotional forces that thunder at their feet.

THE AIR SIGNS

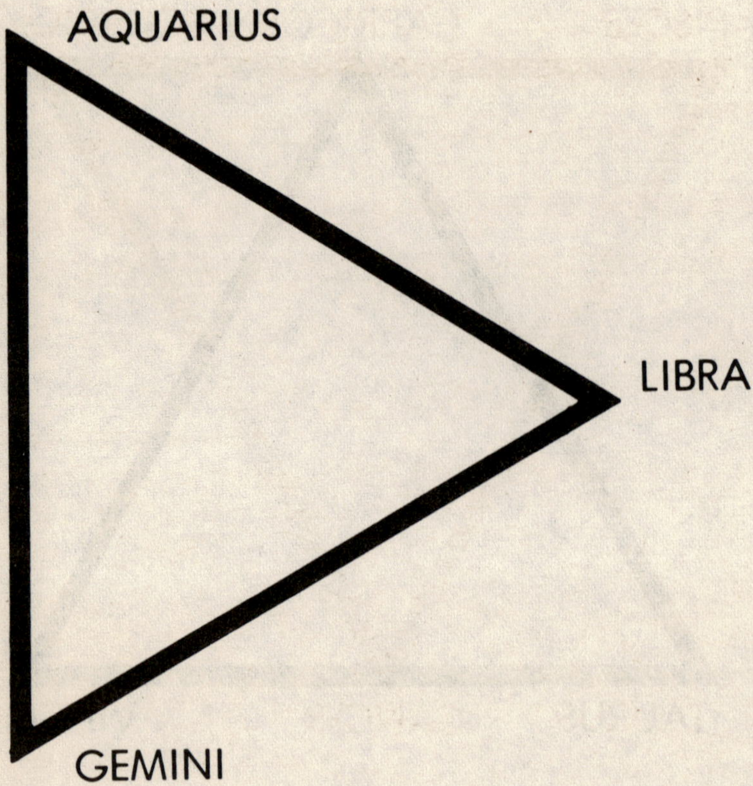

This is the air group. They are light, mental creatures desirous of contact, communication and relationship. They are involved with people and the forming of ties on many levels. Original thinkers, they are the bearers of human news. Their language is their sense of word, color, style and beauty. They provide an atmosphere suitable and pleasant for living. They add change and versatility to the scene, and it is through them that we can explore new territory of human intelligence and experience.

THE WATER SIGNS

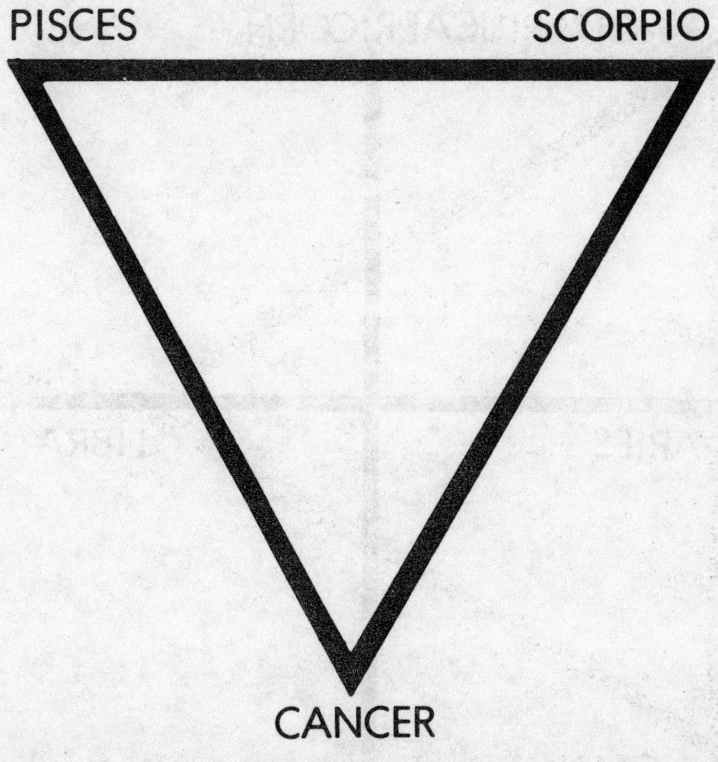

This is the water group. Through the water people, we are all joined together on emotional, non-verbal levels. They are silent, mysterious types whose magic hypnotizes even the most determined realist. They have uncanny perceptions about people and are as rich as the oceans when it comes to feeling, emotion or imagination. They are sensitive, mystical creatures with memories that go back beyond time. Through water, life is sustained. These people have the potential for the depths of darkness or the heights of mysticism and art.

THE CARDINAL SIGNS

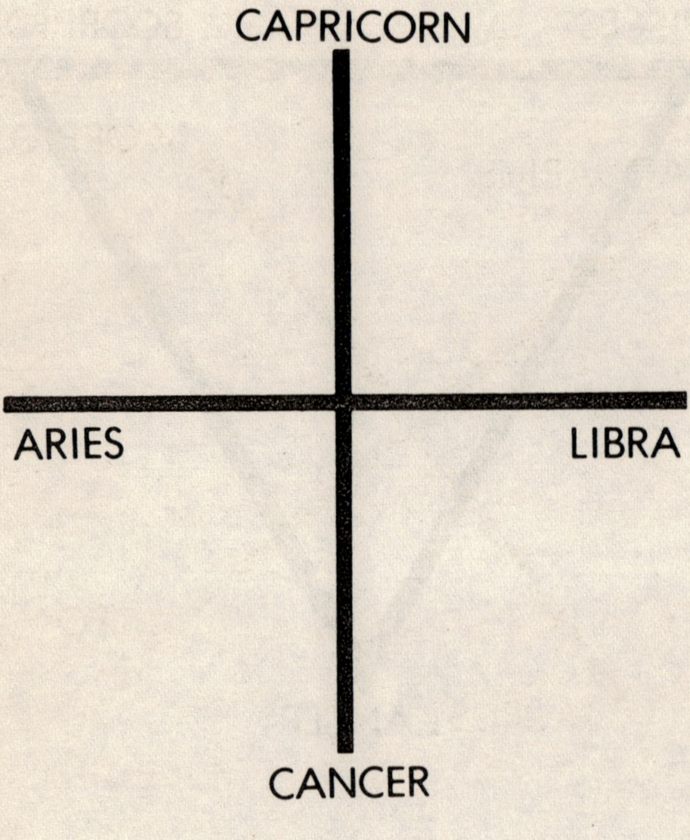

Put together, this is a clear-cut picture of dynamism, activity, tremendous stress and remarkable achievement. These people know the meaning of great change since their lives are often characterized by significant crises and major successes. This combination is like a simultaneous storm of summer, fall, winter and spring. The danger is chaotic diffusion of energy; the potential is irrepressible growth and victory.

THE FIXED SIGNS

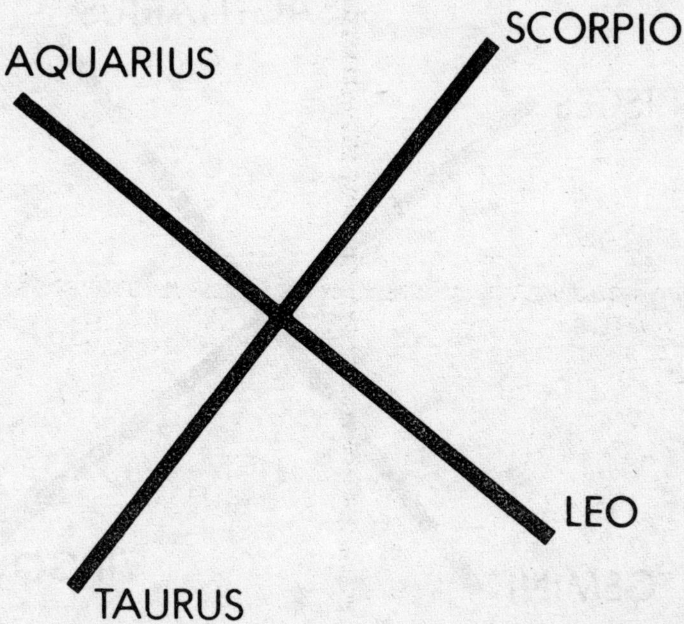

Fixed signs are always establishing themselves in a given place or area of experience. Like explorers who arrive and plant a flag, these people claim a position from which they do not enjoy being deposed. They are staunch, stalwart, upright, trusty, honorable people, although their obstinacy is well-known. Their contribution is fixity, and they are the angels who support our visible world.

THE MUTABLE SIGNS

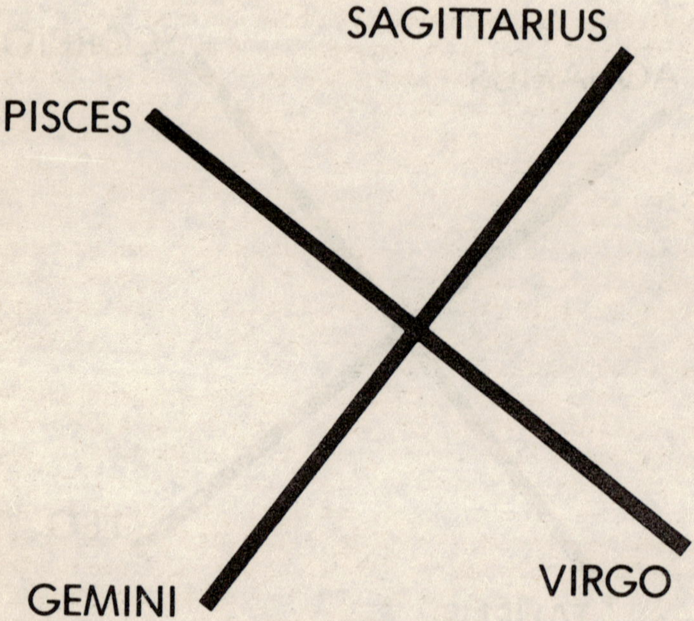

Mutable people are versatile, sensitive, intelligent, nervous and deeply curious about life. They are the translators of all energy. They often carry out or complete tasks initiated by others. Combinations of these signs have highly developed minds; they are imaginative and jumpy and think and talk a lot. At worst their lives are a Tower of Babel. At best they are adaptable and ready creatures who can assimilate one kind of experience and enjoy it while anticipating coming changes.

HOW TO APPROXIMATE YOUR RISING SIGN

Apart from the month and day of birth, the exact *time* of birth is another vital factor in the determination of an accurate horoscope. Not only do the planets move with great speed, but one must know how far the Earth has turned during the day. That way you can determine exactly where the planets are located with respect to the precise birthplace of an individual. This makes *your* horoscope *your* horoscope. In addition to these factors, another grid is laid upon that of the Zodiac and the planets: the houses. After all three have been considered, specific planetary relationships can be measured and analyzed in accordance with certain ordered procedures. It is the skillful translation of all this complex astrological language that a serious astrologer strives for in his attempt at coherent astrological synthesis. Keep this in mind.

The horoscope sets up a kind of framework around which the life of an individual grows like wild ivy, this way and that, weaving its way around the trellis of the natal positions of the planets. The year of birth tells us the positions of the distant, slow-moving planets like Jupiter, Saturn, Uranus and Pluto. The month of birth indicates the Sun sign, or birth sign as it is commonly called, as well as indicating the positions of the rapidly moving planets like Venus, Mercury and Mars. The day of birth locates the position of our Moon, and the moment of birth determines the houses through what is called the Ascendant, or Rising Sign.

As the Earth rotates on its axis once every 24 hours, each one of the twelve signs of the Zodiac appears to be "rising" on the horizon, with a new one appearing about every two hours. Actually it is the turning of the Earth that exposes each sign to view, but you will remember that in much of our astrological work we are discussing "apparent" motion. This *Rising Sign* marks the Ascendant and it colors the whole orientation of a horoscope. It indicates the sign governing the first house of the chart, and will thus determine which signs will govern all the other houses. The idea is a bit complicated at first, and we needn't dwell on complications in this introduction, but if you can imagine two color wheels with twelve divisions superimposed upon each other, one moving slowly and the other remaining still, you will have some idea of how the signs keep shifting the "color" of the houses as the Rising Sign continues to change every two hours.

The important point is that the birth chart, or horoscope, actually does define specific factors of a person's makeup. It contains a picture of being, much the way the nucleus of a tiny cell contains the potential for an entire elephant, or a packet of seeds contains a rosebush. If there were no order or continuity to the world, we could plant roses and get elephants. This same order that gives continuous flow to our lives often annoys people if it threatens to determine too much of their lives. We must grow from what we were planted, and there's no reason why we can't do that magnificently. It's all there in the horoscope. Where there is limitation, there is breakthrough; where there is crisis, there is transformation. Accurate analysis of a horoscope can help you find these points of breakthrough and transformation, and it requires knowledge of subtleties and distinctions that demand skillful judgment in order to solve even the simplest kind of personal question.

It is still quite possible, however, to draw some conclusions based upon the sign occupied by the Sun alone. In fact, if you're just being introduced to this vast subject, you're better off keeping it simple. Otherwise it seems like an impossible jumble, much like trying to read a novel in a foreign language without knowing the basic vocabulary. As with anything else, you can progress in your appreciation and understanding of astrology in direct proportion to your interest. To become really good at it requires study, experience, patience and above all—and maybe simplest of all—a fundamental understanding of what is actually going on right up there in the sky over your head. It is a vital living process you can observe, contemplate and ultimately understand. You can start by observing sunrise, or sunset, or even the full Moon.

In fact you can do a simple experiment after reading this introduction. You can erect a rough chart by following the simple procedure below:

1. Draw a circle with twelve equal segments.

2. Starting at what would be the nine o'clock position on a clock, number the segments, or houses, from 1 to 12 in a *counterclockwise direction.*

3. Label house number 1 in the following way: 4 A.M.-6 A.M.

4. In a counterclockwise direction, label the rest of the houses: 2 A.M.-4 A.M., MIDNIGHT-2 A.M., 10 P.M-MIDNIGHT, 8 P.M.-10 P.M., 6 P.M.-8 P.M., 4 P.M.-6 P.M., 2 P.M.-4 P.M., NOON-2 P.M., 10 A.M.-NOON, 8 A.M.-10 A.M., and 6 A.M.-8 A.M.

5. Now find out what time you were born and place the sun in the appropriate house.

6. Label the edge of that house with your Sun sign. You now have a description of your basic character and your fundamental drives. You can also see in what areas of life on Earth you will be most likely to focus your constant energy and center your activity.

7. If you are really feeling ambitious, label the rest of the houses with the signs, starting with your Sun sign, in order, still in a *counterclockwise direction.* When you get to Pisces, start over with Aries and keep going until you reach the house behind the Sun.

8. Look to house number 1. The sign that you have now labeled and attached to house number 1 is your Rising sign. It will color your self-image, outlook, physical constitution, early life and whole orientation to life. Of course this is a mere approximation, since there are many complicated calculations that must be made with respect to adjustments for birth time, but if you read descriptions of the sign preceding and the sign following the one you have calculated in the above manner, you may be able to identify yourself better. In any case, when you get through labeling all the houses, your drawing should look something like this:

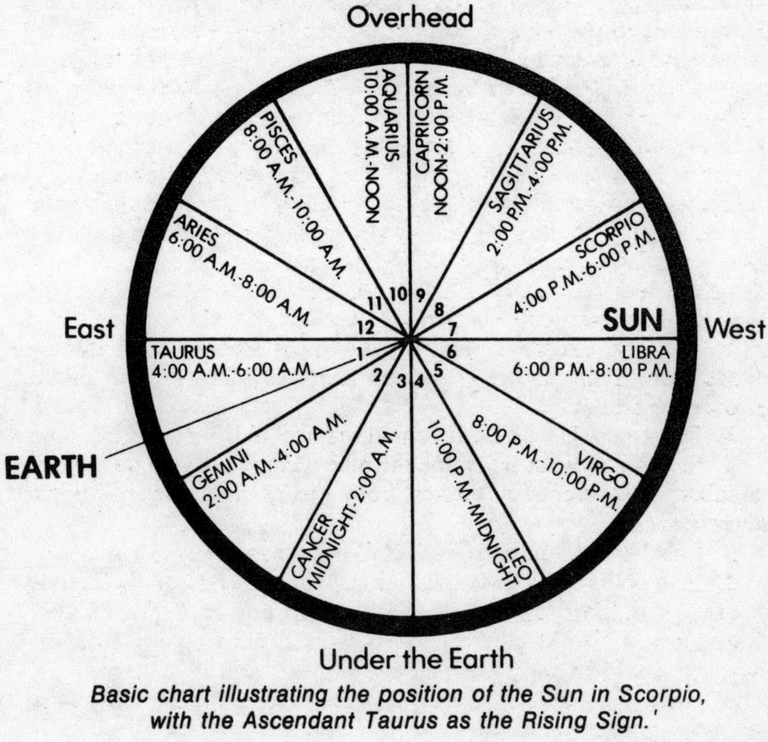

Basic chart illustrating the position of the Sun in Scorpio, with the Ascendant Taurus as the Rising Sign.'

This individual was born at 5:15 P.M. on October 31 in New York City. The Sun is in Scorpio and is found in the 7th house. The Rising sign, or the sign governing house number 1, is Taurus, so this person is a blend of Scorpio and Taurus.

Any further calculation would necessitate that you look in an ephemeris, or table of planetary motion, for the positions of the rest of the planets for your particular birth year. But we will take the time to define briefly all the known planets of our Solar System and the Sun to acquaint you with some more of the astrological vocabulary that you will be meeting again and again. (See page 21 for a full explanation of the Moon in all the Signs.)

THE PLANETS AND SIGNS THEY RULE

The signs of the Zodiac are linked to the planets in the following way. Each sign is governed or ruled by one or more planets. No matter where the planets are located in the sky at any given moment, they still rule their respective signs, and when they travel through the signs they rule, they have special dignity and their effects are stronger.

Following is a list of the planets and the signs they rule. After looking at the list, go back over the definitions of the planets and see if you can determine how the planet ruling *your* Sun sign has affected your life.

SIGNS	RULING PLANETS
Aries	Mars, Pluto
Taurus	Venus
Gemini	Mercury
Cancer	Moon
Leo	Sun
Virgo	Mercury
Libra	Venus
Scorpio	Mars, Pluto
Sagittarius	Jupiter
Capricorn	Saturn
Aquarius	Saturn, Uranus
Pisces	Jupiter, Neptune

THE PLANETS OF THE SOLAR SYSTEM

Here are the planets of the Solar System. They all travel around the Sun at different speeds and different distances. Taken with the Sun, they all distribute individual intelligence and ability throughout the entire chart.

The planets modify the influence of the Sun in a chart according to their own particular natures, strengths and positions. Their positions must be calculated for each year and day, and their function and expression in a horoscope will change as they move from one area of the Zodiac to another.

Following, you will find brief statements of their pure meanings.

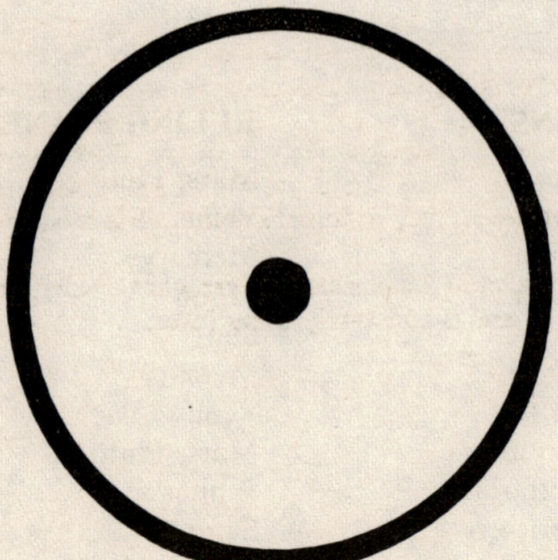

THE SUN

SUN

This is the center of existence. Around this flaming sphere all the planets revolve in endless orbits. Our star is constantly sending out its beams of light and energy without which no life on Earth would be possible. In astrology it symbolizes everything we are trying to become, the center around which all of our activity in life will always revolve. It is the symbol of our basic nature and describes the natural and constant thread that runs through everything that we do from birth to death on this planet.

To early astrologers, the sun seemed to be another planet because it crossed the heavens every day, just like the rest of the bodies in the sky.

It is the only star near enough to be seen well—it is, in fact, a dwarf star. Approximately 860,000 miles in diameter, it is about ten times as wide as the giant planet Jupiter. The next nearest star is nearly 300,000 times as far away, and if the Sun were located as far away as most of the bright stars, it would be too faint to be seen without a telescope.

Everything in the horoscope ultimately revolves around this singular body. Although other forces may be prominent in the charts of some individuals, still the Sun is the total nucleus of being and symbolizes the complete potential of every human being alive. It is vitality and the life force. Your whole essence comes from the position of the Sun.

You are always trying to express the Sun according to its position by house and sign. Possibility for all development is found in the Sun, and it marks the fundamental character of your personal radiations all around you.

It is the symbol of strength, vigor, wisdom, dignity, ardor and generosity, and the ability for a person to function as a mature individual. It is also a creative force in society. It is consciousness of the gift of life.

The underdeveloped solar nature is arrogant, pushy, undependable and proud, and is constantly using force.

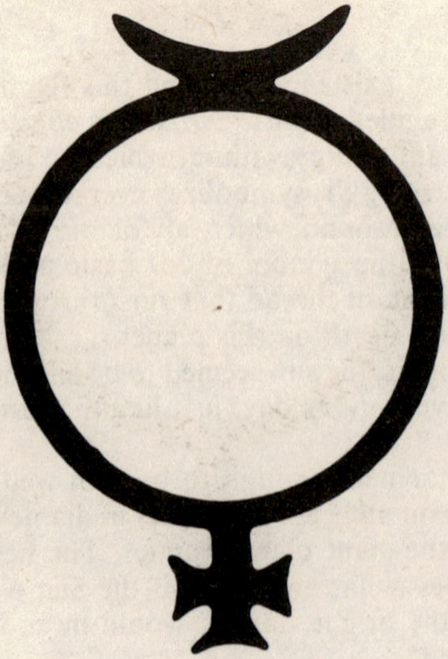

MERCURY

Mercury is the planet closest to the Sun. It races around our star, gathering information and translating it to the rest of the system. Mercury represents your capacity to understand the desires of your own will and to translate those desires into action.

In other words it is the planet of Mind and the power of communication. Through Mercury we develop an ability to think, write, speak and observe—to become aware of the world around us. It colors our attitudes and vision of the world, as well as our capacity to communicate our inner responses to the outside world. Some people who have serious disabilities in their power of verbal communication have often wrongly been described as people lacking intelligence.

Although this planet (and its position in the horoscope) indicates your power to communicate your thoughts and perceptions to the world, intelligence is something deeper. Intelligence is distributed throughout all the planets. It is the relationship of the planets to each other that truly describes what we call intelligence. Mercury rules speaking, language, mathematics, draft and design, students, messengers, young people, offices, teachers and any pursuits where the mind of man has wings.

VENUS

Venus is beauty. It symbolizes the harmony and radiance of a rare and elusive quality: beauty itself. It is refinement and delicacy, softness and charm. In astrology it indicates grace, balance and the aesthetic sense. Where Venus is we see beauty, a gentle drawing in of energy and the need for satisfaction and completion. It is a special touch that finishes off rough edges. It is sensitivity, and affection, and it is always the place for that other elusive phenomenon: love. Venus describes our sense of what is beautiful and loving. Poorly developed, it is vulgar, tasteless and self-indulgent. But its ideal is the flame of spiritual love—Aphrodite, goddess of love, and the sweetness and power of personal beauty.

MARS

This is raw, crude energy. The planet next to Earth but outward from the Sun is a fiery red sphere that charges through the horoscope with force and fury. It represents the way you reach out for new adventure and new experience. It is energy and drive, initiative, courage and daring. The power to start something and see it through. It can be thoughtless, cruel and wild, angry and hostile, causing cuts, burns, scalds and wounds. It can stab its way through a chart, or it can be the symbol of healthy spirited adventure, well-channeled constructive power to begin and keep up the drive. If you have trouble starting things, if you lack the get-up-and-go to start the ball rolling, if you lack aggressiveness and self-confidence, chances are there's another planet influencing your Mars. Mars rules soldiers, butchers, surgeons, salesmen—any field that requires daring, bold skill, operational technique or self-promotion.

JUPITER

This is the largest planet of the Solar System. Scientists have recently learned that Jupiter reflects more light than it receives from the Sun. In a sense it is like a star itself. In astrology it rules good luck and good cheer, health, wealth, optimism, happiness, success and joy. It is the symbol of opportunity and always opens the way for new possibilities in your life. It rules exuberance, enthusiasm, wisdom, knowledge, generosity and all forms of expansion in general. It rules actors, statesmen, clerics, professional people, religion, publishing and the distribution of many people over large areas.

Sometimes Jupiter makes you think you deserve everything, and you become sloppy, wasteful, careless and rude, prodigal and lawless, in the illusion that nothing can ever go wrong. Then there is the danger of over-confidence, exaggeration, undependability and over-indulgence.

Jupiter is the minimization of limitation and the emphasis on spirituality and potential. It is the thirst for knowledge and higher learning.

SATURN

Saturn circles our system in dark splendor with its mysterious rings, forcing us to be awakened to whatever we have neglected in the past. It will present real puzzles and problems to be solved, causing delays, obstacles and hindrances. By doing so, Saturn stirs our own sensitivity to those areas where we are laziest.

Here we must patiently develop *method,* and only through painstaking effort can our ends be achieved. It brings order to a horoscope and imposes reason just where we are feeling least reasonable. By creating limitations and boundary, Saturn shows the consequences of being human and demands that we accept the changing cycles inevitable in human life. Saturn rules time, old age and sobriety. It can bring depression, gloom, jealousy and greed, or serious acceptance of responsibilities out of which success will develop. With Saturn there is nothing to do but face facts. It rules laborers, stones, granite, rocks and crystals of all kinds.

The Outer Planets

The following three are the outer planets. They liberate human beings from cultural conditioning, and in that sense are the law breakers. In early times it was thought that Saturn was the last planet of the system—the outer limit beyond which we could never go. The discovery of the next three planets ushered in new phases of human history, revolution and technology.

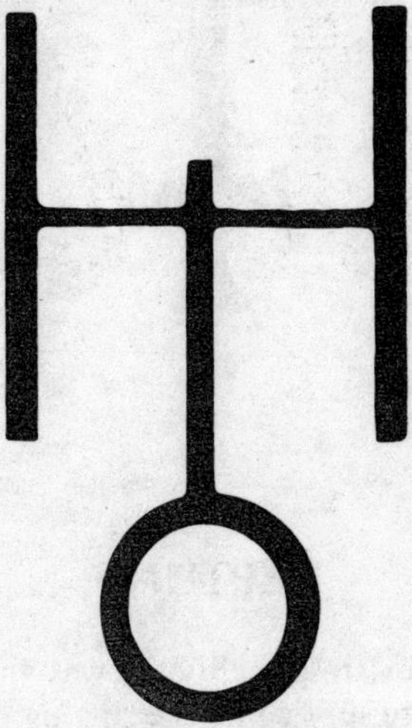

URANUS

Uranus rules unexpected change, upheaval, revolution. It is the symbol of total independence and asserts the freedom of an individual from all restriction and restraint. It is a breakthrough planet and indicates talent, originality and genius in a horoscope. It usually causes last-minute reversals and changes of plan, unwanted separations, accidents, catastrophes and eccentric behavior. It can add irrational rebelliousness and perverse bohemianism to a personality or a streak of unaffected brilliance in science and art. It rules technology, aviation and all forms of electrical and electronic advancement. It governs great leaps forward and topsy-turvy situations, and *always* turns things around at the last minute. Its effects are difficult to ever really predict, since it rules sudden last-minute decisions and events that come like lightning out of the blue.

NEPTUNE

Neptune dissolves existing reality the way the sea erodes the cliffs beside it. Its effects are subtle like the ringing of a buoy's bell in the fog. It suggests a reality higher than definition can usually describe. It awakens a sense of higher responsibility often causing guilt, worry, anxieties or delusions. Neptune is associated with all forms of escape and can make things seem a certain way so convincingly that you are absolutely sure of something that eventually turns out to be quite different.

It is the planet of illusion and therefore governs the invisible realms that lie beyond our ordinary minds, beyond our simple factual ability to prove what is "real." Treachery, deceit, disillusionment and disappointment are linked to Neptune. It describes a vague reality that promises eternity and the divine, yet in a manner so complex that we cannot really fathom it at all. At its worst Neptune is a cheap intoxicant; at its best it is the poetry, music and inspiration of the higher planes of spiritual love. It has dominion over movies, photographs and much of the arts.

PLUTO

Pluto lies at the outpost of our system and therefore rules finality in a horoscope—the final closing of chapters in your life, the passing of major milestones and points of development from which there is no return. It is a final wipeout, a closeout, an evacuation. It is a distant, subtle but powerful catalyst in all transformations that occur. It creates, destroys, then recreates. Sometimes Pluto starts its influence with a minor event or insignificant incident that might even go unnoticed. Slowly but surely, little by little, everything changes, until at last there has been a total transformation in the area of your life where Pluto has been operating. It rules mass thinking and the trends that society first rejects, then adopts and finally outgrows.

Pluto rules the dead and the underworld—all the powerful forces of creation and destruction that go on all the time beneath, around and above us. It can bring a lust for power with strong obsessions.

It is the planet that rules the metamorphoses of the caterpillar into a butterfly, for it symbolizes the capacity to change totally and forever a person's life style, way of thought and behavior.

FAMOUS PERSONALITIES

ARIES: Hans Christian Andersen, Pearl Bailey, Marlon Brando, Wernher Von Braun, Charlie Chaplin, Joan Crawford, Da Vinci, Bette Davis, Doris Day, W. C. Fields, Alec Guinness, Adolf Hitler, William Holden, Thomas Jefferson, Nikita Khrushchev, Elton John, Arturo Toscanini, J. P. Morgan, Paul Robeson, Gloria Steinem, Lowell Thomas, Vincent van Gogh, Tennessee Williams

TAURUS: Fred Astaire, Charlote Brontë, Carol Burnett, Irving Berlin, Bing Crosby, Salvador Dali, Tchaikovsky, Queen Elizabeth II, Duke Ellington, Ella Fitzgerald, Henry Fonda, Sigmund Freud, Orson Welles, Joe Louis, Lenin, Karl Marx, Golda Meir, Eva Peron, Bertrand Russell, Shakespeare, Kate Smith, Benjamin Spock, Barbra Streisand, Shirley Temple, Harry Truman

GEMINI: Mikhail Baryshnikov, Boy George, Igor Stravinsky, Carlos Chavez, Walt Whitman, Bob Dylan, Ralph Waldo Emerson, Judy Garland, Paul Gauguin, Allen Ginsberg, Benny Goodman, Bob Hope, Burl Ives, John F. Kennedy, Peggy Lee, Marilyn Monroe, Joe Namath, Cole Porter, Laurence Olivier, Harriet Beecher Stowe, Queen Victoria, John Wayne, Frank Lloyd Wright

CANCER: "Dear Abby," David Brinkley, Yul Brynner, Pearl Buck, Marc Chagall, Jack Dempsey, Mildred (Babe) Zaharias, Mary Baker Eddy, Henry VIII, John Glenn, Ernest Hemingway, Lena Horne, Oscar Hammerstein, Helen Keller, Ann Landers, George Orwell, Nancy Reagan, Rembrandt, Richard Rodgers, Ginger Rogers, Rubens, Jean-Paul Sartre, O. J. Simpson

LEO: Neil Armstrong, Russell Baker, James Baldwin, Emily Brontë, Wilt Chamberlain, Julia Child, Cecil B. De Mille, Ogden Nash, Amelia Earhart, Edna Ferber, Arthur Goldberg, Dag Hammarskjöld, Alfred Hitchcock, Mick Jagger, George Meany, George Bernard Shaw, Napoleon, Jacqueline Onassis, Henry Ford, Francis Scott Key, Andy Warhol, Mae West, Orville Wright

VIRGO: Ingrid Bergman, Warren Burger, Maurice Chevalier, Agatha Christie, Sean Connery, Lafayette, Peter Falk, Greta Garbo, Althea Gibson, Arthur Godfrey, Goethe, Buddy Hackett, Michael Jackson, Lyndon Johnson, D. H. Lawrence, Sophia Loren, Grandma Moses, Arnold Palmer, Queen Elizabeth I, Walter Reuther, Peter Sellers, Lily Tomlin, George Wallace

LIBRA: Brigitte Bardot, Art Buchwald, Truman Capote, Dwight D. Eisenhower, William Faulkner, F. Scott Fitzgerald, Gandhi, George Gershwin, Micky Mantle, Helen Hayes, Vladimir Horowitz, Doris Lessing, Martina Navratalova, Eugene O'Neill, Luciano Pavarotti, Emily Post, Eleanor Roosevelt, Bruce Springsteen, Margaret Thatcher, Gore Vidal, Barbara Walters, Oscar Wilde

SCORPIO: Vivien Leigh, Richard Burton, Art Carney, Johnny Carson, Billy Graham, Grace Kelly, Walter Cronkite, Marie Curie, Charles de Gaulle, Linda Evans, Indira Gandhi, Theodore Roosevelt, Rock Hudson, Katherine Hepburn, Robert F. Kennedy, Billie Jean King, Martin Luther, Georgia O'Keeffe, Pablo Picasso, Jonas Salk, Alan Shepard, Robert Louis Stevenson

SAGITTARIUS: Jane Austen, Louisa May Alcott, Woody Allen, Beethoven, Willy Brandt, Mary Martin, William F. Buckley, Maria Callas, Winston Churchill, Noel Coward, Emily Dickinson, Walt Disney, Benjamin Disraeli, James Doolittle, Kirk Douglas, Chet Huntley, Jane Fonda, Chris Evert Lloyd, Margaret Mead, Charles Schulz, John Milton, Frank Sinatra, Steven Spielberg

CAPRICORN: Muhammad Ali, Isaac Asimov, Pablo Casals, Dizzy Dean, Marlene Dietrich, James Farmer, Ava Gardner, Barry Goldwater, Cary Grant, J. Edgar Hoover, Howard Hughes, Joan of Arc, Gypsy Rose Lee, Martin Luther King, Jr., Rudyard Kipling, Mao Tse-tung, Richard Nixon, Gamal Nasser, Louis Pasteur, Albert Schweitzer, Stalin, Benjamin Franklin, Elvis Presley

AQUARIUS: Marian Anderson, Susan B. Anthony, Jack Benny, Charles Darwin, Charles Dickens, Thomas Edison, John Barrymore, Clark Gable, Jascha Heifetz, Abraham Lincoln, John McEnroe, Yehudi Menuhin, Mozart, Jack Nicklaus, Ronald Reagan, Jackie Robinson, Norman Rockwell, Franklin D. Roosevelt, Gertrude Stein, Charles Lindbergh, Margaret Truman

PISCES: Edward Albee, Harry Belafonte, Alexander Graham Bell, Frank Borman, Chopin, Adelle Davis, Albert Einstein, Jackie Gleason, Winslow Homer, Edward M. Kennedy, Victor Hugo, Mike Mansfield, Michelangelo, Edna St. Vincent Millay, Liza Minelli, John Steinbeck, Linus Pauling, Ravel, Diana Ross, William Shirer, Elizabeth Taylor, George Washington

LIBRA

CHARACTER ANALYSIS

People born under the sign of Libra are generally quite kind and sympathetic. They dislike seeing others suffer and do what they can to help those in dire straits. Another outstanding characteristic of a Libran is his love of harmony and beauty. He generally has a deep appreciation for all forms of art. He only feels comfortable in places that radiate harmony and beauty. He is often willing to make sacrifices in order to make his environment more suited to his tastes.

Librans like people. They are often afraid of being alone. They love company. Others like them for their charm and gentle ways. They are happiest when with others. A Libran alone is likely to fall into a depressed state rather easily. Being with others help him to keep his spirits up even during difficult moments. A Libran rarely goes through life alone. He is fond of permanent and reliable relationships. Often he marries early in life.

His is a kind and gentle nature. He would never go out of his way to hurt someone. He is considerate of others' feelings. He will always keep up his end of a bargain. He is cooperative and courteous—sometimes to a fault.

The Libra man or woman is someone who is constantly weighing both sides of a problem. He is a difficult person to satisfy. He wants to make sure that he is right in all the decisions he makes. He may take his time before making a decision. He may even change his mind several times. Balance is important to someone born under this sign. Outwardly, the Libran is calm and intelligent. His interest in harmony extends to his social relationships. He seldom holds a grudge. He may not remember things very easily—especially unpleasant things. He forgives and forgets.

Both men and women born under this sign are a bit soft in their dispositions. Sometimes others take advantage of this. The Libra person searches for a world where all things are beautiful and well-balanced—a place where harmony reigns. The Libran—because such a search would be useless in the real world—is given to daydreaming and flights of fancy. The harshness he is sometimes apt to meet in life makes him unhappy. He may have a rather intricate fantasy world where he retreats when the going gets too rough.

He is a gentle, easy-going person. Librans seldom go where they know they are not wanted. Their interest in beauty and art leads them along the less troublesome and conflicting roads of life.

The Libran can often achieve what he wants through friendly persuasion. Because of his calm, others often find him a port in a storm. He will tell people what he knows they want to hear in order to bolster their confidence and to avoid unpleasantness. He is tactful and knows how to use his gentleness to his own advantage; others may try to take advantage of him, but when he has his wits about him, this is rather difficult. Even when others think they see through him, they find him a difficult nut to crack. He is so strong in his ways of persuasion that he is almost never undermined.

The Libra man or woman is even-tempered generally, but he can flare up when cornered. Still and all, he cools off quite rapidly and is willing to let bygones be bygones. The Libran understands others quite deeply because of his sympathetic nature; it is quite easy for him to put himself in another's place. He is considerate of other people's opinions no matter how wrong they may seem.

The Libran is fair-minded. He dislikes it when someone is mistreated or cheated out of a chance that is rightfully his. Injustice infuriates him. In all matters, he tries to make the right decision. He may take his time about coming to a conclusion.

In most social affairs, the Libran is quite popular and charming. People like him because of his pleasantness and easy-going ways. Most Librans have a lot of friends. All kinds of people attract him. He seldom makes preferences on a superficial basis.

Harmony plays an important part in the life of every Libran. He will try to preserve it at all costs. Harsh realities disturb the Libra man or woman so that he is at times given to lying in order to preserve peace and harmony.

Health

Librans are generally well-groomed and graceful. Their features, for the most part, are small. He is interested in maintaining good health and would never do anything that might encourage illness—even in a slight way. Quite often the man or woman born under this sign is not terribly vigorous and may require lots of rest in order to feel fit. Although he may never say no to a social obligation, the Libran often tires quickly as a result of them. If he does not have his proper rest, he is easily irritated.

Still, the Libran is built well and strongly. In spite of this, he is not what you could really call a strong person. His resistance is not always what it should be; often he falls ill before others when colds are going around. Still, he has remarkable powers of recovery and does not stay out of commission for very long. In spite of the fact that he is delicate, he is surprisingly resilient.

The weakest points of a Libran's body are his kidneys, spine, and loins. When he does fall ill, one of these three points is often affected.

Libra women are often remarkably beautiful. They seldom have problems attracting the opposite sex. Their voices are generally soft and their eyes lively.

Even though the Libra man may not look terribly strong he is often capable of handling work that would exhaust someone who is bigger or seemingly more vigorous. They often know how to use what strength they have to effective advantage.

All in all, the Libra person is good-natured and easy-going. He may, however, become somewhat out of sorts if he is ill. Being sick tends to make him finicky and ill-humored. He likes sympathy when he is in this condition and when his whims are not satisfied he is likely to complain about being neglected or unloved.

Occupation

The Libra man or woman is usually pleasant to work with. He likes to cooperate with others. He will not oppose authority unless he feels that it is unjust. The Libran is flexible. It is not difficult for him to shift from one phase of an operation to another. Environment may have an uncommonly strong influence on the Libran; it may spur him on to greater heights or slow him down. Sometimes he needs to be inspired by the activities of those working in his immediate vicinity. He will sometimes look at the other fellow to see how he is working before he begins on his own.

The Libra person likes to work in pleasant surroundings. He abhors filth and disorder. He does what he can to bring about the working conditions that are best suited to his nature. Libra people are not attracted to work that is likely to be strenuous or untidy.

Libra people make good business partners. They are quite good at making the proper decisions at the right time. The person born under this sign knows how to weigh the pros and cons of an argument or problem. People often turn to him to make the right decision. Others find it easy to believe in his powers for reasoning. He seldom makes a wrong move. He can always be relied upon to do what is proper.

On the whole the Libran is rather moderate or conservative in most things; this stems from his desire to avoid extremes —especially if they are apt to bring about controversy. Secrets are safe with the Libran, especially if they might do someone some harm.

The person born under this sign is often quite intelligent. He has the ability to reason well and to analyze. Philosophical argument does not frighten him and he can hold his own in almost any intellectual debate. He has a talent for objectivity; he can put himself in another's shoes quite easily. As a mediator he is excellent. People born under this sign also make good diplomats.

He can view things calmly when necessary. He is not easily swayed by his emotions if the truth or justice is at stake. He wants what is good for everybody concerned. He tends to look at things the way they are. He is not one to make a mountain out of a molehill. In moments of confusion, his mind is as clear as a bell. In law, the Libran can often be of service to many. He makes a competent judge or lawyer. He knows how to criticize without hurting and, therefore, he could do well as a reviewer of plays or books. Some Librans turn out to be admirable scientists and physicists.

Most Librans are good in creative matters. Anything to do with art or aesthetics appeals to them most of the time. Some of them make good painters, writers, or musicians. The person under this sign sometimes ignores surges of inspiration when they overcome him for fear of being too self-indulgent, but the strong Libran knows how to seize these moments to further his aims and interests. Some of the greatest painters in the world were born under the sign of Libra.

Because the Libra person is good at persuasion, he makes an invaluable salesman. He is in possession of so much charm that his customers often buy more than they originally intended. Because of their rare beauty, Libra women often do well in the field of modeling or acting.

The Libran is capable of spending more money than he actually has. During his lifetime, great sums are apt to come into his hand. He does not care too much about money, though. He is generous to a fault, and finds it hard to refuse people who claim they are in need. The Libran usually has expensive tastes. He finds it hard to save money. Because he likes people and a busy social life, the person born under this sign often spends considerable sums in entertainment. Luxuries are as important to him at times as necessities are to someone else.

In spite of his light ways with money, the Libran is no fool. He knows well how to discourage someone who is only interested in him for his finances.

Home and Family

Home is important to the average Libran. It must be a place where he can relax and feel comfortable. It must radiate charm, beauty, and harmony. A popular person, the Libra man or woman loves to entertain. Nothing excites him more than company of good friends and acquaintances. He usually makes a good host; he knows how to put his guests at ease. People like to visit him because of his charming and easy-going ways.

The furnishings in a Libran's home are usually of excellent taste. They like ornamental furnishings; things that are often a bit ostentatious. No Libra home is without its paintings or pieces of sculpture. The Libra woman is often excellent at interior decorating. She may have a habit of changing the interior of her house quite often.

The Libra person is refined in nature and is not fond of getting his hands soiled. He'd rather leave the rough tasks for others to do. If he has money enough he'll see to it that someone comes to the house several times a week to clean up after him. There are always flowers and plants in the Libra home. In general, he is fond of light gardening.

There is usually a definite relationship between the Libra woman and her home. It usually complements or supplements her charm and personality.

The person born under this sign is generally a good parent. He or she does what he can to bring up the offspring properly. He never tries to influence his children unnecessarily. He lets them develop along natural lines, never forcing them into a mold he has designed. One thing a Libran respects in a child is originality and individuality. The Libran parent is far from strict, yet his children seldom turn out spoiled. The Libra mother or father will correct or punish whenever it is absolutely necessary. Most of the time, the children listen to him because of his calm sure way. They have faith in their Libra parent and usually respect his judgement. Children like being with Libra adults because in them they have a sympathetic friend—someone who can understand their point of view.

Librans as children are often happy and friendly. Parents find them ideal because they are so agreeable and cooperative. They never challenge their parents' authority and do what is expected of them most of the time. Libra children are often creative. Whenever they show signs of artistic ability they should be encouraged. Some of them are great daydreamers at school and have to be encouraged and inspired in order to do their best.

Social Relationships

The Libra man or woman usually makes a good friend because of his even disposition and easy-going ways. Others turn to him in time of need. He always is able to advise someone in a helpful manner. Generally he is honest and sincere in his dealings with his associates and friends. However, the Libra person may feel a bit envious if his friends have things that are nicer than his. Librans do not enjoy being alone and perhaps this is the reason they are so friendly. They enjoy being popular and well-liked. They seldom disappoint people who believe in them. All in all, they are quite cooperative and easy to get along with. They can be counted on to do the right thing at all times.

The person born under this sign usually becomes angry rather quickly. However, he quickly gets over it and is willing to kiss and make up within a short time after his explosion. Whatever he does he will try to avoid hurting someone else's feelings. He is not cruel or petty. That is not his nature.

The Libra person is a good conversationalist. Often at parties he's the center of attention. People generally have the impression that he is well-informed and rather aristocratic. At times he is upset or disturbed but does what he can not to let it show.

LOVE AND MARRIAGE

In matters of love and romance, the Libran is without equal. He is usually well up on everything that has to do with romance. Love is important to him. He is affectionate and gentle—considerate of his mate or lover.

At times, the Libra man or woman may be uncertain of his feelings. He may go through a series of love affairs before he really knows what he is looking for in a mate. He is rather fickle. He can be quite passionate in a love affair, then some days later break it off or lose interest for no apparent reason. It is just one of Libra's ways—difficult as it may be to understand.

He is easily attracted to members of the opposite sex and enjoys their company immensely. Others find his charm difficult to resist. Some people born under this seventh sign of the Zodiac are somewhat sentimental and are easily moved; this quality often appeals to their lovers or admirers. When he desires to transfer his affection he usually does so with much tact and consideration.

Librans are often passionate lovers in spite of their calm and gentle ways. Their calm fronts often hide a hot temperament. When in love he'll forsake his usual lamb-like ways for those of a lion.

The Libra woman expects to be handled with kid gloves by the man who professes to love her. She enjoys small courtesies and enjoys having things done for her.

Libra people are generally quite well suited for marriage or permanent love relationships. Although they may go from one romance to the other quite easily, what they are always in search of is permanent union. They are quite domestic by nature and enjoy setting up house and attending to family affairs. Some of them marry quite young. Although they may not be faithful at all times, they are honest in their intention of being steadfast.

The Libra person enjoys homelife. A place for entertaining and sharing the company of those he loves, the home is something rather special for him. He is usually a very considerate partner. His mate may find it a difficult task keeping up with him. His ease in social relationships is a quality that is rare to come by.

In spite of an occasional post-marital fling that he may find difficult to pass up from time to time, the Libran shuns all thoughts of divorce or separation. He does what he can to keep his marriage together and will try to keep his more serious faults to himself. He is not likely to be open about his indiscretions with his mate for fear of upsetting her and the relationship.

Romance and the Libra Woman

Libra women are quite passionate and affectionate. Most of them possess a mysterious charm which makes them much in demand with the opposite sex. The Libra woman is never short of admirers. She may have a difficult time trying to make up her mind about which one to settle down with, but she does what she can to enjoy herself during her state of indecision. She may go from one affair to the other without any regrets or misgivings. Others may accuse her of being a great flirt, but in all love relationships she is quite sincere. She is changeable though and impulsive and this makes it hard for her to be consistent in her affections at times.

The Libra woman adjusts to married life very well. When she has found the right man she is willing to do all she can to keep their life a peaceful and harmonious one. In spite of her inclination to flirt, the Libra woman usually remains faithful after she has married. At times, she may find herself strongly attracted to another man but she knows how to control herself and would do nothing that might jeopardize her marriage.

The Libra woman is usually poised and charming—in a rather standoffish way; underneath, however, she may be very passionate and loving. Her husband may find her more romantic than he expected. She is the kind of woman most men adore. There is something helpless yet seductive about her. She is not the sort of woman who would like to wear the pants in the family. She is only too glad to let someone else manage everything; she likes being taken care of.

Although she may seem terribly dependent and clinging, when the situations calls for her to take things over, she can do this quite ably. She's the kind of a woman who generally gets things her own way; her charm and beauty are indeed irresistible.

The Libra woman makes an ideal wife. She knows how to arrange things in a home so that they radiate peace, harmony, and beauty. When guests arrive, she knows how to make them fee comfortable immediately. She makes an excellent hostess. Her husband is apt to find her an invaluable companion. He can discuss things with her at his ease. The Libra woman is quite intelligent and has no difficulty in discussing matters that many women fail to understand or master.

She is a lover of a busy social life; however, she would be willing to give up all the glitter and laughter of party going if it interfered with her duties as a wife or mother.

The Libra woman makes an understanding mother. It is important to her that her children get a chance to develop their real personalities. She is quite persuasive in a gentle way.

Her tastes are rather expensive. She may run up bills without giving it much thought. If her husband can afford her extravagance, chances are he won't complain. He is apt to feel that his charming wife is worth the extra expense.

Romance and the Libra Man

Libra men have no trouble at all in attracting members of the opposite sex. Women find them charming and handsome. They are usually quite considerate of their women friends and know how to make them feel important and loved. The Libra man is quite a lover. He is not at a loss when it comes to romancing, for he finds love one of the most important things there is about life.

One fault, however, is the Libra man's ability to change from one love to another with appalling ease. He is always sincere in his love interests, but sometimes he finds it difficult to remain in love with the same person for a long period of time.

Women like him because he seems to know what is right; he never does the wrong thing, no matter what the occasion. His interest in the arts and such matters impress women. His sensitivity is another quality they often admire. The Libra man does not stint when it comes to demonstrating his affection for the woman he believes he loves; however, he is quite crestfallen if the woman should indicate that she is not ready to reciprocate.

Once he settles down, the Libra man makes a good husband and father. He is well suited to family life. Home is important to him. He likes to entertain close friends and relatives frequently. He is generally a very considerate and lively host. It is important that the Libra man find the right woman for his married life. If he has selected someone who finds it difficult to show the same interest in him that he shows in her, he will begin to look elsewhere for companionship. However, he is interested in having stability in his home and will do what he can to keep things in order.

He may be rather difficult to please at times, particularly if his wife does not share his refined tastes. If his wife has a practical mind, so much the better—for generally speaking, the Libran has a poor head for financial matters and is apt to let money slip through his fingers like water.

As a father he is quite considerate and encouraging. He is anxious to see his children express themselves as they desire; yet he will not tolerate spoiled behavior. Children understand him generally, and do what they can to please him.

Woman—Man

LIBRA WOMAN ARIES MAN

In some ways, the Aries man resembles an intellectual mountain goat leaping from crag to crag. He has an insatiable thirst for knowledge. He's ambitious and is apt to have his finger in many pies. He can do with a woman like you—someone attractive, quickwitted, and smart.

He is not interested in a clinging-vine kind of wife, but someone who is there when he needs her; someone who listens and understands what he says; someone who can give advice if he should ever need it—which is not likely to be often. The Aries man wants a woman who will look good on his arm without hanging on it too heavily. He is looking for a woman who has both feet on the ground and yet is mysterious and enticing—a kind of domestic Helen of Troy whose face or fine dinner can launch a thousand business deals if need be. That woman he's in search of sounds a little like you, doesn't she? If the shoe fits, put it on. You won't regret it.

The Aries man makes a good husband. He is faithful and attentive. He is an affectionate kind of man. He'll make you feel needed and loved. Love is a serious matter for the Aries man. He does not believe in flirting or playing the field—especially after he's found the woman of his dreams. He'll expect you to be as constant in your affection as he is in his. He'll expect you to be one hundred percent his; he won't put up with any nonsense while romancing you.

The Aries man may be pretty progressive and modern about many things; however, when it comes to pants wearing, he's downright conventional: it's strictly male attire. The best position you can take in the relationship is a supporting one. He's the boss and that's that. Once you have learned to accept that, you'll find the going easy.

The Aries man, with his endless energy and drive, likes to relax in the comfort of his home at the end of the day. The good homemaker can be sure of holding his love. He's keen on slippers and pipe and a comfortable armchair. If you see to it that everything in the house is where he expects to find it, you'll have no difficulty keeping the relationship on an even keel.

Life and love with an Aries man may be just the medicine you need. He'll be a good provider. He'll spoil you if he's financially able.

He's young at heart and can get along with children easily. He'll spoil them every chance he gets.

LIBRA WOMAN
TAURUS MAN

If you've got your heart set on a man born under the sign of Taurus, you'll have to learn the art of being patient. Taureans take their time about everything—even love.

The steady and deliberate Taurus man is a little slow on the draw; it may take him quite a while before he gets around to popping that question. For the woman who doesn't mind twiddling her thumbs, the waiting and anticipating almost always pays off in the end. Taurus men want to make sure that every step they take is a good one—particularly if they feel that the path they're on is one that leads to the altar.

If you are in the mood for a whirlwind romance, you had better cast your net in shallower waters. Moreover, most Taureans prefer to do the angling themselves. They are not keen on women taking the lead; once she does, he's liable to drop her like a dead fish. If you let yourself get caught on his terms, you'll find that he's fallen for you—hook, line and sinker.

The Taurus man is fond of a comfortable home life. It is very important to him. If you keep those home fires burning you will have no trouble keeping that flame in your Taurean's heart aglow. You have a talent for homemaking; use it. Your taste in furnishings is excellent. You know how to make a house come to life with colors and decorations.

Taurus, the strong, steady, and protective Bull may not be your idea of a man on the move, still he's reliable. Perhaps he could be the anchor for your dreams and plans. He could help you to acquire a more balanced outlook and approach to your life. If you're given to impulsiveness, he could help you to curb it. He's the man who is always there when you need him.

When you tie the knot with a man born under Taurus, you can put away fears about creditors pounding on the front door. Taureans are practical about everything including bill paying. When he carries you over that threshold, you can be certain that the entire house is paid for, not only the doorsill.

As a housewife, you won't have to worry about putting aside your many interests for the sake of back-breaking house chores. Your Taurus hubby will see to it that you have all the latest time-saving appliances and comforts.

Your children will be obedient and orderly. Your Taurus husband will see to that.

LIBRA WOMAN
GEMINI MAN

The Gemini man is quite a catch. Many a woman has set her cap for him and failed to bag him. Generally, Gemini men are intelligent, witty, and outgoing. Many of them tend to be rather versatile. The Gemini man could easily wind up being your better half.

One thing that causes a Twin's mind and affection to wander is a bore, and it is unlikely that an active woman like you would ever allow herself to be accused of being that. The Gemini man that has caught your heart will admire you for your ideas and intellect —perhaps even more than for your homemaking talents and good looks.

The woman who hitches up with a Twin needn't feel that once she's made her marriage vows that she'll have to store her interests and ambition in the attic somewhere. The Gemini man will admire you for your zeal and liveliness. He's the kind of guy who won't scowl if you let him shift for himself in the kitchen once in a while. In fact, he'll enjoy the challenge of wrestling with pots and pans himself for a change. Chances are, too, that he might turn out to be a better cook than you—that is, if he isn't already.

The man born under the sign of the Twins is a very active person. There aren't many women who have enough pep to keep up with him, but this should be no problem for a spry woman like you. The Gemini man is a dreamer, planner and idealist. A woman with a strong personality could easily fill the role of rudder for her Gemini's ship-without-a-sail. If you are a cultivated, purposeful woman, he won't mind it too much. The intelligent Twin is often aware of his shortcomings and doesn't resent it if someone with better bearings than himself gives him a shove in the right direction—when it's needed. The average Gemini does not have serious ego-hangups and will even accept a well-deserved chewing out from his mate quite good-naturedly.

When you team up with a Gemini man, you'll probably always have a houseful of people to entertain—interesting people, too; Geminis find it hard to tolerate sluggish minds and dispositions.

People born under Gemini generally have two sides to their natures, as different as night and day. It's very easy for them to be happy-go-lucky one minute, then down in the dumps the next. They hate to be bored and will generally do anything to make their lives interesting, vivid, and action-packed.

Gemini men are always attractive to the opposite sex. He'll flirt occasionally but it will never amount to anything serious.

As a father, he's a pushover; he loves children so much that he lets them do what they want.

LIBRA WOMAN
CANCER MAN

Chances are you won't hit it off too well with the man born under Cancer if your plans are love, but then, Cupid has been known to do some pretty unlikely things. The Cancer man is very sensitive—thin-skinned and occasionally moody. You've got to keep on your toes—and not step on his—if you're determined to make a go of the relationship.

The Cancer man may be lacking in some of the qualities you seek in a man, but when it comes to being faithful and being a good provider, he's hard to beat.

The perceptive woman will not mistake the Crab's quietness for sullenness or his thriftiness for pennypinching. In some respects, he is like that wise old owl out on a limb; he may look like he's dozing but actually he hasn't missed a thing. Cancer people often possess a well of knowledge about human behavior; they can come across with some pretty helpful advice to those in trouble or in need. He can certainly guide you in making investments both in time and money. He may not say much, but he's always got his wits about him.

The Crab may not be the match or catch for a woman like you; at times, you are likely to find him downright dull. True to his sign, he can be fairly cranky and crabby when handled the wrong way. He is perhaps more sensitive than he should be.

If you're smarter than your Cancer friend, be smart enough not to let him know. Never give him the idea that you think he's a little short on brain power. It would send him scurrying back into his shell—and all that ground lost in the relationship will perhaps never be recovered.

The Crab is most himself at home. Once settled down for the night or the weekend, wild horses couldn't drag him farther than the gatepost—that is, unless those wild horses were dispatched by his mother. The Crab is sometimes a Momma's boy. If his mate does not put her foot down, he will see to it that his mother always comes first. No self-respecting wife would ever allow herself to play second fiddle—even if it's to her old gray-haired mother-in-law. With a little bit of tact, however, she'll find that slipping into that number-one position is as easy as pie (that legendary one his mother used to bake).

If you pamper your Cancer man, you'll find that "Mother" turns up increasingly less—at the front door as well as in conversations.

Cancer men make protective, proud, and patient fathers.

LIBRA WOMAN
LEO MAN

For the woman who enjoys being swept off her feet in a romantic whirlwind fashion, Leo is the sign of love. When the Lion puts his mind to romancing, he doesn't stint. It's all wining and dining and dancing till the wee hours of the morning.

Leo is all heart and knows how to make his woman feel like a woman. The girl in constant search of a man she can look up to need go no farther: Leo is ten-feet tall—in spirit if not in stature. He's a man not only in full control of his faculties but in full control of just about any situation he finds himself in. He's a winner.

The Leo man may not look like Tarzan, but he knows how to roar and beat his chest if he has to. The woman who has had her fill of weak-kneed men, finds in a Leo someone she can at last lean upon. He can support you not only physically but spiritually as well. He's good at giving advice that pays off.

Leos are direct people. They don't believe in wasting time or effort. They almost never make unwise investments.

Many Leos rise to the top of their professions; through example, they often prove to be a source of great inspiration to others.

Although he's a ladies' man, the Leo man is very particular about his ladies. His standards are high when it comes to love interests. The idealistic and cultivated woman should have no trouble keeping her balance on the pedestal the Lion sets her on. Leo believes that romance should be played on a fair give-and-take basis. He won't stand for any monkey business in a love relationship. It's all or nothing.

You'll find him a frank, off-the-shoulder person; he generally says what is on his mind.

If you decide upon a Leo man for a mate, you must be prepared to stand behind him full-force. He expects it—and usually deserves it. He's the head of the house and can handle that position without a hitch. He knows how to go about breadwinning and, if he has his way (and most Leos do have their own way), he'll see to it that you'll have all the luxuries you crave and the comforts you need.

It's unlikely that the romance in your marriage will ever die out. Lions need love like flowers need sunshine. They're ever-amorous and generally expect like attention and affection from their mates. Leos are fond of going out on the town; they love to give parties, as well as go to them.

Leos make strict fathers, generally. They love their children but won't spoil them.

LIBRA WOMAN
VIRGO MAN

The Virgo man is all business—at least he may seem so to you. He is usually very cool, calm, and collected. He's perhaps too much of a fussbudget to wake up deep romantic interests in a woman like you. Torrid romancing to him is just so much sentimental mush. He can do without it and can make that quite evident in short order. He's keen on chastity and, if necessary, he can lead a sedentary, sexless life without caring too much about the fun others think he's missing. In short, you are liable to find him a first-class dud. He doesn't have much of an imagination; flights of fancy don't interest him. He is always correct and likes to be handled correctly. Almost everything about him is orderly. "There's a place for everything . . ." is likely to be an adage he'll fall upon quite regularly.

He does have an honest-to-goodness heart, believe it or not. The woman who finds herself strangely attracted to his cool, feet-flat-on-the-ground ways, will discover that his is a constant heart, not one that goes in for flings or sordid affairs. Virgos take an awfully long time to warm up to someone. A practical man, even in matters of the heart, he wants to know just what kind of person you are before he takes a chance on you.

The impulsive girl had better not make the mistake of kissing her Virgo friend on the street—even if it's only a peck on the cheek. He's not at all demonstrative and hates public displays of affection. Love, according to him, should be kept within the confines of one's home—with the curtains drawn. Once he believes that you are on the level with him as far as your love is concerned, you'll see how fast he can lose his cool. Virgos are considerate, gentle lovers. He'll spend a long time, though, getting to know you. He'll like you before he loves you.

A romance with a Virgo man can be a sometime—or, rather, a onetime—thing. If the bottom ever falls out, don't bother reaching for the adhesive tape. Nine times out of ten he won't care about patching up. He's a once-burnt-twice-shy guy. When he crosses your telephone number out of his address book, he's crossing you out of his life—for good.

Neat as a pin, he's thumbs-down on what he considers "sloppy" housekeeping. An ashtray with just one stubbed out cigarette in it can annoy him even if it's only two seconds old. Glassware should always sparkle and shine if you want to keep him happy.

If you marry him, keep your sunny-side up.

Your children should be kept as spotless as your house. Kids with dirty faces and hands displease him. Train them to be kind and courteous.

LIBRA WOMAN
LIBRA MAN

If there's a Libra in your life, you are most likely a very happy woman. Men born under this sign have a way with women. You'll always feel at ease in a Libra's company; you can be yourself when you're with him.

The Libra man can be moody at times. His moodiness is often puzzling. One moment he comes on hard and strong with declarations of his love, the next moment you find that he's left you like yesterday's mashed potatoes. He'll come back, though; don't worry. Libras are like that. Deep down inside he really knows what he wants even though he may not appear to.

You'll appreciate his admiration of beauty and harmony. If you're dressed to the teeth and never looked lovelier, you'll get a ready compliment—and one that's really deserved. Libras don't indulge in idle flattery. If they don't like something, they are tactful enough to remain silent.

Libras will go to great lengths to preserve peace and harmony—even tell a fat lie if necessary. They don't like showdowns or disagreeable confrontations. The frank woman is all for getting whatever is bothering her off her chest and out into the open, even if it comes out all wrong. To the Libra man, making a clean breast of everything seems like sheer folly sometimes.

You may lose your patience while waiting for your Libra friend to make up his mind. It takes him ages sometimes to make a decision. He weighs both sides carefully before committing himself to anything. You seldom dillydally—at least about small things—and so it's likely that you will find it difficult to see eye to eye with a hesitating Libran when it comes to decision-making methods.

All in all, though, he is kind, considerate, and fair. He is interested in the "real" truth; he'll try to balance everything out until he has all the correct answers. It's not difficult for him to see both sides of a story.

He's a peace-loving man. The sight of blood is apt to turn his stomach.

Librans are not showoffs. Generally, they are well-balanced, modest people. Honest, wholesome, and affectionate, they are serious about every love encounter they have. If he should find that the girl he's dating is not really suited to him, he will end the relationship in such a tactful manner that no hard feelings will come about.

The Libra father is firm, gentle, and patient.

LIBRA WOMAN
SCORPIO MAN

Many find the Scorpio's sting a fate worse than death. When his anger breaks loose, you had better clear out of the vicinity.

The average Scorpio may strike you as a brute. He'll stick pins into the balloons of your plans and dreams if they don't line up with what he thinks is right. If you do anything to irritate him—just anything—you'll wish you hadn't. He'll give you a sounding out that would make you pack your bags and go back to mother—if you were that kind of a girl.

The Scorpio man hates being tied down to homelife—he would rather be out on the battlefield of life, belting away at whatever he feels is a just and worthy cause, instead of staying home nestled in a comfortable armchair with the evening paper. If you are a girl who has a homemaking streak—don't keep those home fires burning too brightly, too long; you may just run out of firewood.

As passionate as he is in business affairs and politics, the Scorpio man still has plenty of pep and ginger stored away for lovemaking.

Most women are easily attracted to him—perhaps you are no exception. Those who allow a man born under this sign to sweep them off their feet, shortly find that they are dealing with a cauldron of seething excitement. The Scorpio is passionate with a capital P, you can be sure of that. But he's capable of dishing out as much pain as pleasure. Damsels with fluttering hearts who, when in the embrace of a Scorpio, think "This is it," had better be in a position moments later to realize that "Perhaps this isn't it."

Scorpios are blunt. An insult is likely to whiz out of his mouth quicker than a compliment.

If you're the kind of woman who can keep a stiff upper lip, take it on the chin, turn a deaf ear, and all that, because you feel you are still under his love spell in spite of everything: lots of luck.

If you have decided to take the bitter with the sweet, prepare yourself for a lot of ups and downs. Chances are you won't have as much time for your own affairs and interests as you'd like. The Scorpio's love of power may cause you to be at his constant beck and call.

Scorpios like fathering large families. They love children but quite often they fail to live up to their responsibilities as a parent.

LIBRA WOMAN
SAGITTARIUS MAN

If you've set your cap for a man born under the sign of Sagittarius, you may have to apply an awful lot of strategy before you can persuade him to get down on bended knee. Although some Sagittarians may be marriage-shy, they're not ones to skitter away from romance. You'll find a love relationship with a Sagittarian—whether a fling or "the real thing"—a very enjoyable experience.

As a rule, Sagittarians are bright, happy, healthy people. They have a strong sense of fair play. Often they are a source of inspiration to others. They are full of drive and ideas.

You'll be taken by the Sagittarian's infectious grin and his lighthearted friendly nature. If you do wind up being the woman in his life, you'll find that he's apt to treat you more like a buddy than the love of his life. It's just his way. Sagittarians are often more chummy than romantic.

You'll admire his broadmindedness in most matters—including those of the heart. If, while dating you, he claims that he still wants to play the field, he'll expect you to enjoy the same liberty. Once he's promised to love, honor, and obey, however, he does just that. Marriage for him, once he's taken that big step, is very serious business.

The Sagittarius man is quick-witted. He has a genuine interest in equality. He hates prejudice and injustice. Generally, Sagittarians are good at sports. They love the great out-of-doors and respect wild life in all its forms.

He's not much of a homebody. Quite often he's occupied with faraway places either in his daydreams or in reality. He enjoys being on the move. He's got ants in his pants and refuses to sit still for long stretches at a time. Humdrum routine—especially at home—bores him.

At the drop of a hat, he may ask you to whip off your apron and dine out for a change. He likes to surprise people.

He'll take great pride in showing you off to his friends. He'll always be considerate where your feelings are concerned; he will never embarrass or disappoint you intentionally.

His friendly, sun-shiny nature is capable of attracting many people. Like you, he's very tolerant when it comes to friends. You will most likely spend a great deal of time helping him entertain people.

Sagittarians are all thumbs when it comes to tiny tots. They develop an interest in children when they grow older and wiser.

LIBRA WOMAN
CAPRICORN MAN

A with-it girl like you is likely to find the average Capricorn man a bit of a drag. The man born under the sign of the Goat is often a closed person and difficult to get to know. Even if you do get to know him, you may not find him very interesting.

In romance, Capricorn men are a little on the rusty side. You'll probably have to make all the passes.

You may find his plodding manner irritating and his conservative, traditional ways downright maddening. He's not one to take chances on anything. "If it was good enough for my father, it's good enough for me" may be his motto. He follows a way that is tried and true.

Whenever adventure rears its tantalizing head, the Goat will turn the other way; he's just not interested.

He may be just as ambitious as you are—perhaps even more so—but his ways of accomplishing his aims are more subterranean or, at least, seem so. He operates from the background a good deal of the time. At a gathering you may never even notice him, but he's there, taking in everything, sizing everyone up—planning his next careful move.

Although Capricorns may be intellectual to a degree, it is not generally the kind of intelligence you appreciate. He may not be as quick or as bright as you; it may take him ages to understand a simple joke.

If you do decide to take up with a man born under this sign, you ought to be pretty good in the "Cheering Up" department. The Capricorn man often acts as though he's constantly being followed by a cloud of gloom.

The Capricorn man is most himself when in the comfort and privacy of his own home. The security possible within four walls can make him a happy man. He'll spend as much time as he can at home. If he is loaded down with extra work, he'll bring it home instead of working overtime at the office.

You'll most likely find yourself frequently confronted by his relatives. Family is very important to the Capricorn—*his* family that is. They had better take a pretty important place in your life, too, if you want to keep your home a happy one.

Although his caution in most matters may all but drive you up the wall, you'll find that his concerned way with money justified most of the time. He'll plan everything right down to the last penny.

He can be quite a scold with children. You'll have to step in and smooth things out.

LIBRA WOMAN
AQUARIUS MAN

Aquarians love everybody—even their worst enemies sometimes. Through your love relationship with an Aquarian you'll find yourself running into all sorts of people, ranging from near-genius to downright insane—and they're all friends of his.

As a rule, Aquarians are extremely friendly and open. Of all the signs, they are perhaps the most tolerant. In the thinking department, they are often miles ahead of others.

You'll most likely find your relationship with this man a challenging one. Your high respect for intelligence and imagination may be reason enough for you to set your heart on a Water-Bearer. You'll find that you can learn a lot from him.

In the holding-hands phase of your romance, you may find that your Water-Bearing friend has cold feet. Aquarians take quite a bit of warming up before they are ready to come across with that first goodnight kiss. More than likely, he'll just want to be your pal in the beginning. For him, that's an important first step in any relationship—love included. The "poetry and flowers" stage—if it ever comes—will come later. The Aquarian is all heart; still, when it comes to tying himself down to one person and for keeps, he is almost always sure to hesitate. He may even try to get out of it if you breathe down his neck too heavily.

The Aquarius man is no Valentino and wouldn't want to be. The kind of love life he's looking for is one that's made up mainly of companionship. Although he may not be very romantic, the memory of his first romance will always hold an important position in his heart. Some Aquarians wind up marrying their childhood sweethearts.

You won't find it difficult to look up to a man born under the sign of the Water-Bearer, but you may find the challenge of trying to keep up with him dizzying. He can pierce through the most complicated problem as if it were a matter of 2 + 2. You may find him a little too lofty and high-minded, but don't judge him too harshly if that's the case; he's way ahead of his time—your time, too, most likely.

If you marry this man, he'll stay true to you. Don't think that once the honeymoon is over, you'll be chained to the kitchen sink forever. Your Aquarius husband will encourage you to keep active in your own interests and affairs. You'll most likely have a minor tiff now and again but never anything serious.

Kids love him and vice-versa. He'll be as tolerant with them as he is with adults.

LIBRA WOMAN
PISCES MAN

The man born under Pisces is quite a dreamer. Sometimes he's so wrapped up in his dreams that he's difficult to reach. To the average, ambitious woman, he may seem a little sluggish.

He's easy-going most of the time. He seems to take things in his stride. He'll entertain all kinds of views and opinions from just about anyone, nodding or smiling vaguely, giving the impression that he's with them 100 percent while that may not be the case at all. His attitude may be "why bother" when he is confronted with someone wrong who thinks he's right. The Pisces man will seldom speak his mind if he thinks he'll be rigidly opposed.

The Pisces man is oversensitive at times—he's afraid of getting his feelings hurt. He'll sometimes imagine a personal affront when none's been made. Chances are you'll find this complex of his maddening; at times, you may feel like giving him a swift kick where it hurts the most. It won't do any good, though. It would just add fuel to the fire of his complex.

One thing you will admire about this man is his concern for people who are sickly or troubled. He'll make his shoulder available to anyone in the mood for a good cry. He can listen to one hard-luck story after another without seeming to tire. When his advice is asked, he is capable of coming across with some pretty important words of wisdom. He often knows what's bugging someone before that person is aware of it himself. It's almost intuitive with Pisces, it seems. Still, at the end of the day, he looks forward to some peace and quiet. If you've got a problem on your mind, don't dump it into his lap at the end of the day. If you do, you're liable to find him short-tempered. He's a good listener but he can only take so much.

Pisces men are not aimless although they may seem so at times. The positive sort of Pisces man is quite often successful in his profession and is likely to wind up rich and influential. Material gain, however, is not a direct goal for a man born under this sign.

The weaker Pisces is usually content to stay put on the level where he happens to find himself. He won't complain too much if the roof leaks or the fence is in need of repair. He'll just shrug it off as a minor inconvenience. He's got more important things to think about, he'll say.

Because of their seemingly laissez-faire manner, people born under this sign are immensely popular with children. For tots they play the double role of confidant and playmate. It will never enter his mind to discipline a child, no matter how spoiled or incorrigible that child becomes.

Man—Woman

LIBRA MAN
ARIES WOMAN

The Aries woman may be a little too bossy and busy for you. Generally speaking, Aries women are ambitious creatures. They tend to lose their patience with thorough and deliberate people who take a lot of time to complete something. The Aries woman is a fast worker. Sometimes she's so fast she forgets to look where she's going. When she stumbles or falls, it would be nice if you were there to grab her. Aries women are proud. They don't like to be told "I told you so" when they err. Tongue-wagging can turn them into blocks of ice. However, don't begin to think that the Aries woman frequently gets tripped up in her plans. Quite often they are capable of taking aim and hitting the bull's-eye. You'll be flabbergasted at times by their accuracy as well as by their ambition.

You are perhaps somewhat slower than the Aries woman in attaining your goals. Still, you are not apt to make mistakes along the way; you're seldom ill-prepared.

The Aries woman is rather sensitive at times. She likes to be handled with gentleness and respect. Let her know that you love her for her brains as well as for her good looks. Never give her cause to become jealous. When your Aries woman sees green, you'd better forget about sharing a rosy future together. Handle her with tender love and care and she's yours.

The Aries woman can be giving if she feels her partner is deserving. She is no iceberg; she responds to the proper masculine flame. She needs a man she can look up to and feel proud of. If the shoe fits, put it on. If not, better put your sneakers back on and quietly tiptoe out of her sight. She can cause you plenty of heartache if you've made up your mind about her and she hasn't made up hers about you. Aries women are very demanding at times. Some of them tend to be high-strung. They can be difficult if they feel their independence is being hampered.

The cultivated Aries woman makes a wonderful homemaker and hostess. You'll find that she's very clever in decorating; she knows how to use colors. Your house will be tastefully furnished; she'll see to it that it radiates harmony. Friends and acquaintances will love your Aries wife. She knows how to make everyone feel at home and welcome.

Although the Aries woman may not be keen on burdensome responsibilities, she is fond of children and the joy they bring.

LIBRA MAN
TAURUS WOMAN

The woman born under the sign of Taurus may lack a little of the sparkle and bubble you often like to find in a woman. The Taurus woman is generally down-to-earth and never flighty. It's important to her that she keep both feet flat on the ground. She is not fond of bounding all over the place, especially if she's under the impression that there's no profit in it.

On the other hand, if you hit it off with a Taurus woman, you won't be disappointed in the romance area. The Taurus woman is all woman and proud of it, too. She can be very devoted and loving once she decides that her relationship with you is no fly-by-night romance. Basically, she's a passionate person. In sex, she's direct and to-the-point. If she really loves you, she'll let you know she's yours—and without reservations.

Better not flirt with other women once you've committed yourself to her. She's capable of being very jealous and possessive.

She'll stick by you through thick and thin. It's almost certain that if the going ever gets rough, she won't go running home to her mother. She can adjust to the hard times just as graciously as she can to the good times.

Taureans are, on the whole, pretty even-tempered. They like to be treated with kindness. Pretty things and soft objects make them purr like kittens.

You may find her a little slow and deliberate. She likes to be safe and sure about everything. Let her plod along if she likes; don't coax her, but just let her take her own sweet time. Everything she does is done thoroughly and, generally, without mistakes.

Don't deride her for being a slowpoke. It could lead to flying pots and pans and a fireworks display that could put Bastille Day to shame. The Taurus woman doesn't anger readily but when prodded often enough, she's capable of letting loose with a cyclone of ill will. If you treat her with kindness and consideration, you'll have no cause for complaint.

The Taurean loves doing things for her man. She's a whiz in the kitchen and can whip up feasts fit for a king if she thinks they'll be royally appreciated. She may not fully understand you but she'll adore you and be faithful to you if she feels you're worthy of it.

The Taurus woman makes a wonderful mother. She knows how to keep her children well-loved, cuddled, and warm. She may have some difficult times with them when they reach adolescence, though.

LIBRA MAN
GEMINI WOMAN

You may find a romance with a woman born under the sign of the Twins a many-splendoured thing. In her you can find the intellectual companionship you often look for in a friend or mate. A Gemini girl friend can appreciate your aims and desires because she travels pretty much the same road as you do intellectually—that is, at least part of the way. She may share your interest but she will lack your tenacity.
she travels pretty much the same road as you do intellectually—that is, at least part of the way. She may share your interest but she will lack your tenacity.

She suffers from itchy feet. She can be here, there . . . all over the place and at the same time, or so it would seem. Her eagerness to move about may make you dizzy, still you'll enjoy and appreciate her liveliness and mental agility.

Geminis often have sparkling personalities; you'll be attracted by her warmth and grace. While she's on your arm you'll probably notice that many male eyes are drawn to her—she may even return a gaze or two, but don't let that worry you. All women born under this sign have nothing against a harmless flirt once in a while. They enjoy this sort of attention; if she feels she is already spoken for, however, she will never let it get out of hand.

Although she may not be as handy as you'd like in the kitchen, you'll never go hungry for a filling and tasty meal. She's as much in a hurry as you are, and won't feel like she's cheating by breaking out the instant mashed potatoes or the frozen peas. She may not be much of a good cook but she is clever; with a dash of this and a suggestion of that, she can make an uninteresting TV dinner taste like something out of a Jim Beard cookbook. Then, again, maybe you've struck it rich and have a Gemini girl friend who finds complicated recipes a challenge to her intellect. If so, you'll find every meal a tantalizing and mouth-watering surprise.

When you're beating your brains out over the Sunday crossword puzzle and find yourself stuck, just ask your Gemini girl; she'll give you all the right answers without batting an eyelash.

Like you, she loves all kinds of people. You may even find that you're a bit more particular than she. Often all that a Gemini requires is that her friends be interesting . . . and stay interesting. One thing she's not able to abide is a dullard.

Leave the party-organizing to your Gemini sweetheart or mate and you'll never have a chance to know what a dull moment is. She'll bring the swinger out in you if you give her half a chance.

A Gemini mother enjoys her children. Like them, she's often restless, adventurous, and easily bored.

LIBRA MAN
CANCER WOMAN

If you fall in love with a Cancer woman, be prepared for anything. They are sometimes difficult to understand when it comes to love. In one hour, she can unravel a whole gamut of emotions; it will leave you in a tizzy. She'll always keep you guessing, that's for sure.

You may find her a little too uncertain and sensitive for your liking. You'll most likely spend a good deal of time encouraging her—helping her to erase her foolish fears. Tell her she's a living doll a dozen times a day and you'll be well loved in return.

Be careful of the jokes you make when in her company—don't let any of them revolve around her, her personal interests, or her family. If you do, you'll most likely reduce her to tears. She can't stand being made fun of. It will take bushels of roses and tons of chocolates—not to mention the apologies—to get her to come back out of her shell.

In matters of money-managing, she may not easily come around to your way of thinking. Money will never burn a hole in her pocket book. You may get the notion that your Cancer sweetheart or mate is a direct descendant of Scrooge. If she has her way, she'll hang onto the first dollar you earned. She's not only that way with money, but with everything right on up from bakery string to jelly jars. She's a saver; she never throws anything away, no matter how trivial.

Once she returns your "I love you," you'll find you have an affectionate, self-sacrificing, and devoted woman on your hands. Her love for you will never alter unless you want it to. She'll put you up on a high pedestal and will do everything—even if it's against your will—to keep you there.

Cancer women love homelife. For them, marriage is an easy step to make. They're domestic with a capital D. She'll do her best to make your home comfortable and cozy. The Cancer woman is more herself at home than in strange surroundings. She makes an excellent hostess. The best in her comes out when she's in her own environment.

Cancer women make the best mothers of all the signs of the Zodiac. She'll make every complaint of her child a major catastrophe. With her, children come first. If you're lucky, you'll run a close second. You'll perhaps see her as too devoted to the children. You may have a hard time convincing her that her apron strings are too long.

LIBRA MAN
LEO WOMAN

If you can manage a girl who likes to kick up her heels every now and again, then the Leo woman was made for you. You'll have to learn to put away jealous fears when you take up with a woman born under this sign, as she's often the kind that makes heads turn and tongues wag. You don't necessarily have to believe any of what you hear—it's most likely just jealous gossip or wishful thinking.

The Leo girl has more than a fair share of grace and glamour. She knows it, generally, and knows how to put it to good use. Needless to say, other women in her vicinity turn green with envy and will try anything, short of shoving her into the nearest lake, in order to put her out of the running.

If she's captured your heart and fancy, woo her full-force if your intention is to eventually win her. Shower her with expensive gifts and promise her the moon—if you're in a position to go that far—then you'll find her resistance beginning to weaken. It's not that she's such a difficult cookie—she'll probably make a lot over you once she's decided you're the man for her—but she does enjoy a lot of attention. What's more: she feels she's entitled to it. Her mild arrogance, however, is becoming. The Leo woman knows how to transform the crime of excessive pride into a very charming misdemeanor. It sweeps most men right off their feet—rather, all men. Those who do not succumb to her leonine charm are few and far between.

If you've got an important business deal to clinch and you have doubts as to whether you can bring it off as you should, take your Leo wife along to the business luncheon and it'll be a cinch that you'll have that contract—lock, stock, and barrel—in your pocket before the meeting is over. She won't have to say or do anything . . . just be there at your side. The grouchiest oil magnate can be transformed into a gushing, obedient schoolboy if there's a Leo woman in the room.

If you're rich and want to see to it that you stay that way, don't give your Leo spouse a free hand with the charge accounts and credit cards. When it comes to spending, Leos tend to overdo. If you're poor, you have no worries because the luxury-loving Leo will most likely never recognize your existence—let alone, consent to marry you.

As a mother, she's both strict and easy. She can pal around with her children and still see to it that they know their places. She won't spoil them but she'll be a loving and devoted parent.

LIBRA MAN
VIRGO WOMAN

The Virgo woman may be a little too difficult for you to understand at first. Her waters run deep. Even when you think you know her, don't take any bets on it. She's capable of keeping things hidden in the deep recesses of her womanly soul—things she'll only release when she's sure that you're the man she's been looking for. It may take her some time to come around to this decision. Virgo girls are finicky about almost everything; everything has to be letter-perfect before they're satisfied. Many of them have the idea that the only people who can do things correctly are Virgos.

Nothing offends a Virgo woman more than slovenly dress, sloppy character, or a careless display of affection. Make sure your tie is not crooked and your shoes sport a bright shine before you go calling on this lady. Keep your off-color jokes for the locker room; she'll have none of that. Take her arm when crossing the street. Don't rush the romance. Trying to corner her in the back of a cab may be one way of striking out. Never criticize the way she looks—in fact, the best policy would be to agree with her as much as possible. Still, there's just so much a man can take; all those dos and don'ts you'll have to observe if you want to get to first base with a Virgo may be just a little too much to ask of you. After a few dates, you may come to the conclusion that she just isn't worth all that trouble. However, the Virgo woman is mysterious enough, generally speaking, to keep her men running back for more. Chances are you'll be intrigued by her airs and graces.

If lovemaking means a lot to you, you'll be disappointed at first in the cool ways of your Virgo girl. However, under her glacial facade there lies a hot cauldron of seething excitement. If you're patient and artful in your romantic approach, you'll find that all that caution was well worth the trouble. When Virgos love, they don't stint. It's all or nothing as far as they're concerned. Once they're convinced that they love you, they go all the way, right off the bat—tossing all cares to the wind.

One thing a Virgo woman can't stand in love is hypocrisy. They don't give a hoot about what the neighbors say, if their hearts tell them "Go ahead." They're very concerned with human truths . . . so much so that if their hearts stumble upon another fancy, they're liable to be true to that new heartthrob and leave you standing in the rain.

She's honest to her heart and will be as true to you as you are with her, generally. Do her wrong once, however, and it's curtains.

She's both strict and tender with children. As a mother she'll try to bring out the best in her children.

LIBRA MAN
LIBRA WOMAN

You'll probably find that the girl born under the sign of Libra is worth more than her weight in gold. She's a woman after your own heart.

With her, you'll always come first—make no mistake about that. She'll always be behind you 100 percent, no matter what you do. When you ask her advice about almost anything, you'll most likely get a very balanced and realistic opinion. She is good at thinking things out and never lets her emotions run away with her when clear logic is called for.

As a homemaker she is hard to beat. She is very concerned with harmony and balance. You can be sure she'll make your house a joy to live in; she'll see to it that the house is tastefully furnished and decorated. A Libran cannot stand filth or disarray—it gives her goose-bumps. Anything that does not radiate harmony, in fact, runs against her orderly grain.

She is chock-full of charm and womanly ways. She can sweep just about any man off his feet with one winning smile. When it comes to using her brains, she can outthink almost anyone and, sometimes, with half the effort. She is diplomatic enough, though, never to let this become glaringly apparent. She may even turn the conversation around so that you think you were the one who did all the brainwork. She couldn't care less, really, just as long as you wind up doing what is right.

The Libra woman will put you up on a pretty high pedestal. You are her man and her idol. She'll leave all the decision-making—large or small—up to you. She's not interested in running things and will only offer her assistance if she feels you really need it.

Some find her approach to reason masculine; however, in the areas of love and affection the Libra woman is *all* woman. She'll literally shower you with love and kisses during your romance with her. She doesn't believe in holding out. You shouldn't either, if you want to hang on to her.

She is the kind of girl who likes to snuggle up to you in front of the fire on chilly autumn nights . . . the kind of girl who will bring you breakfast in bed Sunday. She'll be very thoughtful about anything that concerns you. If anyone dares suggest you're not the grandest guy in the world, she'll give that person what-for. She'll defend you till her dying breath. The Libra woman will be everything you want her to be.

She'll be a sensitive and loving mother. Still, you'll always come before the children.

LIBRA MAN
SCORPIO WOMAN

The Scorpio woman can be a whirlwind of passion—perhaps too much passion to really suit you. When her temper flies, you'd better lock up the family heirlooms and take cover. When she chooses to be sweet, you're apt to think that butter wouldn't melt in her mouth . . . but, of course, it would.

The Scorpio woman can be as hot as a tamale or as cool as a cucumber, but whatever mood she's in, she's in it for real. She does not believe in posing or putting on airs.

The Scorpio woman is often sultry and seductive—her femme-fatale charm can pierce through the hardest of hearts like a laser ray. She may not look like Mata Hari (quite often Scorpios resemble the tomboy next door) but once she's fixed you with her tantalizing eyes, you're a goner.

Life with the Scorpio woman will not be all smiles and smooth-sailing; when prompted, she can unleash a gale of venom. Generally, she'll have the good grace to keep family battles within the walls of your home. When company visits, she's apt to give the impression that married life with you is one great big joyride. It's just one of her ways of expressing her loyalty to you—at least in front of others. She may fight you tooth and nail in the confines of your living room, but at a ball or during an evening out, she'll hang onto your arm and have stars in her eyes.

Scorpio women are good at keeping secrets. She may even keep a few buried from you if she feels like it.

Never cross her up on even the smallest thing. When it comes to revenge, she's an eye-for-an-eye woman. She's not too keen on forgiveness—especially if she feels she's been wronged unfairly. You'd be well-advised not to give her any cause to be jealous, either. When the Scorpio woman sees green, your life will be made far from rosy. Once she's put you in the doghouse, you can be sure that you're going to stay there awhile.

You may find life with a Scorpio woman too draining. Although she may be full of the old paprika, it's quite likely that she's not the kind of girl you'd like to spend the rest of your natural life with. You'd prefer someone gentler and not so hot-tempered, someone who can take the highs with the lows and not bellyache, someone who is flexible and understanding. A woman born under Scorpio can be heavenly, but she can also be the very devil when she chooses.

As a mother, a Scorpio is protective and encouraging.

LIBRA MAN
SAGITTARIUS WOMAN

You'll most likely never come across a more good-natured girl than the one born under the sign of Sagittarius. Generally, they're full of bounce and good cheer. Their sunny disposition seems almost permanent and can be relied upon even on the rainiest of days.

Women born under this sign are almost never malicious. If ever they seem to be it is only seeming. Sagittarians are often a little short on tact and say literally anything that comes into their pretty little heads—no matter what the occasion. Sometimes the words that tumble out of their mouths seem downright cutting and cruel. Still, no matter what she says, she means well. The Sagittarius woman is quite capable of losing some of her friends—and perhaps even some of yours—through a careless slip of the lip.

On the other hand, you are liable to appreciate her honesty and good intentions. To you, qualities of this sort play an important part in life. With a little patience and practice, you can probably help cure your Sagittarian of her loose tongue; in most cases, she'll give in to your better judgement and try to follow your advice to the letter.

Chances are she'll be the outdoors type of girl friend. Long hikes, fishing trips, and white-water canoeing will most likely appeal to her. She's a busy person; no one could ever call her a slouch. She sets great store in mobility. Her feet are itchy and she won't sit still for a minute if she doesn't have to.

She is great company most of the time and, generally, lots of fun. Even if your buddies drop by for poker and beer, she won't have any trouble fitting in.

On the whole, she is a very kind and sympathetic woman. If she feels she's made a mistake, she'll be the first to call your attention to it. She's not afraid to own up to her faults and shortcomings.

You might lose your patience with her once or twice. After she's seen how upset her shortsightedness or tendency to blabber has made you, she'll do her best to straighten up.

The Sagittarian woman is not the kind who will pry into your business affairs. But she'll always be there, ready to offer advice if you need it. If you come home with red stains on your collar and you say it's paint and not lipstick, she'll believe you.

She'll seldom be suspicious; your word will almost always be good enough for her.

She is a wonderful and loving friend to her children.

LIBRA MAN
CAPRICORN WOMAN

If you are not a successful businessman or, at least, on your way to success, it's quite possible that a Capricorn woman will have no interest in entering your life. Generally speaking, she is a very security-minded female; she'll see to it that she invests her time only in sure things. Men who whittle away their time with one unsuccessful scheme or another, seldom attract a Capricorn. Men who are interested in getting somewhere in life and keep their noses close to the grindstone quite often have a Capricorn woman behind them, helping them to get ahead.

Although she is a kind of "climber" she is not what you could call cruel or hard-hearted. Beneath that cool, seemingly calculating, exterior, there's a warm and desirable woman. She just happens to think that it is just as easy to fall in love with a rich or ambitious man as it is with a poor or lazy one. She's practical.

The Capricorn woman may be keenly interested in rising to the top, but she'll never be aggressive about it. She'll seldom step on someone's feet or nudge competitors away with her elbows. She's quiet about her desires. She sits, waits, and watches. When an opening or opportunity does appear, she'll latch onto it lickety-split. For an on-the-move man, an ambitious Capricorn wife or girlfriend can be quite an asset. She can probably give you some very good advice about business matters. When you invite the boss and his wife for dinner, she'll charm them both right off the ground.

The Capricorn woman is thorough in whatever she does: cooking, cleaning, making a success out of life . . . Capricorns make excellent hostesses as well as guests. Generally, they are very well mannered and gracious, no matter what their backgrounds are. They seem to have a built-in sense of what is proper. Crude behavior or a careless faux pas can offend them no end.

If you should marry a woman born under Capricorn you need never worry about her going on a wild shopping spree. Capricorns are careful with every cent that comes into their hands. They understand the value of money better than most women and have no room in their lives for careless spending.

Capricorn girls are usually very fond of family—their own, that is. With them, family ties run very deep. Don't make jokes about her relatives; she won't stand for it. You'd better check her family out before you get down on bended knee; after your marriage you'll undoubtedly be seeing lots of them.

Capricorn women make loving mothers. They train their children to be polite and respectful.

LIBRA MAN
AQUARIUS WOMAN

If you find that you've fallen head over heels for a woman born under the sign of the Water-Bearer, you'd better fasten your safety belt. It may take you quite a while to actually discover what this girl is like—and even then, you may have nothing to go on but a string of vague hunches. The Aquarian is like a rainbow, full of bright and shining hues; she's like no other girl you've ever known. There is something elusive about her—something delightfully mysterious. You'll most likely never be able to put your finger on it. It's nothing calculated, either; Aquarians don't believe in phony charm.

There will never be a dull moment in your life with this Water-Bearing woman; she seems to radiate adventure and magic. She'll most likely be the most open-minded and tolerant woman you've ever met. She has a strong dislike for injustice and prejudice. Narrow-mindedness runs against her grain.

She is very independent by nature and quite capable of shifting for herself if necessary. She may receive many proposals for marriage from all sorts of people without ever really taking them seriously. Marriage is a very big step for her; she wants to be sure she knows what she's getting into. If she thinks that it will seriously curb her independence and love of freedom, she's liable to shake her head and give the man his engagement ring back—if indeed she's let the romance get that far.

The line between friendship and romance is a pretty fuzzy one for an Aquarian. It's not difficult for her to remain buddy-buddy with an ex-lover. She's tolerant, remember? So, if you should see her on the arm of an old love, don't jump to any hasty conclusions.

She's not a jealous person herself and doesn't expect you to be, either. You'll find her pretty much of a free spirit most of the time. Just when you think you know her inside-out, you'll discover that you don't really know her at all.

She's a very sympathetic and warm person; she can be helpful to people in need of assistance and advice.

She'll seldom be suspicious even if she has every right to be. If she loves a man, she'll forgive him just about anything. If he allows himself a little fling, chances are she'll just turn her head the other way. Her tolerance does have its limits, however, and her man should never press his luck at hanky-panky.

She makes a big-hearted mother; her good qualities rub off on her children.

LIBRA MAN
PISCES WOMAN

Many a man dreams of a Pisces kind of a girl. You're perhaps no exception. She's soft and cuddly—very domestic. She'll let you be the brains of the family; she's contented to just lean on your shoulder and let you be the master of the household.

She can be very ladylike and proper. Your business associates and friends will be dazzled by her warmth and femininity. Although she's a charmer, there is a lot more to her than just a pretty face. There is a brain ticking away behind that soft, womanly facade. You may never become aware of it—that is, until you're married to her. It's no cause for alarm, however; she'll most likely never use it against you.

If she feels you're botching up your married life through careless behavior or if she feels you could be earning more money than you do, she'll tell you about it. But any wife would, really. She will never try to usurp your position as head of the family.

No one had better dare say one uncomplimentary word about you in her presence. It's liable to cause her to break into tears. Pisces women are usually very sensitive beings. Their reaction to adversity, frustration, or anger is just a plain, good, old-fashioned cry. They can weep buckets when inclined.

She'll have an extra-special dinner waiting for you when you come home from an important business meeting. Don't bother to go into any of the details about the meeting, though, at the dinner table; she doesn't have much of a head for business matters, usually, and is only too happy to leave that up to you.

She can do wonders with a house. She is very fond of soft and beautiful things. There will always be plenty of fresh-cut flowers around the house. She'll see that you always have plenty of socks and underwear in that top drawer of your dresser.

Treat her with tenderness and your relationship will be an enjoyable one. She's most likely fond of chocolates. A bunch of beautiful roses will never fail to make her eyes light up. See to it that you never forget her birthday or your anniversary. She won't. If you are patient and kind, you can keep a Pisces woman happy for a lifetime. She is, however, not without her faults. Her "sensitivity" may get on your nerves after a while. You may find her lacking in imagination and zest. You may even feel that she only uses her tears as a method of getting her own way.

She makes a strong, self-sacrificing mother. She'll find it difficult to refuse her children anything.

LIBRA

LIBRA

YEARLY FORECAST: 1994

Forecast for 1994 Concerning Business and Financial Affairs, Job Prospects Travel, Health, Romance and Marriage for Those Born with the Sun in the Zodiacal Sign of Libra. September 23-October 22

For the harmony-loving Libra, 1994 promises opportunity to expand from your own circle of family and friends outward into the community and beyond. You will be in a leadership position that allows you to make decisions rather than accept another's as in the past years. Ideas that you propose are likely to be accepted and acted upon, with results giving you a sense of pride and accomplishment. This is an outstanding year to reach out to people who lack your vision and positive outlook. You are ready to take on more responsibility and carry through to the results you want. Where you have been unsure and uncertain you now are increasingly confident. Small self-doubts that have kept you from embracing controversial ideas can be swept aside. You will have the stamina to compete for an elected office or to go beyond what is expected in an appointed position. You have a perfect combination of past experience combining with independent thinking and the ability to get along with people from all walks of life. You can practice the art of the possible this year while maintaining that unmatched Libra idealism that sets you above and apart.

Work and business affairs should benefit significantly from the energy you have to expend on your assignments. A piece of the action is not enough for you in 1994; you want to be in the thick of things from start to finish. Superiors will be sitting up and taking notice. Romance, too, benefits from the center-stage position of Libras in the coming year. Whether married or single, you can expect to attract attention from the opposite sex. Friendships will increase, with love growing slowly but steadily from that seed. More travel is foreseen, probably on short notice during the middle third of 1994. Your ability to adapt to foreign ways helps you overcome cultural barriers and be readily accepted. Both romance and business opportunity exist at a distance. The year is good for financial affairs, although you may not see immediate results of your efforts in the form of a paycheck. Your generous nature is likely to give away much of what you earn with no regrets. As long as the basics are taken care of, there is no need to accumulate wealth in order to feel happy and fulfilled. A partnership with someone who is possession-oriented could be one of the most difficult aspects of the year. Unless this basic disagreement is worked out you may come to a parting of the ways. Your ideas are apt to rub off, however, without the relationship reaching the breaking point. You know when to back down and when, in good conscience, you must stand your ground. Libra instincts will not play you false.

Although money is not a dominant consideration it can be a stumbling block. Pay more attention to money matters so that lack of funds does not thwart your efforts. Look for ways to cut costs by making do with what you already have rather than buying and stockpiling. Pare your budget to necessities with a few frills for good measure. You can please family members and friends in many important ways that money cannot buy. Living within your means is vital; otherwise you may devote an increasing amount of time and energy to juggling funds and financial acrobatics. Through your regular work you stand the best chance of steady income. Put more of yourself into every assignment. Let your Libra creativity take you beyond the ordinary and set you apart. Higher-ups are both aware and appreciative of your abilities. A higher-paying position is likely to be offered to you early in the year or during the last two months. Whether or not you take it will depend on family considerations. You value private time and cannot be satisfied if making money becomes the prime pursuit. Part-time income is foreseen through expanding a hobby, especially an artistic one. New investment is worthwhile based on a hunch about a friend's business or employment. Do not put money into an unknown offering where the management philosophy may go against your ideals. You can reap a good rate of return in insured accounts that give you peace of mind.

Frequent travel may be necessary this year in connection with family matters as well as work. Events occurring at a distance have a definite impact on all of your affairs. The influence is likely to be mutual. You should be in close cooperation by midyear with a person whose background is quite different from your own. Keep your passport at the ready; you will be using it more often than in the past few years. Frequent flyer miles are going to accumulate rapidly. It is better to travel with a companion who can act as an extra set of eyes and ears for you. In person you can be especially persuasive, getting your ideas across and waylaying objections. Because you will not be as good a communicator in writing or through electronics, it is important to get out and about. An emissary could be useful at times, but people who are depending on you want to meet you in person. There is a special opportunity to forge an alliance that extends beyond the boundaries of your own country. A business merger or sale could open a whole new world of opportunity. From March 14 to May 23 is best for taking a trip with a definite purpose; summer months are apt to be the least effective period. Travel purely for pleasure should be relegated to off-peak tourist times if possible. You will not enjoy being one of a crowd. This is a year to go beyond where you have been. Your influence as well as your interests will be expanding.

Easygoing harmony is unlikely at home for most of the year. You will have your differences with your mate or other family members, especially the older generation. But throughout you know that they are behind you and will not let you down when you need them most. Your leadership role forces you to do a lot of cajoling and convincing; you are not going along with the consensus, but rather setting it yourself in many areas. Maintain your enthusiasm even when you are faced with opposition. Winning over people whose views are not like your own at the outset can be inspiring as well as energizing. You have the stamina to make some significant changes at home to accommodate the other changes in your life. It is a propitious year to relocate or move in your own community to larger quarters. There may be an addition to the family circle, most likely one that takes you a little by surprise. January, February and October are the best times to purchase a home.

Libra singles not interested in settling down must be wary throughout 1994. Your central position, as you gain power and predominance, makes you a natural attraction for the opposite sex. You are apt to be chased more than the one to be doing the chasing. Lack of sincerity could characterize a relationship that begins early in the year. It will take you a month or longer to recognize what is going on. Even then you will want to ease out of the affair rather than break it off abruptly. No matter what a family member or friend says, you have to find out for yourself and make up your own mind when it comes to an affair of the heart. You enjoy a variety of people and experiences, and this year you are expanding more than ever before. Relax and enjoy the attention. Avoid getting seriously involved unless you know that you are ready to make a lifelong commitment. For the Libra who has been hurt in a love affair, the last quarter of the year brings release from the ties holding you to the past. By November you are prepared to be open and eager again for emotional bonding.

Health should not be a problem except during June, when you may have to take a few days off in order to restore your energy. You will have more stamina than usual and can do more than you ever thought possible. Home and work and outside commitments will meld into a wholesome whole. Relationships are apt to overlap and flow together. You should be able to get by on less sleep and never miss it. Nutrition and exercise have to be monitored, however; it is easy to overlook being good to yourself when others are depending on you. A pain that persists more than a few days should be discussed with a doctor. Do not trust home remedies when other help is available. Your emotional balance is at peak this year. Arguments and disagreements, that in past years you would have avoided to your own detriment, are now a challenge that you will enjoy. When you can openly discuss how you feel and can listen to what others have to say with an open mind, you are in a very healthy state.

There is no stopping Libras when it comes to work and business advancement in 1994. Past experience has given you a good basis for moving forward. A hobby may come into play with your regular work, putting you ahead of the competition. A pay raise or promotion is foreseen, although you could have some reservations if relocating is part of the deal. For many Libras this is a year for a job switch, perhaps to an entirely new line of work. You are not content to be stagnant. Opportunity not only beckons but compels you. Returning to school can open up even more possibilities. It is important to become a specialist in at least one area. A scientific or artistic breakthrough is foreseen during the third quarter, which can lead to an award or other recognition. Work that involves helping people, especially teaching or the medical professions, is starred. With Venus as your ruling planet, you are bestowed with the desire and ability to serve others as a means of enriching your own life.

DAILY FORECAST

January–December 1994

JANUARY

1. SATURDAY. Mixed. You may have the urge to start checking items off your priority list, but the vitality is not there today. Rest and take care of yourself. Handle only what is necessary; leave the rest until you are more energetic. Family members are willing to pitch in with work around the house. Clean off surfaces and get the kitchen back in good order. Drop-in guests may take you by surprise. Come up with a potluck meal for them, or order a few pizzas and forget about cooking. Do not be reluctant to take credit for what you have been doing. Blow your own horn so that friends and relatives sit up and take notice. You want to please yourself, but pleasing others is part of that mix.

2. SUNDAY. Variable. Activities with other people are favored throughout the day. Alone you may begin to feel sorry for yourself or let a problem build out of proportion. Offer to help a friend or family member without waiting to be asked. Pitch right in and do what you can. It is a starred time to teach your mate or steady date the rules of a game you enjoy, then work to better their techniques. Make music a part of your day as well. Check the newspapers to see if tickets are available for a concert to be performed tonight or in the coming week. Buy the best seats you can afford. If travel is on the agenda today, take special precautions. Be sure to allow ample time to reach your destination. Hurrying can make it difficult to avoid an accident.

3. MONDAY. Inactive. You still have not reached your pre-New Year's pace and should not push yourself. Tackling one or two routine jobs is enough now. Teamwork can be useful providing it is a true partnership endeavor. You will not relish being in the role of cheerleader and prime authority. Libras are more comfortable following along and helping out wherever needed.

Being useful gives you a good feeling. Go out of your way to welcome a newcomer who is feeling uncertain; you may make a new friend in the process. Someone you think you do not have much in common with may surprise you with their hidden interests and talents. Romance can blossom in the most unlikely situation.

4. TUESDAY. Good. The past has a strange way of catching up with you, and today you will welcome a phone call or letter from someone who was once an active participant in your life. Reliving old times, if only in memory, is sure to bring a smile to your lips. Emphasize balance in your everyday affairs. Avoid overdoing in any one area, including looking back instead of ahead. Find a way to include family as well as friends in your evening agenda. Children need extra attention from their Libra parent or relative. You can help them stay on track by being more involved in their school assignments. Dinnertime is not the moment to discuss anything negative. Keep the conversation neutral until you are alone with the one who deserves a comeuppance.

5. WEDNESDAY. Pleasant. Relationships are back on an even keel, thanks to your honesty in expressing what has been on your mind. Vow not to allow a problem to fester, especially if lack of communication is what drove you apart from your mate or partner. There are expansion plans under consideration that involve you in a very direct way. Before even being consulted, think about your own wants and whether you are willing to put in extra hours on the job in return for higher pay and a promotion. An offer may be flattering, but not right for you just now. Having time for your own interests is vital. This is a fine evening to go out for dinner and a long conversation. If you have a question, now is the time; the answer will delight you.

6. THURSDAY. Fortunate. Everything is beginning to fall into place quite nicely, but do not become too complacent. Continue working toward a long-term goal. A strong element of good fortune is a special boon now. You may have a chance to talk with an important person who can put in a good word for you with those in charge of granting exemptions or permits. To reach the pinnacle that is your aim, you need a dose of luck as well as hard work and dedication. Libras are fortunate in maintaining friendships that go back often as far as school days. These contacts can open doors on your behalf, sometimes without your being aware of it. Love life is beginning to take an exciting new shape.

7. FRIDAY. Cautious. Protect yourself from getting stuck in a rut. Break out of old familiar patterns and try something new and a little daring. Contented Libras can become bored and boring. Investigate a group that is just forming; you could be in on its inception and help shape it to your own needs. It is also a positive time to consider signing up to take a course or to return to school as a degree-seeking student. A few less honest types are around. Be leery of getting involved with them on a personal or business basis. Trust your instincts when it comes to loaning money or anything else of value. You do not have to come up with a good excuse for saying no, unless your boss poses the question.

8. SATURDAY. Difficult. It is all too easy today to become obsessed with minor matters and miss the big picture entirely. Be guided by your mate or other family member; they have a clearer vision of what lies ahead. Go along willingly with their plans. What does not appeal to you at first may become more interesting once you get into it. Do not put up any impenetrable barriers to love, friendship or other emotion. Deciding beforehand the qualities you are looking for in a mate, date or friend can eliminate just those people who might be best for you. Someone considerably older or younger is about to come into your life. Lack of available money necessitates changing evening plans.

9. SUNDAY. Unsettling. A friend's reluctance to go along with your plans could force you to put them on hold. Do not convert maybe into yes as an answer to an important question. Someone is trying to let you down gently without hurting your feelings. Look around for a new companion to fill the hours now available. A family member could be a good substitute if you have an extra ticket to a show or sports event. A younger relative is turning to you for ideas and is copying what you do. Set a good example in your conduct as well as your words. If an in-law or other older relative is interfering in your life, tell them firmly but politely to back off and leave you alone.

10. MONDAY. Variable. You are apt to be caught in a tug-of-war between what you want to do and what you are being told to do. Try to figure out a compromise so that at least some of your desires are fulfilled. This is a starred day to volunteer to work with a group striving to better themselves in some way. You may be able to provide practical help in a teaching role. A financial contribution would undoubtedly be easier for you than a gift of time. A long-lost item may turn up unexpectedly. Vow to try to take better care of what is precious to you. Anything sent in the mail should be insured if it is valuable. Evening favors a trip down memory lane with old photos or film classics as your entertainment.

11. TUESDAY. Pleasant. A relationship that is very important to you is moving up to a higher plane. Avoid asking too many questions about what was in the past. Concentrate on the future and all that it holds for you with this particular person at your side. You may be breaking out of one mold and headed for another. Try not to get into a new rut. Keep all of your options wide open. There is no one to bother you today unless and until you ask for assistance. Then you should have no trouble getting all the help you need. In-laws and other older relatives may be having a direct impact on your work. You can rely on their experience as a clue to what you could be doing.

12. WEDNESDAY. Disconcerting. An unexpected visit can disrupt your thought processes and set you spinning. Be wary if the boss or another higher-up drops by to see you rather than calling you to the office. Trouble is brewing behind the scenes, and your name may be coming up in the conversation. Keep track of what people say to you and what promises have been made. Also be sure to hold onto receipts and other proof of current expenses, especially if you are disbursing money belonging to someone else. There could be a claim of some wrongdoing that you must refute. Stay far clear of a courtroom or lawyer. Anything with legal ramifications can trap you in a tangled web.

13. THURSDAY. Excellent. Libra intuition will not play you false today. Go with your first impression in sizing up a newcomer on the scene. There is opportunity for new friendship with a person unlike you in almost every way. The exception is the most important trait that you look for but seldom find. Physical power is at a peak. This is the day to use your hands and muscles and let your brain take a rest. Pitch in to help where needed; do not wait to be invited. All forms of physical exercise are favored. If you are a member of a health club, plan on a workout before you go to work, or drop by on your way home. Swimming is especially good for toning your body.

14. FRIDAY. Successful. Dig deep into your personal resources and you will have the strength to be successful today. Someone is putting you to the test; do not let them or yourself down. Be more daring than usual, but in a controlled manner. Do not allow anyone to goad you into taking action that goes against your better judgment. Be true to the basic principles that have stood the test of time. Working conditions are good. The boss knows what you are capable of doing and what you could achieve if given the opportunity. That chance is not far off. Keep on the good side of higher-ups; do nothing that might cause them to have second thoughts about your judgment.

15. SATURDAY. Productive. Use your skills around the house or helping a friend. The more experience you get, the better you become. Do not try to save your strength for a rainy day; use it or you could lose it. Everyone around the house is preoccupied and unable to help except for short spurts of time. Whatever is accomplished has to be done primarily on your own. A local store owner can offer worthwhile advice, especially if you are buying tools, paint or other items to use in beautifying your living quarters. Stop by a florist and get a bunch of flowers to brighten the kitchen table. If evening plans are postponed, come up with an alternative plan. It is likely to work out even better than your original intention.

16. SUNDAY. Mixed. Far-off places have special appeal. Although you may not be able to get away on vacation now, you can begin planning a trip or merely dreaming up a once-in-a-lifetime sojourn. Check out the travel section of your local newspaper for ideas of where you might go for a complete change of pace and climate. Look into alternative travel arrangements such as a tramp steamer or a caravan tour. Let your mind rule your actions throughout the day. Do not get carried away with a fanciful idea. Friends may laugh at your latest version of what has been happening. You are not seeing eye-to-eye when viewing the same scene. A loved one, too, is on a different wave length.

17. MONDAY. Buoyant. Communications from someone at a distance cheer you up and put you in a much better frame of mind by noontime. Good news is likely regarding an investment in a multinational company. Or you may get word of a buyout or merger that promises to return a good dividend for you. Libras looking for work should check again with the employment division of a large corporation. Practice taking a test or performing work that you know is in demand. Academic training could also be worthwhile, especially if you were recently laid off or are returning to the job market after time away from it. An older relative has you in mind for an inheritance.

18. TUESDAY. Changeable. There is some jealousy interfering with a relationship that you value. Your mate or another family member may feel that you spend most of your waking time thinking about work. Try to be more understanding. Verbalize your feelings instead of assuming that they are understood. All conditions are in flux. Work that has become routine will soon be taken over by a machine or a younger colleague, leaving you to use more brainpower than muscle. Getting away from everyday duties for a while helps you gain better perspective of where you fit into the overall scheme of things. You may be dwelling on minor matters and missing the main point entirely.

19. WEDNESDAY. Difficult. Ignore a rumor that is making the rounds at work or in your neighborhood. What is being said is only half the truth at best. If someone you know is being mentioned unfavorably, stand up and support the person as forcibly as you can. You might also have to defend some of your own recent actions that are being questioned. Romance is not on today's agenda. That special person in your life may be out of town or otherwise occupied, leaving you to fend for yourself. Libras who want a shoulder to cry on should turn to a longtime friend, not a recent acquaintance. Imagination is giving you more worry than you deserve. Be realistic in assessing current goings-on.

20. THURSDAY. Frustrating. Yesterday's upsets spill over into today, making this another period when you do not quite know which way to turn. New alliances are being formed. Working as part of a team is favored, but you will not have as much say as you want. It is a time when you are forced to be a follower instead of a leader. Beware of taking on the moods of those you are working with. You have enough on your mind without getting involved with their difficulties and projecting them as your own. You can empathize without becoming emotional. Rejection of a recent application, especially by a banker, could force you back to square one as you struggle to come up with an operative plan.

21. FRIDAY. Lucky. Conditions are doing an abrupt about-face. A person who has been causing you aggravation is starting to understand your reasons and accept them. Welcome a former antagonist as a new ally. It is an especially lucky day for new partnership of a personal or business nature. Working as part of a tight team gives you special advantages impossible as an individual. You will also find that there is strength in numbers. Changes that you hope to see enacted can be hurried along by organizing a petition drive or a march to show support. Get in touch with an elected representative to put the ball in motion. A letter to the editor could also help you stir up support.

22. SATURDAY. Outstanding. Sports have a special place in the day, although Libras may be on the sidelines as officials or bona fide rooters. You will enjoy direct competition more from a distance than as an active participant. Your love of harmony makes it hard to accept beating someone for the top spot, and you also hate to lose; competition thus becomes a no-win situation for you. Do not allow the weather to put a damper on your plans. Switch from one location to a better protected one, if necessary. A friend is worried that you are going in over your head in a new job or a new romance. Find time to have a long chat to allay their concerns and express your happiness.

23. SUNDAY. Cautious. Avoid making any new commitment or becoming involved with a person or group whose aims are very different from your own. You can easily be swept along in a tide of excitement, then suddenly stop short and wonder why in the world you are with these people. Libras can be led, but only to a point; after that you dig your heels in and will not budge. Be wary of contributing either time or money to a cause that is not spelled out clearly. Check the reliability of a charity, particularly one that collects furniture or other items for resale. Pay outstanding bills, but leave something in the bank for that proverbial rainy day. If you do not have the money in hand, do not buy now.

24. MONDAY. Variable. Someone you have been corresponding with on a regular basis may announce intentions to visit. This could make you a little uneasy, especially if you have been inclined to exaggerate by phone or letter. There is no turning back now, however. Results of a face-to-face meeting are apt to be much happier than you envision. It is a starred day for Libras acting as middlemen. In your capacity as a mover and shaker, you can be a power broker in business or a marriage broker in your own family. A friend is waiting for you to nudge them into action. You are seeing the overall situation while they see only a small fraction of it. Dinner is a good time to make introductions.

25. TUESDAY. Changeable. Ambition is not enough now as you strive to get ahead. You should also upgrade your skills or acquire new ones. Learning on the job can be best, especially if your line of work is specialized. Pay close attention to a co-worker who is highly regarded. Analyze their way of operating, but do not be too obvious about it. They may fear that you are after their job. It is not surprising that you have been falling behind. Other people may be getting some off-hours help from a higher-up who has more than an employment interest in their advancement. You are bucking some strong odds, but can come out on top if you apply yourself to the task more than other people are doing.

26. WEDNESDAY. Satisfactory. Emotional reaction is not a reliable guide in making up your mind. Let your reasoning take charge and remain in charge. Weigh the pros and cons carefully. What you perceive as a negative can be given a little twist and turned to your advantage. Someone you worked with in the past is a good source of inside information. You appreciate the company of other people, but can get by on your own if necessary. Avoid joining a group just to add your name to the membership roll. If you have no intention of being a fully participating member, stay away. An older person has practical advice to offer if you ask for it directly.

27. THURSDAY. Profitable. It may not be income that makes this day profitable, but Libras can look forward to a new relationship or additional responsibility. Extra income is foreseen as the result of what you are currently undertaking. Partnership is favored providing you remain in control. Do not relinquish that control to anyone, even for a day. Once you slip back it may be almost impossible to work your way back to the top of the heap. Your patience can be put to the test. Someone is vowing to outlast you by hanging on longer than you are wiling to do. Keep a sense of humor. Laugh at yourself, not at anyone else. News from a family member gives you a sense of pending excitement.

28. FRIDAY. Quiet. A sociable Friday is on tap, with little chance of accomplishing much work after the noontime break. Squeeze in serious concentration between breakfast and the first coffee break of the day. A discussion then can resolve a matter without being turned into a federal case. Have a heart-to-heart talk with the boss or another person in charge. Find out what they really want, not what they are publicizing. You are like a magnet to dreamers whose idea of reality is what they have seen in movies. But when they explain their ideas you may begin to see realistic possibilities. Planning is favored over action, at least until next month. Consider potential financial backers and how best to get them to part with their money.

29. SATURDAY. Mixed. Family plays the dominant role today. Stay within the confines of your own home most of the time. Do not venture far away from your mate or another family member at your side. Married Libras have an opportunity to draw closer to their mate by sharing work around the house. A major project, especially redecorating or adding on a porch or patio, can be started now. You do not have to hire a professional if you have at least some experience. A good how-to manual can be the best guide, and a cheaper one than any so-called expert. Choose your own materials and colors from a list of suggestions. Be sure to obtain any necessary permits or permissions.

30. SUNDAY. Easygoing. Stay in bed late, or plan on taking a long siesta during the afternoon hours. Your physical strength is at a low point for the month. Turn down any offers that would involve lifting or carrying. What you would like to do is not in tune with your capacity now. A family member is likely to bring a problem out into the open. You can be blunt and truthful with this person without worrying about hurt feelings. Relationships at home are easygoing. The day is starred for welcoming a new addition to the family circle, either the two-legged or four-legged variety. A child craves love and attention, so do not stint on either. The more you give, the more they learn.

31. MONDAY. Rewarding. It may be difficult to separate romance and finance. Lucky is the Libra whose mate or steady date comes with an inheritance or trust fund. Or it may be that a promotion puts this person ahead of you on the salary scale. Instead of feeling threatened, count your lucky stars and be grateful. Even recently graduated Libras can begin now to plan for eventual retirement. Look into alternative savings programs that help your money to grow ahead of the inflation index. Savings in a bank account can be eaten up with taxes and stagnation. A friend's insight could make the idea of backtracking appealing as a way for you to switch to a different approach.

FEBRUARY

1. TUESDAY. Pleasant. If you look back you may stumble trying to move forward. Keep your sights firmly set on the goal that you are trying to achieve. There are likely to be problems along the way, but none you cannot resolve amicably. All personal relationships are happy today. It may be easier getting along with someone you argued with recently than it is with a usually calm and placid family member. A good airing of views helps you know where you stand and how far you dare to go. Control your own emotional responses. Allow extra time to let a different point of view sink in and to digest it. You may discover that what is foreign to you today becomes ordinary by month's end.

2. WEDNESDAY. Satisfactory. Let other people take the ball and run with it today. You will be content and useful staying in the background of all that is going on. Work from a position of influence behind the scenes. Pull some strings based on who you know on a personal basis. You should try to get your thoughts in order, your ducks in a row. When you have reached a decision you can act, but not before then. Turn over a complex problem to a specialist who is equipped to handle it. Any complicated repair job should be handled by a professional whose reputation is well known. If you do not know who to call, ask a friend or co-worker for a recommendation. Love makes tonight take on a special glow.

3. THURSDAY. Good. Be practical when it comes to saving money as well as earning it. Do not give away what you could sell for a profit. Before buying anything that costs a lot, check around to see if you could borrow or rent it. It is not smart to clutter up your life with one-use-only purchases. Libra intuition is right on target today. Someone who is new on the scene is trying hard to impress you. Do not be turned off by their eagerness to please. A recent dream is a good guide to future actions. Jot down notes of what you can recall from the nocturnal playacting. Figure out what it means in connection with a current problem situation just beginning to emerge.

4. FRIDAY. Mixed. Some expenditures cannot be put off even though you do not want to spend the money you have in your savings account. Small repair jobs should be taken care of now before they become major problems. Check the newspaper for an advertised sale or a money-off coupon. A major purchase, perhaps a car or a home, is also looming on the horizon. Begin to investigate potential sources of funding, starting with a well-to-do family member who might be willing to back you. Timing is all important when you are making a long-term commitment. A small difference in interest rates can be a major sum. Accept advice offered by a friend who has more experience than you.

5. SATURDAY. Rewarding. A personal relationship with someone who is older and wiser promises to be especially rewarding. Learn all that you can by asking questions and absorbing the answers. Someone you have never considered as a potential partner may be sparking your interest now. Romance or a business relationship can result; if you are lucky, the two can be combined. Do some maneuvering behind the scenes to stage a meeting that may seem accidental, but is actually well planned. You may receive an offer today that is too good to refuse. Family members will relish a special treat this evening. Plan on going out for dinner and then to a show or concert.

6. SUNDAY. Pleasant. Entertainment suggested by your mate or steady date is sure to be enjoyable. Dress up so that you stand out in a crowd. It is also an excellent day to shop for bargains in handcrafted items at a boutique or through a private sale. You can add to a collection by way of careful shopping and bargaining. Do not pay full retail price for anything. If you cannot get the price down now, wait for a sale to be announced. What is new and unusual strikes your fancy. Be a trendsetter instead of a follower. Socializing deserves high priority. If you aim to know co-workers and higher-ups on a personal basis, your career will benefit. New friendship is also foreseen.

7. MONDAY. Difficult. Struggle to catch up with work that you have been putting off. Get an early start and dig right in. Tackle the easiest of the lot first, then move right on to the next and the next assignments. Do not take time off in between to congratulate yourself. There is a lot to be done and no spare time for lolling around. Frustration comes easily today. You will not be satisfied with less than the best that you can do. But when you are under pressure you are prone to make careless mistakes, which other people pick up on quickly. Check and recheck, using a calculator, dictionary or other available aids for accuracy. Libras in charge can expect little cooperation of the willing variety.

8. TUESDAY. Stressful. Volunteer for a job that no one else seems to want. Prove that it can help your career by doing more than is expected. This is a fortuitous time to sign a contract or conclude a deal that has been in the negotiating stage since early in the year. Make some concessions in order to break a stalemate. When you give in a little, you will undoubtedly get a lot in return. Do not allow anyone to know what your bottom line really is. Be wary around people with whom you have little in common. It pays to listen more than you talk. There is also a lot to learn through out-of-town travel. If you expect to be away from home overnight, be sure to pack more than one of everything.

9. WEDNESDAY. Unsettling. The first three days of this week are a challenge to the most adept Libra. Today you may have to put up with interference from a person who knows less than you, but also thinks you are old-fashioned. Do not try to prove anything to this person. Instead, let him or her have their say, doing it their way, and then turning to you for help. You may be in charge, but that does not give you absolute guarantees. A new employee who is not working out as expected should be let go before anyone is upset by their leaving. It is not a good day to hire or to apply for a job. You are unsure of yourself now and cannot project a very positive image. Stay home tonight with a book for company.

10. THURSDAY. Fortunate. Results are beginning to come in from your recent efforts on the job. Do not let up one iota; keep pushing ahead with vim and vigor. Focus on long-term objectives. More and more people are beginning to sit up and take notice of what you are doing. Help is more readily available. Financing can also be obtained, but not the amount you would like. Accept a meager offer in hopes of a better one to come as you continue to prove yourself. It could be that you are asked to take over work started by another person. Try to build on what they have done instead of going back to square one. There is opportunity for worthwhile new investment in a business close to home.

11. FRIDAY. Variable. How you look affects how you feel, which, in turn, puts you into the swing of all that is going on. A new outfit or a special piece of jewelry should be worn to good advantage today. Dress to impress; it cannot hurt your chances. Trying hard is no guarantee of success. Who you know, and who recognizes your abilities, are important ingredients in the mix that will push you to the top. Try to be more self-reliant when it comes to making decisions. Follow orders, but add your special Libra talent to make an indelible mark on all that you are doing. Love life is looking positive. Tonight is prime time for stargazing with that special person, as long as there are clear skies.

12. SATURDAY. Sensitive. Personal relationships at home are at the sensitive stage. If you offended a family member, especially unintentionally, make a full and wholehearted apology at the start of the day. By afternoon you should feel tempers easing and harmony returning. You are not fearful of being alone, but would rather have company than not. Make it clear that you are extending an open invitation to anyone who would like to take part in your planned activities, then sit back and see who joins in. A young person understands your motives at least as well as you do. Out of the mouths of babes may come a truth you have not faced squarely. You will enjoy being part of a crowd tonight.

13. SUNDAY. Promising. Try to get a friend to go along with your plans if a family member has turned you down. Maintain your optimism despite initial rejection. Your ideas are promising for long-term success; immediate gratification is out of the question. Some revisions and changes may become necessary as you proceed. Be prepared to keep a secret longer than you thought would be necessary. It is possible that you have been assuming too much or expecting more than any single person can give. If lack of cooperation is hampering your efforts, break the job down into small segments and try to get those handled by others. Only you have to keep overall control.

14. MONDAY. Rewarding. You can proceed faster and more efficiently as part of a team than on your own. Individual effort only goes so far; there are some areas where you lack skill or talent. Pair up with a person whose abilities complement your own. It can be helpful to hitch your wagon to a rising star at work. Becoming indispensable to a busy executive gives you access to information that others would pay a high price to obtain. Guard against downplaying anyone else's abilities in order to magnify your own. It is performance that counts, not words or promises. The less critical you are, the more acceptance you will win from the people who can advance your cause.

15. TUESDAY. Routine. This is a wait-and-see day even though you had hoped to make some significant progress. A promise may not be fulfilled, leaving you waiting for a phone call or letter. Put all of your energy into ordinary pursuits that have to be handled sooner or later. Get them out of the way now so that the decks are cleared for the remainder of the week. Exercise is a valuable release of pent-up tension. Take a long walk at lunchtime, or plan on stopping off to swim after work. Keep close tabs of all expenditures. When you know where your money is going, you can begin to figure out how to save more of it. A romantic fiction novel can give you some new ideas.

16. WEDNESDAY. Misleading. As the Moon enters stubborn Taurus today, you may encounter a bullheaded person born under that Sign. Be ready to counter opposition with good reasons that not only sound legitimate but are. It does not pay to make up an excuse or try to invent a ready alibi. Cutting corners in your work can backfire also. Hard work is the order of the day. Put more of yourself into everything that you are doing. Dredge up some expertise from younger days when you were more willing to try new things. What worked well then can be adapted to the current dilemma with good results. If an unconventional idea is rejected by those in charge, go ahead on your own in a low-key manner so as not to defy anyone.

17. THURSDAY. Excellent. A combination of luck and your dogged determination helps you make significant progress today. Do not give up easily; in fact, there is no reason to give up at all in trying to resolve a situation that has been causing you headaches for a while. Look for a new way to approach the problem and you will find the elusive answer. Get in touch with a former schoolmate or teacher if you need specific information not available to the general public. This is an excellent time to make a firm commitment with long-range implications. Socializing can provide some surprising benefits. Begin to plan a party or other gathering designed to impress as well as entertain.

18. FRIDAY. Ordinary. What is interesting to you may be a big yawn to a family member or co-worker. Do not talk endlessly about your own work or after-hours interests. Instead, pay attention to what is compelling to other people. At first you may have to feign interest, but you will get caught up in their enthusiasm. It is likely that you are taking some matters much too seriously. Look on the light, bright side. Find the spark of optimism in an otherwise humdrum situation. Handling ordinary chores is necessary now. Take care of paperwork, especially bills. Get in touch with an insurance agent to review coverage. The fewer people involved in evening plans, the less chance for a mix-up.

19. SATURDAY. Fair. Tackle one repair job at home that you know you can complete successfully. Constant upkeep helps avoid a major overhaul that would require the services of a highly paid professional. This is also a good time to consider redecorating. A new easychair or couch can add to your comfort as well as the appearance of your living room. Your friends will be impressed. Go through a recipe book in search of a different meal to prepare this evening. Shopping at a market carrying foreign food can be inspiring. Gourmet cooking could become a most welcome hobby that the whole family enjoys. Guard against feelings of jealousy, especially if a neighbor shows up with a new car or other luxury item you have long desired.

20. SUNDAY. Enjoyable. A personal relationship has reached a plateau that is comfortable, but perhaps a little too ordinary for you. Try to add some new zest by suggesting a trip or other outing. For married Libras, a second honeymoon could be just what the doctor ordered. Be wary of taking a loved one for granted. Children rate extra attention as well. You may want to volunteer to lead a Scout group or coach a sports team. Get more involved with school activities so that you know what is going on. You have the will power now to eliminate a habit you know is unhealthy. Find a substitute that helps you over the initial hump of giving up and feeling deprived. Your efforts will earn you a gold star from family members and friends.

21. MONDAY. Challenging. Find a way to maneuver around a stumbling block instead of charging right at it. Patience and perseverance pay off with handsome dividends. Play up to a person who wields power behind the scenes. Become acquainted on a personal basis through extracurricular activity you know they are involved in. Prove that you are intent on being a member of the team, not a loner. To obtain financial support, you may have to wade through a lot of red tape. Fill out forms as thoroughly as possible; you will then not be delayed by having to redo them. Start now to collect information for preparing your tax returns. A financial planner can help you find ways to save more by sound investing.

22. TUESDAY. Variable. Nothing is proceeding exactly as you had outlined it, but there should be no major blips. Be open to new suggestions, especially from someone just arrived on the scene. What has been in vogue in a different part of the country is just beginning to become a trend in your area. You can be one of the first to latch on to the new idea. This is a starred day to negotiate the fine points of a new contract or other obligation. Libra job hunters can have success by holding out for a little more than is initially offered. Do not undersell yourself or your services. Unless you value yourself, no one else is going to do so.

23. WEDNESDAY. Satisfactory. Take the reins of a project that has been drifting along under someone else's supervision. Once you become involved, you can go straight to the finish line without having to worry about how other people may react. Your ability to harmonize divergent interests is a great asset today. With your intervention you can bring together opposing forces that have been blocking progress. Emphasize organization and action geared for results. There is no need to deal through middlemen; face-to-face talks help you break a stalemate. When asking questions, be wary of revealing your intentions. There is a certain group who tends to tell what they believe you want to hear, whether or not they believe it to be the truth.

24. THURSDAY. Mixed. A major domestic adjustment is taking place. Be prepared to give more than you expect to get. Libras are at the turning point of change now; they can tip the balance either way. Guard against allowing emotion to dictate your choices. Use all of your intellectual powers to weigh options and figure out which are most promising. Then test them one by one. You cannot hope to achieve the success you want if you are building barriers against certain people or certain actions. Combine your good ideas with those of a person who has been on the opposite side for a while. Together you make an unbeatable partnership. Learning a foreign language can prove invaluable before year's end.

25. FRIDAY. Uncertain. Step in quickly if you begin to suspect someone is going behind your back and trying to subvert your intentions. Do not allow the situation to go on, with the hope that it will peter out. Someone you are counting on as a supporter or helper has to be given extra strokes and heaps of praise. Be wary of taking this person for granted. It is not smart now to make any long-term promises. If you have to go back on your word later, your reputation could suffer. Unexpected visitors may annoy you, but be gracious nevertheless. What seems to be a purposeless conversation may have more meaning than you know. You are being evaluated for an important assignment.

26. SATURDAY. Changeable. Resist an urge to tell off a friend or neighbor. Instead, work to find common ground on which to build better understanding. Conditions are changing faster than you can keep up with them. New advances could leave you feeling outdated and out of style. Look into brush-up courses being offered by a community college or other institution. You may be able to get your employer to pay part or all of the cost of the course. Self-study manuals can also be worthwhile if you have sufficient dedication to plow through them chapter by chapter. The easy way out is not likely to work for you. Diligence will take you where you want to be. Go out tonight and kick up your heels.

27. SUNDAY. Good. Time spent at home may be necessary if you hope to avert a minor skirmish between relatives on opposite sides. Strive to bring harmony to the mix by emphasizing the advantages of working together. You may want to call in a mediator if your efforts prove less than successful, but first give it a try. Travel is favored today or in the coming week. Getting away from the site of ongoing friction gives you a much needed break and can cool hot tempers. People at or from a distance are having a definite impact on your options. Read a news report thoroughly about conditions in a part of the world where you do business or hope to travel as a tourist.

28. MONDAY. Variable. Come to know a new neighbor or colleague whose background is far different from your own. Be the first to initiate friendship by inviting this person to lunch or to sit together at an open meeting. Resist the temptation to tell the boss what you think should be done. You may be surprised when an idea that is not your own proves successful. If your superior is the understanding type, suggest a trial where two plans are tested simultaneously. An offer from a friend is too good to resist. Arrange for time off so that you can go along on a trip or a shopping excursion. Romance is high on your list of priorities. Let that special person know that your thoughts are with them even if you cannot be.

MARCH

1. TUESDAY. Pleasant. Congratulations are coming your way for a job well done. Accept them graciously, giving full credit to other people who were also active participants in the project. This is a starred day to round up a new team in preparation for launching another major undertaking. Do not rest on your laurels; look ahead expectantly. Your recent work warrants praise, and perhaps a pay raise as well. Press the advantage while you have it. A talk with the boss can make it clear that you are anxious to get ahead financially. Shopping could be worthwhile later. An advertised sale is too good to resist. Snap up a bargain while it is available. Buy in bulk if the price is right.

2. WEDNESDAY. Satisfactory. Negotiations and making deals are very promising now. Know what you are willing to accept, but do not reveal this information to anyone else. You will be most successful doing your own bargaining. Avoid dealing through intermediaries if possible. A lawyer can wind up costing you more than you win because you pay so much for his or her professional services. There is opportunity to conclude a deal with a major company, possibly one that is foreign-based. A handshake is not enough; get all the particulars in writing for future reference. Libras looking for a job should be concentrating on large corporations. You will excel in an interview situation.

3. THURSDAY. Variable. Combine mental effort with physical exertion for a winning combination. Focus your efforts on one task at a time. If you try to handle too much, you can wind up doing a haphazard job. Co-workers are applying pressure on you to change your mind or to reverse a recent decision already being implemented. Hold out a little longer to see if you were right. Do not be so stubborn, though, that you are willing to compromise if that becomes obviously necessary. Being right but not being accepted will get you nowhere fast. Teamwork is not favored today. Independent action gives you an opening to test a theory without having to justify your reasons for doing so.

4. FRIDAY. Mixed. Someone you are counting on for help, especially a loan, should be informed of your progress. Keeping them in the dark may cause them to lose interest. Avoid making any promises today that you might regret later on. Long-term commitments have a way of catching up with you at the worst possible time. Agree to consider a new proposal without setting any limits. Anything underhanded is likely to backfire. You do not have the basic cunning necessary to carry off a deal that is just short of breaking the law. Keep everything open and aboveboard. Stay within the confines of rules and regulations without expecting an exception to be made for you.

5. SATURDAY. Demanding. It is unwise today to carry a lot of money in your wallet. If you go shopping, plan on paying with a check or credit card. You have the will power to resist buying unless certain you want and need the item. For Libras who must be on the job, this is a time to be more aggressive and assertive. It may surprise you that when you make a demand instead of a request you are given greater credence. Pretend to know a little more than you really do, particularly about a situation that is just beginning to brew. A knowing smile can cover lack of accurate inside information. Put off a face-to-face meeting by conferring over the phone or sending a long letter. Put on the ritz if going out tonight; do nothing halfheartedly.

6. SUNDAY. Changeable. Intuition is not totally reliable today. Someone who does not appeal to you on first meeting could begin to grow in your favor. Try harder to keep an open mind. Be sure to remember names and faces of those to whom you are introduced. Be wary if shopping. An aggressive salesperson could sway you against your better judgment. Appearances can be deceiving. What is advertised may not be the merchandise shown in the store at the sale price. Change is the order of the day. Home relationships are in flux. A younger family member could soon be an ally as you work out a solution with a parent or in-law. Avoid any new commitment of time, or of money, especially.

7. MONDAY. Variable. Do not make up rules for yourself as you go along. Operate according to well-established rules and regulations that apply to everyone equally. Even a friend is unlikely to make exceptions for you. Opportunity exists if you play fair and square. Look for ways to cut costs by trimming excesses from your personal spending or a work project. You can make do with materials and equipment already on hand. Speed may be reduced, but quality will be up to your high standards. Friendship does not have to be expensive. You cannot buy lasting love or attention. Actively seek to expand your circle of friends and acquaintances by joining a group of people who share your interests.

8. TUESDAY. Outstanding. Do some deep thinking about current plans and projects. You may decide to abandon one or two that no longer appeal to you or are not consistent with your needs. Guard against becoming so stubborn that you will not give up in the face of inevitable loss. There is always a different way to approach a problem or to obtain what you want. Sneaking up on it can be better sometimes than a frontal assault. If you wait for volunteers to step forward with an offer of help, you could be waiting a very long time. Independent action is favored. Results of your own work will be outstanding and merit favorable attention from those at the top of the heap.

9. WEDNESDAY. Uncertain. You cannot accomplish much if you spend the day dreaming about what might have been or what might be in the future. Operate in the here and now. Look for a new way to achieve a goal that is proving elusive. Someone you have never worked with before may make the best team member. Align yourself with those who share your desire to get to the top without gouging anyone else. Definite goals could bring fortunate results. The more people you come to know, the more potential help and information is available to you. Make good use of a written report that outlines how a project was done; build on that instead of going back to the beginning and, in effect, reinventing the wheel.

10. THURSDAY. Mixed. An announcement made today may not be what you wanted to hear, but you can learn to live with it. Look for help at a distance. Someone with whom you used to work, or a former schoolmate, may surface as a surprising ally. Make good use of publicity outlets such as a letter to the editor or a notice on the community bulletin board. Publicize your discontent and others who feel the same way will join forces with you. It is up to you to set the tone. Libras can be torn between family responsibilities and outside interests. Find a balance that everyone can accept even if they are not totally pleased. A short trip could help you get necessary information.

11. FRIDAY. Promising. Open your mind to a new suggestion from a person who usually follows instead of leads. You can benefit from expanding beyond your usual base of operations. Shake up normal operating procedures to put some renewed excitement into what has become routine. This is an excellent day for Libras to add on a new employee or team member. Enthusiasm can be as important as formal training. A relationship that has been stagnating can be given new life if you are open about your needs and willing to listen to the needs of others. Bring a problem out in the open and examine it from all angles. You have ample energy for all that you want to do.

12. SATURDAY. Ordinary. Concentrate on household tasks that cannot be put off if you are to be comfortable at home. Do some weeding out of closets and drawers to give yourself more space. Plan on giving away what you do not want to a charitable organization instead of tossing the items out with the trash. Money matters can cause some strain with family members. Review the joint budget with your mate to figure out where you can save. You want to have enough for a vacation you hope to take this summer. A major purchase should be carefully budgeted; going head over heels in debt will make you a nervous wreck. You can get by with less than usual if you know you are saving for a special occasion.

13. SUNDAY. Fair. A friend's idea of entertainment may be too expensive or too strenuous for you. Say no without going into too much detail about your reasons. You will not enjoy competition today; win or lose you may feel uncomfortable. Also be wary of anything that puts your hard-earned money at risk. All forms of gambling should be shunned. You are more of a follower than a leader today. Ideas you suggest may meet strong resistance from family members. An older relative deserves a pat on the back and some reassurance. Be the one to offer help without having to be asked. Make no definite decision without first consulting your mate or date.

14. MONDAY. Uncertain. Ease back into work without accepting any additional responsibility. You have plenty to do just picking up the pieces from last week. Try to keep some free time in your schedule for a meeting or other get-together to discuss future planning. Drifting along without definite goals can stifle incentive. Find out what is going on at a distance. If you cannot travel to be there in person, send someone to report events to you. Travel is favorable for Libras without binding family commitments. When it comes to choosing between home and work, however, you will find the choice already made for you. Assert yourself only when positive you are right.

15. TUESDAY. Disconcerting. Do not loan anything of value or ask to borrow. Delegate tasks that do not need your personal touch. It is important today to stay on top of fast-breaking developments. Be ready to come up with a quick alternative when conditions change. A new acquaintance may be steering you in an entirely different direction. Go along for the ride unless and until you begin to feel uncomfortable. You know your own limits, but may not recognize them until you are at that point. You may wish today that the telephone had never been invented. Turn on the answering machine, or refuse to answer the incessant ring while you are busy with another project.

16. WEDNESDAY. Satisfactory. Focus exclusively on work-related matters during daylight hours. Work should go smoothly providing you are available for direct supervision. If you have delegated specific chores, be sure to check on how they are being handled. You should be seeing results of a recent decision and can evaluate them on the spot. Position yourself to exert authority without having to make any threats. Leadership means arousing people to want to perform up to your high standards, and adopt them as their own. Guard against sinking to the lowest common level. Hold out for a little more than you might be willing to accept in a bargaining situation. Your skills are too valuable to give away.

17. THURSDAY. Exciting. Let your good Libra judgment guide all ongoing activities. Avoid anything that could be interpreted as an attempt to evade responsibility. There are exciting possibilities far from your usual arena of operations. Changing conditions at a distance give you a chance to make your presence felt. You can afford to take a risk, providing you have calculated the odds and truly believe them to be in your favor. If you need help from a friend or co-worker, you have only to ask. People are eager to cooperate because it is obvious you are driving to the top. An important breakthrough is foreseen, although you may not recognize it immediately. An elected official is willing to make an exception for you on a one-time-only basis.

18. FRIDAY. Tricky. Stress can make you say one thing when you mean another. Seek ways to calm your racing mind when confronted by a group of people waiting to hear what you have to say. Speaking from a stage or behind a podium can give you butterflies in your stomach. You may want to take a public speaking course to increase your self-confidence. Libra salespeople have a special opportunity now to make a large sale. The trick is to get your foot in the door; after that you should have little trouble. Humor can help you cover nervousness. Creativity gives you a good outlet to release tension. Write a story or create a gift with your own hands. Make up a pattern instead of using a commercial one available to anyone.

19. SATURDAY. Variable. Anything you have for sale is apt to be scooped up by a willing buyer. It is a starred time to get rid of extraneous items that are only gathering dust in your home. Try to sell them yourself, or consign them to a store that does not take too high a commission. You may also want to make a charitable donation of furniture or clothing for needy people who can not afford to buy. You could see some additional profit today if you have invested your money wisely. It's better to be safe than sorry when it comes to savings. Do not gamble any sum you need for everyday expenses. Pay close attention to a legal matter that might produce income for you.

20. SUNDAY. Good. You will enjoy the company of family members more than friends. If you brought work home for this weekend, save it for late in the day so that you can go on an outing. A trip to a museum, zoo or other public place should be special fun for everyone. Sports are also a fine way to interact with those you love providing you do not put the emphasis on winning. The gentle approach is favored in all relationships. You get more from a request than an order. Be especially kind to an older relative who lacks everyday companionship. Listen attentively to what they have to say, even if you have heard it all before. Evening favors close contact with that special person.

21. MONDAY. Easygoing. Reschedule a meeting that you know is otherwise going to be sparsely attended. You may also want to change the time or meeting place if you are going to have lunch or dinner afterward with a friend. Plans do not have to be precise today. You can get by with a vague outline of what you want to do, then follow along with what happens as it develops. Check an electrical appliance for safety; if the cord is frayed, have it replaced. Be sure to use light bulbs that do not exceed the wattage rated for the lamps. Quiet work appeals, especially writing and composing. Music provides the perfect background. This is an excellent day to look for a way to help a needy friend without being obvious about it.

22. TUESDAY. Stressful. Trying to rush through a project may only produce more headaches for you. Take things at a slow, even pace. Patience is not in good supply today for Libras. Be guided by a friend or co-worker who has some hands-on experience in what you are attempting to do. Enthusiasm can sweep you along for a while, but eventually you must stop and take stock. It is important to build a firm foundation. A disagreement regarding time off or vacation scheduling can put you at odds with a person you normally get along with well. Seek a compromise that is acceptable to everyone although delighting no one. Your restlessness makes travel appealing.

23. WEDNESDAY. Changeable. Have facts to back up whatever you intend to do. You may be challenged by a know-it-all, but with perseverance you will manage to wear that person down instead of the other way around. Once you make up your Libra mind it takes a lot to cause a change of heart. First impressions are not necessarily correct. You are likely to have more of an impact on a newcomer than you feel from the encounter. Dress for success today. Play up your best features with color and accessories just right for you. Love life may be complicated by the element of jealousy, especially from a new person on the scene. You have to let go in order to possess.

24. THURSDAY. Fair. Moderation in all things is the order of the day. Guard against overeating or overexerting. Be good to your body and it will respond well when you are ready for action. Pace yourself in work also. New responsibility is a challenge, not a chore. Put more of your creative self into a project that is drifting along as though anyone in the world were in charge of it. Financial affairs require careful scrutiny. Do not pay a bill without an itemized receipt having first been presented. You could wind up paying too much because you are unaware of the going rate. Check around to see what the competition is offering. Run, do not walk, from a fast talker.

25. FRIDAY. Mixed. You may be physically separated from a person you love, but they are close to you in mind and spirit. Proceed as though they were at your side, egging you on. Check that you are eating regular meals and not snacking your way through the day. It is a starred time to make an appointment with your doctor or dentist for a checkup. Pinpointing a small problem can help in curing it the easy way. You should find worries evaporating as you stop sweeping them under the carpet. The direct approach pays off. If shyness has been holding you back, figure out how to make your presence felt in a group. You do not have to stand up and make a fool of yourself in order to be noticed.

26. SATURDAY. Confusing. A cutting remark can hurt, but only if you let it. Turn a deaf ear to a rumor currently making the rounds. Refuse to get involved in any character assassination, especially of a person you admire. Keep politics and religion out of general conversation or you may wind up with a fight on your hands. Home conditions are confusing. Your mate or another relative may be saying one thing, but you know that their intentions are quite different. Some criticism might be valid. If you determine that it is on target, begin to concoct a plan of action to rectify the situation. That special person in your life wants to please you but needs urging.

27. SUNDAY. Starred. Take part in a play or other activity that you would normally avoid. You will get a charge out of putting yourself to the test and proving that you can do it. Interacting with children comes easily now. Make special plans for activity you know they will enjoy. Family should be given first priority. Find a pleasant way to turn down a friend who is asking for a favor or a loan. If you decide to go along with the request, you may wind up kicking yourself for lacking the backbone to say no. Driving demands extra care and caution, particularly on busy thoroughfares. Be alert for youngsters playing ball and not watching where they are going.

28. MONDAY. Fortunate. Understanding the motivation of a co-worker gives you the advantage in dealing with this person. Offer what they want, and in return, you will get what you want. The fact that you will also be helped will not really matter to them one way or the other; do not point it out. Make it appear that you are being generous. When you turn on the Libra charm, you are not going to be refused. Funding is available from an individual, probably someone you know personally. It could be that a friend who always seem short of cash has a fairly good-size bank account. Moreover, he or she would be willing to back your idea in return for a share of potential profits.

29. TUESDAY. Stimulating. Your Libra preference for harmony can help overcome obstacles that would trip up other people. Shy away from a project that has already caused upset before it is even tested. Your own ideas are at least as good as those now being suggested. Speak up and let others consider your plan. Look for ways of hurrying through routine chores so that you have time to concentrate on what is most challenging. You need outside stimulation to set your mind in motion. It is a good day to sign up for a class or to enter a contest. You will stand out in a crowd and impress people who matter. Enjoy flirting, but do not take it seriously or you could imperil a relationship.

30. WEDNESDAY. Satisfactory. Try harder to impress a certain someone who does not even acknowledge your existence at this time. You can make a favorable impression by saying little and listening a lot. The louder you become, the less you are apt to be noticed. Inside information may be revealed to you if you pretend to be ignorant of certain facts. There are indications that you may soon receive special permission or a permit to proceed with a plan that is out of the ordinary. Pay close attention to detail. You are never satisfied with less than the best, including the best that you can do. Steer clear of a person who is coughing or sneezing.

31. THURSDAY. Successful. Changes for the better are beginning to produce desired results. Do not let up if you are an instigator of these changes. Press ahead while you have people's attention. If you are one of those waiting to see what will happen, wait no more. Volunteer to take part in all that is going on. Better late than never when it comes to catching up with the latest trend. There may be a shake-up starting at the top. By this time next month you are apt to have a new boss, or you could be the one at the top. The results of your work during the first quarter of 1994 have had a significant impact on superiors. You can count on a raise, but do not spend the anticipated money until you have it.

APRIL

1. FRIDAY. Productive. Working relations are improving and you should be able to work well as a member of a team. Whatever can be done on your own will be even more successful with group input. Stand up for what you believe is fundamentally right; do not back down in the face of opposition. With your leadership abilities you can persuade others to come around to your point of view with discussion, not confrontation. If someone close to you is going away for the weekend, make plans so that you are not lonely while they are gone. Absence can make the heart grow fonder or freer. Give yourself the opportunity to see which way you go when choices open up.

2. SATURDAY. Outstanding. If romance were a sport, you might be in line for the gold medal. Enjoy all of your relationships, including that special one. This is an outstanding day to make a commitment for the future. Marriage, birth or adoption can be discussed and a mutual decision reached now. Be guided by your strong Libra conscience; it will not mislead you. It is unwise to take anyone or anything for granted, however. A right that you believe is yours could be yanked away if you are not vigilant and protective. Show that you care with action as well as words. A group of people who share your views would provide a good starting point for a campaign to stir fence sitters to action.

3. SUNDAY. Demanding. You could come down to earth with a plop today. Opposition at home is mounting against a decision you made recently. A family member is likely to confront you with an ultimatum. Compromise is the best bet, but finding an area of agreement may take delicate negotiating. An older relative is unlikely to have a change of heart. Health can suffer due to stress. Find an outlet for emotional tension. Outdoor exercise can be useful, or a creative hobby may be right for you. Sympathize with anyone who has had to play a supporting role while their own needs go unnoticed and unmet. Give them the recognition they have earned through self-sacrifice.

4. MONDAY. Variable. Put a dose of imagination into everything that you do. Find a better way, or at least a different way, to accomplish everyday routine. Stirring up feelings at home or at work will get people thinking and reevaluating. There are more options available than you are now considering. Go back to the beginning and look at a situation with a fresh perspective. Choice of teammates is important. Associating with negative thinkers could cause some doors to be slammed in your face. Actions you take now are not going to pass unnoticed. What is lost or given away may never be retrieved. A letter from someone at a distance gives you renewed fighting spirit.

5. TUESDAY. Rewarding. Imagination is flying high right now. You can express yourself most successfully through music or poetry or art. Do what pleases you, not what is currently in vogue. Libra craftspeople who are aiming only at the buying public may not be pleased with their own results. Lack of sales, even interest, may confirm that you were too intent on following a trend instead of setting one. If you begin to feel restless, look for action away from the mainstream. You are ready to talk to anyone. A good argument helps clarify your own views even if not convincing anyone else to change their mind. Pitch in and help where you know you are needed. An invitation is superfluous.

6. WEDNESDAY. Satisfactory. Desire to travel and see the world is natural for Libras. Begin saving now for a special trip that you know will be a lifetime memory. Consider whether to go as part of a group or on your own. Your naturally shy nature makes an organized tour a good option if you intend to be involved in more than mere sightseeing. Brushing up on foreign language skills can be useful personally as well as in your work. The bilingual Libra has special opportunity when an opening comes up overseas. Be stubborn if you are asked to do something you dislike. Stonewalling the request may eventually result in someone else taking on the job with no negative consequences to you.

7. THURSDAY. Pleasant. Plans that you began to formulate yesterday can be taken a step farther now. This is a starred time to make an appointment or reservation. Do not wait to see what a friend or work colleague is going to decide. Act on your own. A sudden bonus is foreseen as the result of past or current work. Or you may receive unexpected income via a tax rebate or a prize. Do not be surprised if someone you argued with recently comes to you for help. Be generous and truthful in the advice you offer. Hold nothing back when it comes to helping anyone in need. Your Libra imagination takes you beyond restrictions learned as a child into the realm of the real world.

8. FRIDAY. Harmonious. An idea that comes to mind while you are otherwise preoccupied may be just the answer you have been seeking. When you are least focused, you may get sudden insight. A dream, too, could be a clue to action that will be useful. Look on the positive side of a situation that has been troubling you. Downplay all that is negative or seemingly impossible. You have more friends and supporters than you imagine. Ask for what you want; you will not be refused without good reason. Good news is coming via the post office. Be on the lookout for an announcement with your name on it. A handshake seals a deal as well as a legal contract.

9. SATURDAY. Cautious. Getting more organized at home could help prevent an accident. Clean off stairs and walkways. Get rid of old paint and other hazardous materials; call a local government agency to see how you should dispose of this waste. Check your car for mechanical problems, and be sure you have enough air pressure in the tires. Proceed cautiously in dealing with an older family member who is making incessant demands. It may be that they need attention far more than any actual help. It is not wise to enter into a neighborhood disagreement, particularly one where children are at the center of the trouble. By the time the kids have worked out their differences, the parents may be embroiled in a full-scale argument.

10. SUNDAY. Buoyant. Today you will have to run the show yourself, organizing and giving orders to keep things hopping. You will enjoy the somewhat unfamiliar role of being in charge. Family members are eager to get out. Check newspaper listings for concerts or shows having available tickets. A group outing is recommended. You enjoy the company of one special person, but you also want to be part of a larger group. Consider joining a guild or other organization whose members are working toward a common goal. Anything musical also appeals, whether you are an amateur performer or an involved listener. Competition can be fun providing there are no significant prizes.

11. MONDAY. Easygoing. Ease back into your normal weekday routine by getting up early and allowing ample time to put yourself in motion. A good breakfast gives you needed mental as well as physical energy. By the time you arrive at work you should be refreshed and ready to go. Ideas are coming to mind one after the other. Quickly analyze and categorize them as to which are immediately useful and which should be filed away for future consideration. You do not have to rely on age-old ways and means. What is considered newfangled can be learned in a few lessons and put to good use. Treat yourself to an appliance or equipment that most of your friends and associates already own.

12. TUESDAY. Mixed. People may be running around in circles, but there is no reason for you to be chasing after them. Be the calm eye in the center of the storm. Take a well-reasoned approach to a problem with emotional overtones. You can surmount obstacles by using your mental or physical agility. Just guard against getting carried away. A plan that is too intricate could backfire. Keeping it simple is the order of the day. Do not breathe a word about a secret that has been entrusted to you. Play dumb when that subject comes up in conversation, and try to change the topic as quickly as possible. Trying to know a newcomer takes extra effort, but could lead to eventual happiness.

13. WEDNESDAY. Satisfactory. Turn on the Libra charm and you stand a good chance of getting your way. Make people understand that what you want is actually in their best interests as well. You will be regarded as a great conversationalist if you listen much more than you talk. Deciding who is trustworthy should not be difficult; your intuition is reliable. Look for clues in body language as well as words. Review a plan that you are about to put into action. Look for small flaws that could be magnified when bunched together. A promise that is not current has to be reconsidered; conditions have changed and a friend may have had a change of heart along the way.

14. THURSDAY. Variable. Morning hours are best for work that requires convincing. You are most persuasive when other people are still rubbing sleep from their eyes. After lunch stay in the background of all that is going on, and tonight you may actually prefer to hide away. A recent purchase that is not performing satisfactorily should be returned for a refund. Do not get involved in repair work; it could go on and on. This is a good time to consider replacing an older model with one that is state of the art. Anything you are sending by mail should be insured for its full value. The promise of a check in the mail may ring false, but actually be right. Meet the postman as he makes his rounds.

15. FRIDAY. Changeable. Be honest and aboveboard in all of your dealings today, even with a person who you feel gypped you in the past. There is little chance of a secret remaining so. You could be put in an awkward position if you talked about someone behind his back, then learned he was told what you said. Offer an explanation to help yourself off the hook, then vow to keep such thoughts to yourself in the future. Do some comparison shopping of price and options. It is a good day to add to a collection by studying classified ads in a newspaper or a magazine. Secondhand items can be particularly good buys.

16. SATURDAY. Tricky. Avoid associating with people who seem to care little about the feelings of others. Hanging around with negative thinkers can diminish your reputation. You have a choice now of companions; you are not being forced to choose one side or the other. An influential person is ready to make some concessions on your behalf in return for promises of future action. Weigh the consequences of being restricted by these ties. Be wary of a neighbor who asks impertinent questions. Do not reveal anything you would not tell a close friend. You might enjoy a movie or theatrical performance staged by an amateur group. Your mate or date could be the star of the show.

17. SUNDAY. Sensitive. Conditions are slow and enthusiasm less than usual. Do not expect cooperation from family members. Work around the house has to be done independently if it is going to be done at all. Even your mate is preoccupied and does not want to be bothered. Nothing is quite good enough for you today. It is easy to find fault, but much harder to rectify the problem. Impatience has to be controlled. It is said that whatever is worth having is worth waiting for. Since you have little choice, test out the adage for yourself. You can work yourself into a tizzy planning and plotting future moves. Someone new is coming into your sphere with a totally different outlook and approach.

18. MONDAY. Mixed. Stay close to the phone. If you must be away from your usual haunts for part of the day, be sure to leave word about how you can be reached. An important phone call is anticipated. People trying to contact you are likely to become frustrated and give up if you are unavailable. Ask if any messages were left for you; do not assume people will pass them on to you. Missing an important meeting could jeopardize your advancement potential. It is important to be in on the initial planning stages of a project so that your input can be considered. You cannot expect to be given serious consideration if you show little interest until a project takes flight.

19. TUESDAY. Quiet. Flow with the tide rather than making any waves today. Be agreeable to a suggestion proposed by a co-worker who you know is after the same promotion you want. The fact that you are willing to cooperate may take them by surprise. The boss is sure to notice your ability to get along well with people from all ranks. You are not in a position to dictate to anyone today. Follow orders to the letter. An unexpected offer confirms that you are being considered for a promotion or job transfer. Libras intent on landing a new job should be pounding the pavement early this morning. Low-key dress makes the best impression in an interview. Stress your willingness to learn as well as your valuable past experience.

20. WEDNESDAY. Satisfactory. Libra should not stray from everyday work habits. Stick with routine that is customary. Once you have made up your mind about a course of action, forge ahead. You can enhance your reputation by proving your loyalty. If offered a new assignment, act decisively. Leadership must be won; it cannot be conferred with a magic wand. You can be especially effective in bringing together two factions that have been at loggerheads, then helping them find common ground. A disagreement among friends can also be resolved if you step in. You may receive an invitation to a special ceremony that you know would never have occurred except for your efforts.

21. THURSDAY. Manageable. The day favors Libras engaged in business far from their usual base of operations. A newcomer is anxious to be included in your plans and planning. Be more outgoing than usual and less secretive. Share your enthusiasm about future work as a means of inspiring those who you hope will join in with you. Be especially alert for danger signals when operating machinery of any type. Wear protective eye coverings or other safety equipment. Driving also demands more attention than usual. Focus your concentration by not listening to the radio or talking on the phone while behind the wheel. Take a philosophical view and ordinary ups and down will not upset you.

22. FRIDAY. Pleasant. A person you have long regarded as a friend may reveal what is in their heart and on their mind. You will be flattered as well as pleasantly surprised. Their announcement could be reason for planning a trip or buying a very special outfit. Guard against becoming single-minded. Diversity keeps away boredom and opens up new possibilities at every turn. Include a former co-worker or boss when deciding who to invite to a party you plan on hosting. Make this a special day for your own lover. Find a way to express how much you appreciate all that is done for you. You may be out in a crowd, but have eyes for only one.

23. SATURDAY. Variable. Do not make any decisions based on appearances alone. With people or potential possessions, take the time to find out more about them. It is a good day for joining a group whose goals coincide with your own interests. Before paying your dues to join, however, attend one or two meetings. If making a major purchase, compare features to find out which are most important to you. It is not smart to pay for a lot of high-tech extras that you will never use. What seems like a negative response could turn out well in the long run. The best-laid plans can be improved with a few changes. Libras are full of ideas and imagination.

24. SUNDAY. Mixed. Trying to enjoy yourself when there are children underfoot could be difficult, whether they are related to you or not. You may be reproached if you attempt to discipline an unruly child who is not your own. Small doses of togetherness are favored today with any relative. You will get more done on your own, but may be urged to join in with family members for part of the day. Outdoor work, especially in the garden, should be enjoyable. It is a starred day to plant flowers or vegetables and also to do some cleanup work. Put your mechanical skill to good use repairing equipment that might otherwise have to be replaced. A neighbor is willing to loan what you need for a short time.

25. MONDAY. Rewarding. Learn from an expert, or be the one to teach if you know as much as anyone else about a subject of interest to a group. Helping others to learn is an ideal to be put into practice today. Libra parents may be involved in their child's school. Or you may have to find a qualified tutor to help bring the student's grades up to standard. Be objective and unemotional when confronted with a problem involving two people who are at each other's throats because of a disagreement. Work to find an amicable solution that everyone can live with comfortably. Reading puts you in a world of your own. Science-fiction or a romance transports you from the present to a special world.

26. TUESDAY. Quiet. Keep a low profile and stay out of the way of the boss or anyone else who might be trying to enlist your help and support. You do not relish any additional responsibilities heaped on you now. Friendships are particularly important. Stay in touch with a person who moved away some time ago. You might even want to arrange a get-together as part of your vacation or a weekend getaway. Concentrate on work that involves attention to intricate details. The day is perfect for expressing yourself in a creative way. You do not need words to convey your feelings to a special person or to the public at large. Art and music are the mediums best suited for your talents.

27. WEDNESDAY. Pleasant. Promote yourself as a candidate for an elective office or a job that involves a pay raise. You could languish in your present comfortable position, but there is a lot more that you can do if you apply yourself to the effort. Break out of a rut. Surprise the boss or your loved one with a burst of enthusiasm. A project that is nearing completion needs only a small push to send it on its way. You have high energy now and should be directing it into useful work. Otherwise you may be viewed as high-strung and even flighty. A subconscious problem that is aired will quickly be resolved. Today you can open a few doors in your mind and see a new vision.

28. THURSDAY. Important. Do not downplay your considerable talents. Let it be known that you want to be promoted to a more visible position at work or in the community. Instead of waiting to be asked, do some campaigning for yourself. A banker or broker may pass on a worthwhile tip; act quickly or you could lose out on the opportunity. New investment is favored now with money you will not need before the end of the year. You are looking for a long-term investment opportunity, not a take-it-or-leave-it gamble. The less you say, the wiser you are thought to be.

Listen and learn from an assortment of people. What you consider a joke could be an affront to a colleague.

29. FRIDAY. Easygoing. You have been on a fast-moving treadmill and should slow the pace and catch up with yourself. Use most of this day to tie up loose ends and contemplate future projects. You may appear to be idle, but your mind is staying in gear. It could be time to let go of a particular task or assignment and let someone else take over. Your methods are good, but are not the only way. Urge others to get involved even if their skills are not currently up to your own high standards. Offer to teach them, or to stay on during a transition period. Keep plans for this evening and the upcoming weekend as simple as possible. Wrap your arms around your loved one and stay close.

30. SATURDAY. Useful. Go out of your way to help a friend or family member going through a difficult period of adjustment. Be available day or night if they want to talk or reminisce. Being a good listener can be more help than any specific aid or advice you could offer. There is a strong element of luck that puts you in the right place at the right time. Be quick to take advantage of it. Some extra money is coming your way as the result of a prize or winning ticket, but you will have already spent it more than once mentally before you ever receive it. Evening entertainment of someone from work can be a wise career move. Work to build up a network of contacts you can call on for assistance.

MAY

1. SUNDAY. Fortunate. Joint effort with a person you have known awhile can be fortunate for both of you. An Aquarius is most likely to figure in your plans, although a Pisces is also becoming dominant. Look for ways to cut costs. Snap up a bargain in quantity if you know it will not go to waste or turn bad before you use it. An exchange of services with a neighbor or a friend can also put more money in your wallet. The social scene is active. Both married and single Libras are eager to expand their circle of acquaintances through group involvement. Enthusiastically take part in a project geared to improve community conditions. A reunion this evening proves the value of friendship.

2. MONDAY. Mixed. Arrange to work closely with a partner even if you must travel some distance in order to do so. Two heads are definitely better than one today, and two pairs of hands will speed all that you have to do. Keep your mate or partner fully informed as you struggle to make a decision. While nobody can make up your mind for you, insightful input can be provided. You should stir this into the mix of information upon which you are going to base your action. A new project launched this week promises a good return. Put more of your Libra creativity into everything that will have your name on it. Step up advertising and publicity in order to attract more attention.

3. TUESDAY. Disconcerting. A light touch can help negotiations proceed without reaching a stalemate. Avoid making demands. All of your statements should be low key. You can be more persuasive with a memo than a shouting confrontation. Facts win the day when all is said and done. Emotion has no role in a business decision. If you feel you are getting in over your head legally, consult an attorney. The fee will be well repaid in peace of mind. An experienced negotiator can also help if you are reworking a contract or going through salary arbitration. A neutral person can hold out for more than you might be able to get independently. You are distressed to find that a co-worker with equal responsibilities is making more money.

4. WEDNESDAY. Satisfactory. Take negative news as a learning experience and vow to do better in the future. Your hopes are on the rise. You should not have much trouble making necessary adjustments to comply with a mandate from the boss or another superior. Be wary of facing future worries now. Concentrate on what must be done today and let tomorrow's frustrations work themselves out. There is no reason to borrow trouble. Once you have made up your mind, stick to it. People are wiling to follow your lead providing they can rely on your word. Your reputation hinges on positive action without any sighs of regret. Sink your teeth into a problem situation and hang on until it is resolved.

5. THURSDAY. Excellent. Continue to participate with members of your family or work team. Guard against alienating yourself from them in any way. Libras have an uncanny knack for getting along with a variety of people holding different views and bringing them together as an unbeatable combination. Much more can be achieved if you are part of a well-knit group. Independent action will not be as effective and certainly will not be as enjoyable. Include a newcomer in your plans. This is also a fine day for affairs of the heart. Love may be blooming in your own backyard. You may soon begin to hear some buzzings about all that is going on when it is supposed no one is noticing.

6. FRIDAY. Good. Matters at work, especially regarding committee action, are taking an upward turn. It is a favored day for signing a contract or other legally binding document. You can rely on the word of a person with whom you have been negotiating, but it is vital to get everything down in black and white. Personal goals deserve extra attention. Make an appointment for a physical evaluation as you strive to get in better shape. A counselor or trainer can help you get on track and stay there. Joining a health club or a swimming association gives you extra incentive when you are inclined to bypass exercise. Agree to attend a sports event accompanied by that special person in your life.

7. SATURDAY. Variable. Conditions at home are not as easygoing as you would like. A disagreement between family members may be forcing everyone to take sides. Try to act as a go-between to ease tension. Finances are restricted now so make no impulsive purchases. If food shopping, have a list of what you intend to buy and stick to it. Look for dinner recipes that you can cook one night, but serve for two nights. Someone new is coming into your sphere from a distance. Gradually build a relationship. If you come on too strong at first, you may scare this person away. Travel is a great way to be alone together with the one who has stolen your heart.

8. SUNDAY. Disconcerting. Libras often overlook health matters, especially of a personal nature. Be good to yourself today. Get extra rest by sleeping late or taking an afternoon snooze. Spruce up your appearance; be sure your nails are in good repair. If you need a haircut, a family member may be able to give you a trim to tide you over until next week. A creative hobby takes your mind off a problem that you cannot do anything about now. Choose your own materials and colors rather than working slavishly from a kit. There are offbeat offers, and perhaps some pressure to take part in a skit. Say no firmly without alienating the person who thought you might be interested. A good book is your best companion tonight.

9. MONDAY. Stimulating. You can talk all you want, but it takes a dedication to action to get anything off the planning board and into production. Ideas are flowing fast and furiously. Turn a concept into a working plan. Round up people whose experience blends well with your own. Working in tandem is recommended; you cannot handle all details on your own. Old friends are especially trustworthy if you yearn to talk about a personal problem. Use them as a sounding board rather than seek specific advice. You may discover that you are being too sensitive. Strive to develop a thick skin so that apparent criticism does not wound you. Departing from traditional methods is favored.

10. TUESDAY. Lucky. A fresh slant on an old problem gives you the edge in resolving it. A degree of secrecy protects your interests now. Do not reveal your intentions to anyone who could conceivably become a competitor. Even a longtime co-worker may have plans to switch jobs; whatever you reveal to this person will be part of the baggage they take along to their next assignment. Someone new on the scene can be fortunate for you. Combining forces with them can pay handsome dividends. Your enterprising nature should be a great help in expanding your career potential. There is opportunity; the trick is to identify it and act quickly. A family member has a worthwhile idea, but lacks necessary money.

11. WEDNESDAY. Satisfactory. Be prepared to take on additional work in order to cover for a colleague who is on sick leave or vacation. Proving that you are capable of doing their work can put you one step higher on the ladder leading toward a promotion. The boss is aware of your abilities and is keeping tabs on your production. Your ability to get along with a wide range of people is especially important. Play the role of mediator or moderator if a situation is heating up at home or at work. It is a starred day to accept nomination as an officer in an organization that would keep you in the social swim. Even if you are unopposed, campaign: state your goals and ideas for change.

12. THURSDAY. Disquieting. An early start enables you to beat a competitor to the punch. Make phone calls at the start of business hours; people are likely to be more relaxed and receptive then. Later in the day you can anticipate some rejection without serious consideration. It is better to take maybe for an answer than to demand a yes or no. Turn a brainstorm into a realistic plan with specific goals and deadlines. Financial assistance may be available through a government program geared to help those who are just starting out in a new career or business. Libras interested in returning to school should also check for financial aid earmarked for special occupations.

13. FRIDAY. Changeable. For the superstitious Libra, this Friday the 13th warns against going back on your word. You can land in trouble if you do not live up to a promise made awhile ago. It is not a good day either to lend or borrow anything of value. Do not breathe a word about a promise made by an older family member or superior at work. A secret that has been entrusted to you must be kept under lock and key. Keep your hard-earned money where you know it is safe, even if it is not earning as much interest as you could get in a riskier investment. If you stick to what you know and can do best, you should not encounter problems today. Accept an offer of help but do not seek it.

14. SATURDAY. Successful. Get your home in better shape for your own enjoyment and pleasure, not to impress anyone else. Storage may be a problem. Check a hardware store for shelving or a ready-to-assemble storage system that would fit in your closet. You may also want to weed out clothes and other items that you no longer use, and donate them to a charity. New colors can perk up a room that is dark and dingy. Invite a few friends to join you in a painting party and you can have the room spic and span with minimum effort. Secondhand furniture can be a budget saver, but shop carefully for quality. A loved one is coming around to your way of thinking; avoid saying I told you so.

15. SUNDAY. Exciting. A family get-together should be enjoyable for all, young and old. Have a bat and ball on hand so that no one is forced to endure daylong conversation; pick teams and stage a sports competition for the fun of it. Be sure to have ample food and drink on hand. If you are a visitor rather than a host, take along a cake, cookies or other dessert to share. Come to know a new family member without asking too many probing questions. You can find out a lot by how this person relates to children and to pets. There may be an announcement that makes you want to stand up and cheer. You could soon be a member of a wedding party or other celebration.

16. MONDAY. Demanding. A co-worker may turn to you for advice, then go and repeat what you have said in a derisive tone. To avoid getting into this situation, offer to listen but not to lead. Many demands are being made on Libras today. You are going to be pulled in two directions at once and must make a choice. Since you cannot please everyone, you are better off pleasing yourself. Reflect on your responsibilities before making any new promises. You can wind up head over heels in debt to someone who you ask to do a favor for you now. They will expect to be repaid many times over. What starts as a small project could escalate into a major time-consumer if you let it.

17. TUESDAY. Fair. There is a lot to be gained from associating with a person who has already earned a degree of success. Adopt some of their ideas and adapt others. Aim for a balance between work and play; too much of either can make you boring to yourself as well as to others. A change is foreseen in your work, probably as the result of a new boss or new management at the top. A merger can be advantageous for you providing you are able to accept new rules and regulations. The only sure thing now is that change is in the air. Pretending to know less than you do is a workable method of finding out what is going on behind the scenes. A friend is only a phone call away if you need advice.

18. WEDNESDAY. Important. Take advantage of increased energy and stamina to tackle a major project. An early start gives you an edge over competitors. Do not let up until you have accomplished everything on your to-do list for the day. There is opportunity to earn a handsome return through new investment. Pay attention to a news announcement about a contract award. A business that you know something about is the best place to put your money for long-term return. Do not allow an investment opportunity to escape your grasp without at least analyzing it. A hot tip, on the other hand, may be too hot to handle. Inside information can backfire if you are not cautious.

19. THURSDAY. Productive. Turn on the Libra charm and you stand a good chance of having things go your way. A person you see daily is about to change to your way of thinking, resulting from facts you have provided. Welcome additional support and help. Playing up to the person in charge can have surprising benefits. It is important to demonstrate that you are ready and willing for additional responsibility even if a pay increase is not part of it. Do not limit yourself in any way. Creativity can cover for lack of experience. You can do better than you may think by following your basic instincts. Someone from the past may appear this evening, or call as they pass through town.

20. FRIDAY. Stressful. Tying up loose ends is the main order of business today. Do not allow a project to dangle unfinished over the weekend ahead. Push to complete it now. Enlist the cooperation of co-workers who are sitting around idly, or at least appear to you to be doing so. Take advantage of the pull you have with certain people in positions of power. Someone you know personally is willing to make an exception or two for you. Rules can be bent if not broken. Travel may be necessary, although the trip is likely to be of a hectic there-and-back variety. A person at a distance wants to gauge your reaction face-to-face. Leave your car at home if you go out tonight.

21. SATURDAY. Harmonious. Work hard to develop a full partnership with your mate or other family members. Share what has to be done around the house as equally as possible. If one person is burdened while the other plays, harmony may be strained. Nothing is cut-and-dried. Be ready to pitch in where needed and to give up a few perks that you have come to take as your right. Someone new is entering the picture. A happy twosome could be disrupted by this person, but only if you allow this to happen. Friends are in high spirits. Activities with them promise special excitement. Be sure to take along a camera if going on an outing with children. Have a light, nourishing meal.

22. SUNDAY. Outstanding. Libras on the move have the advantage today. Sit still and you will not get far. Take a look around the neighborhood for ideas to spruce up your property. A few flowering plants outdoors or on your windowsill will please you as well as passers-by. Social and business affairs can be enhanced by a meeting on neutral territory. Travel is favored, especially a trip to a local tourist attraction that you have never visited before. Pick up a few souvenirs as mementos of the day. Offer a friend a helping hand today and you will have the assistance you need later. Love is a highlight after dark. That special person wants to try something new.

23. MONDAY. Tranquil. This is no time to be making major decisions. Your options are not yet clearly defined. Choosing among the ones available may be difficult because they are so alike. Postpone a decision a few days and you will have a larger menu from which to select. Relationships both at home and on the job are excellent. You can usually get along with anyone, although sometimes you have to bite your tongue or stifle a desire in order to do so. Today, however, there is mutual give-and-take. Conditions are too quiet to begin anything new. Do not venture far from your usual base of operations. Stick to comfortable routine. A change may jar your system and make you uneasy.

24. TUESDAY. Variable. A person you associate with daily is likely to promise one thing, then turn around and do the exact opposite. When you try to find out why, the answer is apt to be vague. Something is going on, but you are not yet aware of what it is. The extent of dissatisfaction may not be apparent to you quite yet. Try to put yourself in the other person's shoes as a means of understanding their viewpoint. Catch up with bill paying and letter writing. Send off an application and keep your fingers crossed for the reply you want. Libra job seekers should have no trouble getting past the initial interview. But competition heats up thereafter and you will have to be well informed to progress.

25. WEDNESDAY. Easygoing. An offer should be gratefully accepted even though you know there are strings attached. You can pull some strings of your own now. Get in touch with an important person who is a personal friend or a friend of your family. Regulations that seem written in stone can be bent without anyone accusing you of cheating. A plan about to be put into action should be scrutinized one last time for possible flaws. You may discover a mathematical error that forces revisions. Plan your moves one step at a time. Make no assumptions without a written commitment. Brooding on past events or what might have been is useless; look to the future.

26. THURSDAY. Misleading. What is already on your agenda is enough to keep you busy. Do not put your fingers in other people's pies. There is an undercurrent of discontent that has to be investigated and resolved. Libras can play the role of meditator with good results, but only after being asked. Otherwise you could be accused of meddling. Keep a close watch on all that is going on. It may pay to stay near the phone. You can deduce a lot even if you only hear one side of a conversation. Strive to distinguish fact from fiction; they may come wrapped in the same disguise. The person who seems most trustworthy is the one to whom you should reveal the least.

27. FRIDAY. Unsettling. It will not be easy to keep your attention riveted on what must be done today. You are thinking ahead and making plans for personal enjoyment. Earning money is probably the least of your concerns now, although you know you have to add to your bank account in order to take a trip. You may have to give away more than you would like in order to get immediate satisfaction. A banker or other money professional is not in a generous frame of mind. What seems like an offer that is too good to be true is probably exactly that. Guard against being duped by an advertisement that is full of half-truths. Do some reading between the lines and you will have better understanding.

28. SATURDAY. Sensitive. Settling down is not easy today. You want to be with someone special, but have to delay gratification due to interference from family members or in-laws. Taking a long walk by yourself can help straighten out your priorities and get your thinking back on track. It may be that you are looking too far into the future. Try to live more for the here and now. Advice that you are given could be inappropriate as no one but you knows the full story yet. If you are the person offering suggestions, you may lack similar knowledge and not be able to make a worthwhile analysis. A child needs extra time and attention to make up for loss of other companionship.

29. SUNDAY. Manageable. Join in the holiday mood that pervades today. It is a favorable time to display your patriotism by flying a flag or wearing a uniform. Show your true emotion without holding anything back. Your imagination is active and full of plans. A companion wants to play a larger role in your activities, but do not get too close too quickly. A friend has good news about setting a date. Begin now to think about a present for a special occasion. An undeveloped talent is waiting to blossom. Look for a creative outlet where your imagination can flower. This is a favorable time to study the life of a person who is a hero to you.

30. MONDAY. Exciting. For Libras who do not have to be at work this Memorial Day, it's a time to seal a romantic partnership or rekindle one that has been burning low. Go out of your way to please your mate or date. Be agreeable to what they suggest, but be ready with ideas of your own if nothing is forthcoming from them. A parade may highlight the day. Whether you are marching along or enjoying being a spectator, you may find renewed reason to be proud of your heritage and country. Be especially cordial to an older relative or friend. Your Libra temperament will not allow them to dull your enthusiasm. Expand your evening plans to include anyone and everyone at home.

31. TUESDAY. Productive. The way ahead is not crystal clear, but neither is it so cloudy that you cannot make plans. Consider options presented by a co-worker or friend. You will be more productive as one of a team than by acting independently. All forms of communication are starred. You can cut to the heart of a problem and find a way to resolve it by talking directly with those involved. Dealing through intermediaries wastes time and energy. As the day progresses your performance improves and your insight clarifies matters. Body language offers good clues to what is going on. A new relationship is forming under your nose; it may even be that you are directly involved.

JUNE

1. WEDNESDAY. Satisfactory. New starts are starred. You have the mental and physical energy to launch a project with the enthusiasm that helps you gather supporters and cooperation. The way ahead is as clear as it can be. Act on a hunch with confidence. Libras are often at their optimum best when the pressure is on and results are expected. Try not only to meet a deadline, but to beat it. As the day progresses you may have to step in to referee a disagreement between co-workers or family members. A generational gap may be presenting a major obstacle to success. There is no best way to accomplish what has to be done; select what seems right to you, not what others demand.

2. THURSDAY. Productive. Go out of your way to please loved ones. Purchase a new electrical or mechanical piece of equipment that some may view as a toy. But there is also an educational advantage to keep up with the latest technology. Libras must balance an urge to save with willingness to get pleasure from the profits of your work. Do not keep track of everything you spend; allow some leeway for spur-of-the-moment purchases. An unexpected offer can be rewarding in the long run; a quick return is unlikely, however. Do not invest money that you know you are going to need for everyday living expenses. Look for a bargain in food that can be cooked, frozen and stored.

3. FRIDAY. Disconcerting. Flow with the tide rather than making any waves. Go along with suggestions from your mate; if the boss asks a favor, you have little choice but to agree. You are not in a position today where you can dictate terms to others. What is being offered on the bargaining table is the best you are going to get. Avoid being so hardheaded that you lose out to a competitor. Orders have to be followed precisely. It is not smart to bend rules for one person; others will hear about it and expect the same treatment for themselves. You could be kept waiting by a doctor or other professional. Stay calm and cool by reading a magazine or contemplating a new project.

4. SATURDAY. Good. There is a lot to be done around the house, but nothing so important that you are locked into doing it if a tempting offer comes along. Socializing with neighbors and co-workers can be useful as well as enjoyable. Find out what is going on at a distance. A new trend is beginning to emerge that could make you richer or more famous if you latch on to it right away. Break with tradition if you think you have come up with an innovative plan. What has worked in the past is no guarantee of success in the future. Learn more about advanced technology from a person who is not afraid to experiment. What you do not know will not hurt you when it comes to a family member's past.

5. SUNDAY. Harmonious. For the Libra in love, this is a propitious day to ask that all-important question. Do not dance around the subject with hints and innuendos; come right out and say what is on your mind and in your heart. The future is opening up right before your eyes. It is also an excellent time for all Libras to get closer to those they love through better communication and sharing of feelings as well as ideas. Set aside some special time for a heart-to-heart talk with an older relative. Working as part of a group is favored if you are trying to raise money or the public consciousness. Whatever can be achieved individually can be even more effective as part of a concerted effort.

6. MONDAY. Rewarding. You may be full of pride about a recent success, but not yet able to tell anyone because you have been sworn to secrecy. Try to keep from blurting out what you want them to know. Offering hints can be a problem as they begin making wild guesses you must refute. It is all too easy now to be fussy and overly concerned with picky details. Take a long-range overview of all that is going on. Welcome a newcomer on the scene with open arms. Share what you know and loan what you own. Rewards are foreseen as the result of your generosity. Break your normal routine and become involved in a new undertaking with great promise. A change of scenery will waken your senses.

7. TUESDAY. Variable. Deciding to hide away can be worthwhile if you are mentally exhausted and do not want to answer any questions. Keep a low profile even if you are on the job or in your regular haunts. Listen more than you talk. Be available to hear the whole story a friend wants to tell. You know you are only getting one side, but be sympathetic and understanding. Too much objectivity can make you seem cool and remote. An argument is possible if you refuse to believe what you are being told by a person who has never been known to distort the truth. The unusual could become routine now. Skip socializing tonight so that you can wash clothes and get to bed early.

8. WEDNESDAY. Mixed. Cooperation is yours for the asking. But once you make a request you cannot then turn around and change your mind. Be sure you want what you claim to be after. Do not ask too many questions of a superior; their answers may not please you. It is up to you today to prove that you are capable of taking on greater responsibility, which should lead to a pay raise. Hold personal spending to necessities only. You may have to refuse a charitable request because you do not have enough money to contribute. Instead, consider giving a few hours of your time in lieu of it. If you are not appreciated in one group, find another where your talents are needed.

9. THURSDAY. Changeable. Role reversals are foreseen at home or on the job. You may have to step in and handle work normally done by someone considerably younger or less experienced than you. There is also a small chance of being asked to fill in for a superior who has been called away. Recognize that these changes are short term; treat them as an opportunity. Practice the fine art of diplomacy with everyone you meet. You can twist any situation to put a positive light on it. Emphasize what is good and advantageous, then quickly add what you believe could make it even better. Avoid listening to people who are full of bright ideas about how you should handle your life, your job or your money. You alone know what is best for you.

10. FRIDAY. Easygoing. The day favors Libras trying to find solutions and work out amicable agreements. Your easygoing mood puts others at ease as well. Leapfrog over a problem and go on to the next topic. By the time a discussion is concluded, you may discover that the original bone of contention is already resolved. People are likely to be adamant if they believe their rights are being trampled upon. Point out their freedom of choice, even if you know it is a limited option. You do not want to know what is going on with a younger family member who is under no obligation to report in to you. Watch what you put in writing or you may have to do some serious explaining later.

11. SATURDAY. Excellent. Set the pace for others to follow today. Your leadership is at full throttle. People, especially family members, are ready to go along with your plans. Conditions are ripe for making some major changes at home. It may be that you want to redecorate or do some outdoor landscaping. Or you may have other changes to put into effect involving household chores and how they are to be divided. Shaking up the normal weekend routine is advisable to keep anyone from growing bored and stale with their responsibilities. Travel is favored, particularly to visit someone you see far too infrequently. Instead of driving, use public transportation if available.

12. SUNDAY. Pleasant. Unexpected news is likely from a family member or a friend of the family. It may be that you are in line to inherit money or property eventually from a favorite relative. Entering a contest can be lucky for you. Your skills are good and your creativity excellent. Look for a way to combine these into one eye-catching project. Libras who play an instrument will enjoy putting together an impromptu concert or perhaps a band. Listening is sure to be a pleasure as well. An outdoor performance will be fun for the whole family. Anything offered for sale through a telephone solicitation should be carefully investigated first; make no promises to a stranger.

13. MONDAY. Productive. A short trip promises results providing you have set up the meeting ahead of time. Have facts and figures at your fingertips to support your stand. Express your ideas in as few words as possible; the more you say, the more you will tend to turn off your audience. Use pictures and diagrams to good advantage. Your optimism can encourage support from the ranks of the undecided. Ingenuity is on an equal footing with financial aid now. Make do with materials already on hand; do not purchase anything that is an option. A certain matter that has been languishing on the shelf for too long can be dusted off and brought to completion by day's end.

14. TUESDAY. Satisfactory. Being single-minded can help you accomplish all that you want to do. Tackle one project at a time. Work on it till you reach a dead end or a logical stopping point, and only then turn to the next item on your list. Try to master the art of relaxation in between strenuous activity. A quick catnap can restore your energy better than a jolt of chocolate or caffeine. Accept an invitation from a person you barely know. Branching out in a new direction can be useful. As the day progresses, concentration becomes increasingly difficult. This evening you will be happy to plop down in front of the television set and put all concerns aside.

15. WEDNESDAY. Good. Turn over a complex problem to a specialist with particular training. Most things you can handle, but it is important to know when you are getting out of your depth. Any complicated repair job should be referred to a person with a license so that you can be assured of competent work. If you meddle where you are not qualified, you can easily make matters worse. Conditions are good on the job. Superiors recognize your abilities and are prepared to reward you accordingly. Continue to reach out to a newcomer who seems shy. Offer some direction and guidance without being overbearing. Accept an invitation to go out tonight, or invite someone yourself.

16. THURSDAY. Changeable. Working as part of a team can help you cope with change. Knowing what has been tried in the past is a clue to the future. You can learn more from a botched job than from one that turned out exactly as planned. Build on both success and failure. There is some danger of Libras feeling under-appreciated, which may make you want to give up trying. Persist and you will please yourself as well as others. Try to see the humorous side of every situation. You may have to relocate temporarily to accommodate another person or group. Or a change of scene can be forced on you by the need to visit a person at a distance. Either way, try to adjust as quickly as possible and then get on with the day's schedule.

17. FRIDAY. Quiet. This is a wait-and-see day for the Libra on the verge of a breakthrough. Other people are dictating the terms now. You will have to be patient until rules are interpreted or permission granted. Trying to speed the process could have the opposite effect. You can be easily steered now, but not forced to do anything that does not seem right. Stay away from a person or a group whose objectives jar with your own. Look into financing options if considering a major purchase such as a car, boat or recreational vehicle. A good secondhand purchase may make more sense economically. Timing is all important in negotiating for the best price. Do not seem too anxious.

18. SATURDAY. Enjoyable. On first meeting someone, you may have trouble finding much to talk about. But persist for a while and you will uncover special areas of mutual interest. Libras can afford to be more aggressive today in pursuing friendship or a deeper relationship. Waiting for people to knock on your door is not recommended; you could be kept cooling your heels for a long time. Instead, go out and mingle. Join a group of people who share a hobby or collection that you enjoy or would like to get involved with. A new relationship, possibly with romantic overtones, is already underway but not obvious even to you. Someone of the opposite sex is hoping you will call.

19. SUNDAY. Happy. A little gamble should not hurt anyone, but be careful not to overdo it. This is a sociable day at home, with drop-in visitors taking you by pleasant surprise. Enlist them in work you are doing outdoors or sports activity you have already planned. Welcome a new addition to the family or to the neighborhood. You may also run into a person you immediately recognize from seeing on television or in the movies. Restrain an urge to ask for an autograph unless others are already doing so. Entertaining can be enjoyable, but do not spend time planning and organizing. Relax and have fun with your guests; just provide food and drink.

20. MONDAY. Stimulating. You should be seeing some initial results from the effort you put into a project earlier in the month. Do not let up now; press ahead harder when you have the advantage. Keep the overall goal in mind while you are working on intermediate steps. More people are beginning to sit up and take notice of what you are doing. Your reputation is growing in just those circles where you want to become better known. Take the time to explain your reasons to a doubting Thomas. You should be especially persuasive in a group. Do not hesitate to take on an assignment being given up reluctantly by someone who has not been able to do the work.

21. TUESDAY. Mixed. Guard against overestimating your worth to an employer or in a potential work situation. You have to settle for a little less than the salary you would like in order to get necessary training or experience. Holding out could spell your defeat. Do your best, but do not expect great rewards. Negotiations are unlikely to go your way. Give a little, get a little is the optimum scenario now. Drop all pretenses and follow your basic Libra instincts. You possess a lot of potential that remains undeveloped. Learning from an expert can have lifelong implications as you move up the ladder of success. Keep a wary eye on a person working with or for you.

22. WEDNESDAY. Satisfactory. Be practical when it comes to money matters. It is not smart to gamble in hopes of a big profit; instead, you could suffer a reversal of fortunes. Distribute your money among banks and investments. Cut back on charge purchases. If you do not have cash in hand, put off buying. Think in long-range terms instead of trying to make a quick buck. Look for ways to save small amounts by taking lunch to work or washing what would otherwise have to be professionally cleaned. At the end of each day, dump the change in your purse into a piggy bank and watch it add up to a significant sum. Bringing pressure to bear on a family member may make you feel guilty.

23. THURSDAY. Sensitive. Dress this morning according to the image you hope to portray. Ideas are basically more important than looks, but now you have first to attract positive attention, then state what is on your mind. Elegance is in; be sure your shoes as well as your choice of jewelry reflect your good taste. Lack of cooperation can hamper your efforts. A past promise may be conveniently forgotten, forcing you to scramble for an alternative. Try to be more self-reliant. You cannot count on others to go out of their way for you even though you may have done so for them. Stick to your guns, but accept alternative methods for reaching cherished objectives. You can be too adamant.

24. FRIDAY. Fair. Catch up with back work before beginning anything new. Do not put away a job only partially finished or you may never get back to it. Volunteering for a task that others are trying to avoid can earn you a few merits with the boss. Listen more than you talk. Ideas being tossed around at home or in a group can inspire you to branch out in a new direction. There is a lot to learn from an out-of-towner. What is just beginning to become a trend in your area may already be established in a foreign country. A trip to see in person what is going on could be an eye-opener. You will not be satisfied with less than the best that you can do.

25. SATURDAY. Outstanding. This is the day to shop for a bargain in high-priced merchandise. Check the newspaper for an advertised sale, but do not stop there. Also study the used-items-for-sale classified ads. You may be able to get a special deal on older equipment that is perfectly adequate for your uses. You do not need state-of-the-art items if you are just learning a technique or plan on sticking to the basics. An outdoor sale could also provide a windfall if you know value when you see it. Take along a knowledgeable friend if you are not too experienced with what you hope to buy. Barter over price; there is no reason to pay full retail.

26. SUNDAY. Fortunate. If a financial problem has been causing you restless nights, this is the day to ask an older relative for a loan. You will not be turned down if they have the money in the bank. Your good mood today is infectious. Family members are agreeable to whatever you suggest. Outdoor activity is starred.

You will enjoy competition providing the sides are even. It is not smart, however, to play for high stakes; win or lose you will feel guilty. A family gathering could be the setting for a surprise announcement that means you will soon be attending a ceremony. Offer heartfelt congratulations without making any doom-and-gloom forecasts about what could happen.

27. MONDAY. Good. This is another day when personal relationships make you feel as though you are on top of the world. Not only are family members agreeable but co-workers and superiors are also clearly on your side. An idea that you propose will quickly be accepted and acted upon. Libras may be surprised by the leadership abilities they possess; you are more respected than you realize. Everything should be going well. Get an agreement in writing, if possible, so that no questions arise in the future as to who said what. It would be most unwise to disappoint a friend or a lover. You have to be as considerate of the special people in your life as you are of associates.

28. TUESDAY. Pleasant. Do not be taken by surprise if your mate or steady date announces plans that you have not been consulted about. Everyone needs their freedom of choice and action. Go along with the plans that are presented without raising objections. Libras, too, should try to be more independent and willing to act on their own if no one else seems interested. There is such a thing as too much togetherness. Be honest without hurting anyone's feelings. Come right out and state a problem that you believe is clouding your relationship. You can clear the air now and reach a higher level of understanding. Go out tonight in a group, not as a twosome.

29. WEDNESDAY. Easygoing. A talent you have been developing on your own in connection with a hobby may become useful in your work as well. The more you are able to contribute, the more valuable you are to a current or potential employer. This is a favorable day for Libras looking for work. You will shine in an interview because you do not seem too intent. Stay low key despite some inner feelings of impatience. An audition should go especially well. Perform in front of an audience as though you were at home singing in the shower or playing for a few close friends. The more you are able to relax, the more successful you will be. You are now laying the groundwork for the future.

30. THURSDAY. Productive. Strive to keep the lines of communication open with your boss as well as those who work for you.

An open-door policy is favored, where grievances can be aired as soon as they start to become a problem. What is kept bottled up can grow out of proportion to the problem. Avoid taking too adamant a stand. There are at least two viewpoints swirling around every action. Often it may be hard to choose which is going to be most effective. There is unusual opportunity at a distance, but also good reason to remain close to your normal base of operations. The phone may be your best friend today. An offer received this afternoon should be snapped up quickly.

JULY

1. FRIDAY. Lucky. The last day of the workweek for many Libras can be a lucky time if you are alert for opportunity. A phone call should galvanize you into action, or you may be the one making the calls and putting together a new group. There is a strong element of luck accompanying your efforts. Do not turn your back on a person who has said no once before. You are at your persuasive best now. Share your plans with those you hope will be a part of them. Urge them to make a decision as soon as possible; time is of the essence in jumping the competition. Evening is a starred time to visit an older friend or a longtime chum.

2. SATURDAY. Unsettling. Nosing around can unearth some information that is distressing. It is not smart to read another person's letter or mail, or to open a diary. You can easily gain the wrong impression, based on feelings expressed at a time of anger or deep sadness. Libras, too, should avoid putting in writing those emotions that are real at the moment, but apt to be fleeting. Choose words in speaking with a loved one with extra care. Do nothing to aggravate a situation that you know is tottering on the brink of an angry eruption. Being with friends gives you a good outlet for emotional tension. Get involved in a sport or other physical activity that you enjoy.

3. SUNDAY. Mixed. Libras on the road today, especially if you are traveling with a companion or a group, should pay special attention to what is going on. Do not allow yourself to be diverted by conversation while you are behind the wheel. It is a good day for a drive with no particular destination in mind. Relax and enjoy the sights; stop at a restaurant that looks appealing. You may discover that flattery is not appreciated, especially if you seem to be offering a compliment in hopes of receiving something in return. Sincere charm can be a moving force, but lack of sincerity will not go unnoticed. Playing a wait-and-see game with a prospective romantic suitor is recommended for the time being.

4. MONDAY. Good. Discuss with someone you trust an idea that you have been contemplating as a way of making some extra money on the side. There is opportunity if you take advantage of a need. Providing a service is the best way to bring in enough to put your budget back in the black. Bills have to be paid. Try to get the balance down to zero, or at least as low as possible. You do not want to be socked with high interest charges. Follow a hunch wherever it leads. Libra determination can reward you handsomely. A gathering with family or friends should be fun. Be sure to record some of the day's events with photographs or a video.

5. TUESDAY. Pleasant. Yesterday's good feelings remain in full force now. Enjoy the company of a person you would like to know better. Go out of your way to be accommodating. Doing a favor for someone now means you will reap extra help when you need it most. People are responding to your enthusiasm about a new project. This is an excellent day to finalize plans, even though there is probably not enough combined energy to set the wheels in full motion. Gauge the chances of success by the way a family member responds when you reveal your ideas. A person who knows you well is not going to pull any punches in offering a frank, honest opinion. Evening favors physical pursuits after dark.

6. WEDNESDAY. Variable. Unfinished business you have been attempting to ignore must be completed before you go on to something new. Hurry through it without agonizing over details. It is better to be finished than to be perfect, although both are ideal whenever possible. Play it straight and by the book if you hope to avoid problems with the boss or another superior. You are unlikely to be given any special permission or exemption from duty. What has worked in the past is only a clue to the future. Modifications are necessary. Stay up to date with technological change. You should not have to use paper and pencil or even refer to a reliable reference book.

7. THURSDAY. Difficult. Walk a thin line to avoid angering a person whose support you need. Compromise is necessary to keep a cooperative effort from unraveling. Avoid expressing what is on your mind, at least in public. Take out frustration by going for a long walk or punching a pillow. A trusted friend understands what you are going through and is ready to help. Guard against a tendency to spend money in an effort to feel better; it will only give you money problems on top of all that is currently worrying you. A new partnership could be the answer, but do not rush into it. Keep people guessing about your future intentions.

8. FRIDAY. Changeable. Suggestions made today may seem far-out, but do not reject them outright. There are worthwhile alternatives that require changing plans but not goals. Advice from a professional could be useful. A do-it-yourself book contains guidelines that can see you through the current difficulties. As the day progresses your concentration improves as well as your mood. A compliment from a person you admire makes you realize that you are appreciated. You may have to talk yourself into going out with a group of friends, but once you are with them you will relax and enjoy yourself. Family members are more negative than your friends, so steer clear of relatives tonight.

9. SATURDAY. Uncertain. Being thrifty now can help you pay for a future purchase with money rather than having to take out a loan. Avoid the pitfalls of jealous reactions. Be appropriately enthused when a friend or neighbor shows off their latest acquisition. Jealousy can interfere in a personal relationship as well. You have to let go in order to grow. A few hours of work this morning will put your home in shape for company. Clear off surfaces by throwing out or piling up newspapers and other accumulations. A hobby can be an enjoyable way to pass the afternoon, especially with a person who shares your interests. Love is beginning to grow, but is not a sure thing.

10. SUNDAY. Excellent. Relax and enjoy company that drops by today. You do not have to plan anything special in order to have a good time. Keep entertaining simple. Your mate or other loved one is tuned in to your needs and anxious to meet them. Children, too, provide some memories today. Write down those cute sayings that come out of the mouths of babes. For Libras in love, this is a prime time to ask that all-important question. The response you receive, which may not be in words alone, is sure to please you. Do not make any plans for more than the week ahead. Conditions are changing and your responsibilities may multiply.

11. MONDAY. Profitable. Unexpected income is coming your way, perhaps as the result of an inheritance. It is more likely to be a reward for work performed earlier in the year, however. A good deed is not going to pass unnoticed. Stay close to the phone this morning until you receive the call you know is coming. Communicate openly and honestly with those in charge of the purse strings. You can also obtain a loan if needed for start-up capital. Libras who will be returning to school should not stop hunting for a scholarship or other financial aid. If you have been considering giving up a goal, promise yourself not to rush to judgment. There are more options than you know about now.

12. TUESDAY. Variable. Something seems to be missing from a relationship that is important to you. Listen more than you talk today. Try to read between the lines and to interpret body language. If presented with a choice, opt for what you believe the other person wants most. For married Libras, there is no reason to try to keep up pretenses in front of friends and older family members. They know what is going on even though you have not spelled it out for them. Your mate, too, understands more than you might like to think. Communicate openly and honestly. Together you can work out a solution that is agreeable to both of you.

13. WEDNESDAY. Satisfactory. Be thankful that the plans you made earlier in the year are giving you a certain degree of freedom of choice now. Options are available, and probably more than you at first imagine. Independent work and thinking are favored. You do not need anyone's approval to move ahead with a project that is important to you. Working together can be useful, but is not vital. Results of your effort should earn you well-deserved recognition before 1994 closes. If you are preparing a report, proposal or other written document, highlight the positive and emphasize possibilities. Choose words with care so that there is no possibility of misinterpretation.

14. THURSDAY. Changeable. Avoid going out on a limb for anyone or anything. Take the conservative approach even while breaking new ground. You cannot rush change. Tried-and-true methods that have worked in the past are the steppingstones to the future. Health requires some extra attention. You may need to see a doctor in order to obtain a prescription refill or a new diagnosis. What you do not know can hurt you; do not put off this appointment. Eyesight should also be checked. You may need glasses that allow you to see clearly what others have no trouble reading. You are missing out on some of what is going on, due to a physical limitation that can be overcome.

15. FRIDAY. Confusing. Nothing is clear-cut or easy to decipher. Look for clues in the way people are acting, not necessarily what they are saying. Control an urge to blurt out a problem to the nearest person who will listen. You must maintain a degree of independence so that your options are not cut off. Certain things are best left unsaid even to a family member or close friend. If you bring up sensitive happenings from the past, you could be reminded of what you would much rather forget. No new worries should be added today. Focus on what is most likely to occur. There is not enough time to consider all possibilities, so limit anxiety by determining likely scenarios.

16. SATURDAY. Mixed. Conditions are coming around to favor your special Libra talents and abilities. Put them on display at home and in your neighborhood. Be generous in sharing what you know. Children have to be given the same attention that you lavish on friends. Your mate or steady date also craves extra attention. Trying to exercise overall control can be frustrating as well as wasteful. Hone in on those changes that you want to make and that are within your power. There are some matters you have to overlook because you are not the person in charge. A loan can be arranged if needed, although terms may crimp your budget for a long time to come. Stay home tonight.

17. SUNDAY. Enjoyable. Your mate or partner, or an older family member, is providing incentive for you to better your physical shape. If they can stick to a diet and exercise program, so can you. Joining forces will provide the incentive you may need now. It is a positive day to give up a habit you know is not good for you. Find an alternative that is healthy. A loved one knows better than you what you really need, so listen to advice offered with love. Stock up on fruit and vegetables for the week ahead. If you do not have high-calorie sweets in your house you cannot be tempted to snack on them. Do not confine your socializing to one particular group or type.

18. MONDAY. Sensitive. If you made a mistake last week, there is no use trying to rectify it all at once. An apology may be due; start with that. Gradually let it be known that you are having a change of heart and would like to be given another chance. Your feelings about a certain person are not set in stone. Their true intentions may be showing through now, much to your surprise. You can afford to be more aggressive in pursuing a business deal than a personal relationship. Diligence is going to pay off. Do not take no for a final answer; assume the word only means maybe. It is up to you to continue to go after what you want. If a door is not opening on the first knock, ring the bell.

19. TUESDAY. Rewarding. Changes coming your way are all for the better. Embrace them without worrying about how you are going to handle additional responsibility. You are likely to amaze yourself with the ability to juggle home, work and personal life without a misstep. Experience is growing as you try new techniques. What is new is not necessarily better, but give it a fair chance. Continue to develop a talent that makes you the envy of co-workers as the spotlight turns on you. Set your sights high. You will be happier climbing a tall ladder to reach your goals than settling for less than you really want. News from a friend gives you good reason to plan a party.

20. WEDNESDAY. Manageable. This is a favorable day to improve what is working well but could be better. A relationship that is plodding along can be given new life if you pay a little more attention and are more forgiving. No one is able to meet your high standards, not even you. Give a little and you are going to get a lot in return. Sincerity is an especially important trait to look for in friends and to offer to them in return. Do not make any promise unless certain you can honor it. Your reputation is a precious possession. Take a few minutes to appreciate your good fortune and to consider what you could do to help someone less fortunate than you. Group action can be effective.

21. THURSDAY. Variable. It might be necessary to seek an opinion from a professional, or at least someone who has more day-to-day experience than you. Do not consider it demeaning to request help and assistance. You cannot do everything yourself, and there are many things that others can do better than you. Use their services to your advantage. You get what you pay for today. Seek a bargain and you are apt to be disappointed with the quality of what you receive. Attempts to dominate a co-worker or a group are not going to be successful. They will not tolerate your interference and may rebel. Children, too, have to be coaxed rather than commanded. A compliment is a good starter.

22. FRIDAY. Difficult. A stalemate can only be broken if you make a move without first seeking a guarantee in return. This is an especially difficult time for the Libra who has been working long and hard for a special goal, only to see others take over and begin to change the agenda. It is important to keep a partnership from breaking up; do all that you can, even if this means giving in more than others seem willing to do. Teamwork is essential to achieving long-term objectives. Your ability to look on the positive side is an important ingredient. Hold down spending personally; insist that your mate or partner gets your approval before taking money out of a joint account.

23. SATURDAY. Mixed. Exercise strong self-control or your temper could flare. Family harmony is in jeopardy. A younger person is testing your resolve to see if you really believe what you have been saying. Do not waver or give in to their demands. Loud music or constant chatter may grate on your nerves. You need a little time alone to restore your perspective about all that is going on. Avoid discussing a personal matter with someone who tends to gossip. An invitation received today may force you to make a choice and both options are attractive. Be swayed by your mate or partner's obvious desires. News from a relative gives you good reason to propose a toast.

24. SUNDAY. Outstanding. A lot can be accomplished without straining yourself or your budget. Put your own special brand of talent on display. Use materials that are already on hand rather than making any new purchases. Teamwork is favored in all activities. Sports may appeal, although you may be torn between rooting for the home team and supporting a player on the opposition. Your interests are coinciding with a trend that is just beginning to emerge. You may be able to turn this to your advantage as a profitable sideline. Join forces with a person you have known awhile. Cooperative effort can bring in extra money without becoming a burden.

25. MONDAY. Disconcerting. Your moods are likely to swing from one to the next quickly, which will keep you from accomplishing much today. Try to direct your attention to one important project and ignore everything else. You can easily be influenced by criticism, but must not give up. If you can get over the current hump, new possibilities will open up for you. Avoid asking for a loan or borrowing anything of value. You should not put yourself in the position of being in someone's debt. A friend has a problem to discuss with you. Listen attentively to what is said and what is only implied. Offer support without giving any specific advice.

26. TUESDAY. Useful. With a shove in the right direction you can get back on track today. Tie up some loose ends by delegating work that others can complete as well as you could. Check rules and regulations to be certain that you are in compliance. By setting a deadline for yourself you can pace your work. Otherwise it is likely to expand and take up all of your time. Compromise is necessary on some issues, but on others you can get your way through persistence. The trick is knowing where you should be holding out. A person who reacts most negatively is the one who is likely to listen to reason. Someone with a low-key approach may be adamant and unmoved by your facts.

27. WEDNESDAY. Routine. Conditions are coming around to favor your interests. Play the waiting game. What is available now is only a small percentage of what will open up for you if you hold out a little longer. Stick to what you know and do best. Do not branch out in a new direction. In the presence of a famous person you are apt to be tongue-tied and could be overlooked; do not take it personally. There is an opportunity to add to a collection through a private purchase. Check newspaper classified ads for merchandise being sold by a collector to raise quick cash. Do not overdo physically. Use mechanical equipment instead of muscle power. A chance encounter late in the day could be the start of a new relationship.

28. THURSDAY. Successful. A co-worker's opposition to your ideas is gradually fading. Be ready to form a new partnership with this person and to let bygones be bygones. There is nothing to be gained from an I-told-you-so attitude. Common goals are a firm bond despite different approaches. This is a most favorable day to talk with the boss about a pay raise or promotion. Let it be known that you are not content to continue doing the same job if there is room for advancement. A newly hired could be seen as a threat. Be sure to push for your own advancement or you can languish while others move ahead. A trip could be worthwhile later.

29. FRIDAY. Good. Dealing with the public should come easily for Libras. You can be an effective speaker without ever taking a public-speaking class. Honesty shines through in all that you say. Stand up in a public meeting and express yourself in terms that everyone can understand. People you hardly know are likely to come up afterward to congratulate you and continue the discussion. There is opportunity to take part in a community effort to raise money without raising taxes. Donate your time to a cause you believe in strongly. Set your sights high and other people will walk a tightrope to follow you. The Libra in love is in for a happy surprise tonight.

30. SATURDAY. Enjoyable. You are on the same wave length as family members. Feelings are running strong and deep. Together you can work out a solution to any problem. Come up with mutual goals as a way of fostering togetherness. Sports may appeal, although you will probably want to take a few lessons from a pro after you see what other people are doing. Winning is not as important to you as playing the game. Look for ways to redecorate your home without buying anything new. Rearranging furniture can be a way of opening up spaces and making your living quarters seem lighter and brighter. Vacationing Libras should be taking in all the tourist sights with a camera at hand.

31. SUNDAY. Variable. You will enjoy social activities that are a little off the beaten track. Get away from your usual Sunday routine. Call a person who you would like to get to know better and make arrangements to meet. Romance is in the air, although it is up to the Libra partner to be more aggressive than usual. You may also meet someone who could be useful to your career advancement. Be sure to remember names and faces. Give yourself a break from serious matters, although they may be in the back of your mind. Enjoy reminiscing about the good old days with a friend or family member. A school yearbook can make you laugh remembering how serious it all seemed then.

AUGUST

1. MONDAY. Promising. Pay more attention to any warning sign of illness that you may be experiencing. Try a home remedy first; but if that is not curing what ails you, make an appointment with your doctor. Focus on nutrition; be sure to eat regularly and to avoid fatty food. Whenever you are thirsty, reach for a glass of water and do not accept any substitute. You can increase your energy by getting more exercise. Walk to work, or use the stairs instead of the elevator. Joining a health club can give you added impetus to exercise regularly. You have the will power now to give up a habit you know is unhealthy. Not only will you benefit, but family members will appreciate your effort as well.

2. TUESDAY. Enjoyable. A bright idea for a money-making venture can be enjoyable as well as profitable. Work today with people whose company you enjoy away from the job as well as from nine to five. A new partnership is especially starred. It is important also to stay on the good side of the boss. You can turn a routine project into one that showcases your talents. Consider taking a course to increase your skills or provide new ones. Do not fall behind in knowledge of state-of-the-art technology. Look into new job possibilities, but be discreet about it. You do not want to let higher-ups know you are at all discontent with current conditions. Love is on the menu tonight.

3. WEDNESDAY. Mixed. A younger family member is giving you something to smile about. Take pride in their accomplishment, and be sure to let them know how you feel. Libras may be showing off recent photos of the newest addition to the family. Everyone cares, but not quite as much as you; guard against overdoing it. Accept an additional work assignment without expecting time off or a bonus. It is important to prove that you are willing to go the extra mile for the company that puts money in your wallet. Doing only what is expected gives you no visibility when raises and promotions are being determined. Do not sign any contract or other legal document without first reading all the fine print.

4. THURSDAY. Tricky. If you are ready for trouble, it will not take you by surprise. A relationship that has been sailing along with a steady breeze could become rocky. Someone you have known a long time feels you are beginning to take advantage of them. Analyze your own motives so that you can make conscious decisions. It may be you who are not getting the appreciation you believe you deserve. You cannot force anyone to recognize all that you do for them, but you may want to stop doing it for a while and see what develops then. Do not lower your own high standards. Hold firm to beliefs that are the basis of all your actions. Someone you thought was on your side may show no interest in your plans. But a newcomer can step in to fill the gap.

5. FRIDAY. Variable. Avoid daydreaming about what might have been if you have made a different choice some time ago. Act in the present. Possibilities look very good today. You have a new opportunity staring you in the face, but if you shut your eyes, it may evaporate. Sign up enthusiastically to participate in a group project. Volunteer effort is sure to be rewarded. A donation of time is more appreciated than money. Focus some attention on a community problem, especially one that involves a certain segment of the population, such as teenagers or the elderly. Find a way to help by speaking out loudly and putting effort into identifying a solution. You have to disrupt surface harmony to get to the heart of the problem and to effect reform.

6. SATURDAY. Disturbing. Envy may rear its ugly head during the day. A neighbor's new acquisition or a recent purchase by a friend may make you dissatisfied with what you have. Guard against making any negative comments to them. Your own financial responsibilities have to be taken care of in the best way you can work them out. What is important to you to own may not appeal to others or they may be jealous. Do not allow that to affect you one way or the other. If you hope to make a major purchase before the end of the year, figure out how to cut back on everyday expenses so that you can save for what you want. It is not smart to add to your debt balance; pay outright or do not buy.

7. SUNDAY. Lucky. In-laws, and other relatives at a distance, could provide a spark of good fortune for you. Keep in contact regularly even if you are not able to visit often. Solicit their opinion about a project you are contemplating. It may come as a surprise to learn of a similar experience that they had, and you can benefit from their advice. Someone to whom you are introduced by a family member, perhaps the parent of your child's friend, could open new doors for you. Go out of your way to socialize. Any disagreement at home can be smoothed over without any formal apology being offered. A most happy reunion is foreseen if your mate or steady date has been absent for a while.

8. MONDAY. Productive. Solve a problem with your brainpower before initiating any action. Thinking comes first, then you can put a plan into motion. Figure out what people are thinking from their body language as well as what they say. Your Libra intuition is the best insight you can have regarding moves that may be in the offing. Look for clues in a report or other written communication; read between the lines. Be honest with yourself and you will not succumb to self-deception. An idea that is too fanciful to work out in the real world should be toned down and modified. Time spent in the library can help you find out what has worked in the past, and especially why it was successful.

9. TUESDAY. Good. Romance is in the air for the young-at-heart Libra. Someone you have known a short time is a likely candidate for flirtation. Do not take the love game too seriously. Relax and have a good time with someone of the opposite sex who obviously finds you attractive. Get better acquainted through shared work or other activities. You may want to plan on getting together in a group so that there is less pressure to keep the conversational ball rolling. Travel can be especially enjoyable if you are not going alone. A companion keeps you alert and aware when new sights begin to be old hat. Try to combine a work trip with a pleasurable few days off for sightseeing.

10. WEDNESDAY. Buoyant. Spread good news whether it involves you or someone you know. You will be especially effective today in the role of publicity agent. Blow your own horn about a recent accomplishment in which you are taking justifiable pride. If you do not let people know what you have been doing, you lose out on a good opportunity. The future is promising and the present is glowing. Your Libra optimism can help you over rough times and make the good ones even better. Focus intently on all that is positive. You can find the kernel of good in any situation. Dream a little, but keep your feet planted firmly on the ground. Pass along an idea that might be useful to a friend.

11. THURSDAY. Demanding. Be open to suggestions from co-workers and friends. Guard against turning a deaf ear to what they have to say. You may not agree with them, but they deserve a fair hearing and consideration. Family members have ideas to pass on as well. These are likely to be less practical, however, because they worry about hurting your feelings. A plan you are about to set in motion can be improved with the adoption of a few new ideas. Avoid rejecting anything as too simple; the simpler the better when it comes to getting results. You could come to regret an answer given in haste. Before withdrawing any money from a joint account, talk it over with your mate or partner and get their okay.

12. FRIDAY. Stressful. When you cannot get in touch with a repairman, you will have to struggle to patch up a problem yourself. Equipment breakdowns are foreseen, especially machinery run by electrical power. Check that cords are not frayed or circuits overloaded. Stock up on batteries for reserve power. Write that letter you have been trying to avoid. Express your views as positively as possible so that you do not turn off the recipient before they reach your closing. Follow through on an order placed earlier in August. You may discover that the package was lost in the mail, but that you are being charged for the merchandise. You are most convincing when you are quietly firm. Yelling gets you nowhere.

13. SATURDAY. Difficult. The weekend does not bring a great deal of relief from the tension that has existed all week.

Family members are apt to get on your nerves without intending to bother you. The harder they try to satisfy you, the more you may resent their apparent freedom while you are struggling with a long list of things to do. Try paring down your schedule to necessities only. You need time for fun and relaxation. After some time off you are going to be much more productive and clearheaded. Restore the garden to better shape by weeding and spreading mulch. Be sure to turn on the sprinkler for a long soaking of parched plants. Share the fruits of your gardening labors with neighbors and friends.

14. SUNDAY. Disappointing. A get-together scheduled for today may have to be canceled due to weather or a health problem. Do not let the moment pass without setting a new date. Opportunity can be lost now unless you are more aggressive than usual. If you wait for other people to make the first move, you could be waiting a long time. Family members are preoccupied. Even a youngster may turn down your suggestion of going to the shopping mall or to a movie. A deal that seems too good to be true is probably exactly that. Avoid buying anything based on an advertisement you see or hear. Check out the product or service personally before parting with your hard-earned money.

15. MONDAY. Rewarding. A dose of your imagination is just what the boss wants at work. Follow instructions closely, but deviate just enough to make the end product a little better than expected. Keep a low profile. Let higher-ups become aware of your abilities through your work, not your words. Bragging can land you in trouble with co-workers. A deal now being finalized in the back room may include you in a starring role. An urge to travel is too strong to resist. If you do not have a chance to take a trip in connection with your job, schedule a weekend for being away. Visiting relatives could be enjoyable as well as a way to save money on lodging. A recent investment is beginning to turn a profit. Do not cash in too hastily.

16. TUESDAY. Lucky. What others may regard as a lucky break for you is actually the result of your careful planning. Do not let anyone in on your little secret; go along with their view that you just happened to be in the right place at the right time. This is a propitious day to take a well-calculated chance at winning a prize, especially a jackpot. Your Libra luck on occasion covers for lack of skill, and this is one of those special times. Consider entering a juried show as well. A hobby can begin to earn you recognition and the possibility of a lucrative sideline if you are willing to sell what you make. Your confidence level is soaring. Only you are standing in your path to success.

17. WEDNESDAY. Mixed. Lack of cooperation can keep you from accomplishing all that should be done now. There is a definite limit to what you can accomplish on your own. Accept an offer of help even if you know the person primarily wants to pick your brain and learn your techniques. Someone from a distance is beginning to exert increasing influence on your options. The longer you take making up your mind, the more limited your choices will be. An outside interest may be taking away from your primary money-making occupation. Guard against mingling work with pleasure, or you could end up with much more time on your hands than you want. Trying hard is not enough now; you should also improve your skills.

18. THURSDAY. Outstanding. Share a secret with that special person in your life. You may discover that they have been having the same thoughts or the same dream. Far-reaching plans can be made. Do not limit yourself to what seems possible right now. A compliment puts you on cloud nine. Someone you hardly know is keeping tabs on your progress and speaking up for you behind the scenes. Do nothing to disappoint a backer. Be true to your word despite the inconveniences that may be involved. Fast-breaking developments give you renewed confidence about what lies ahead. Your predictions are coming true right before your eyes. A winding path could be the quickest route to success.

19. FRIDAY. Disquieting. Transportation delays may make you late for a morning appointment or an evening getaway. Allow ample time to reach your destination. Libras who are driving should check the oil and tire pressure before starting out. Fill up on gas so that you do not have to stop en route. The more you try to hurry, the more frustrated you will become. Maintain a sense of humor while others are bemoaning situations over which they have no control. Leaving earlier than usual can help you escape the crush of vacationers. There is a limit as to what you can hope to accomplish today. Anything requiring teamwork is likely to be put on hold. Willingness to help is not enough; you lack the expertise that comes with experience.

20. SATURDAY. Fortunate. There should be a significant drop in pressure placed on you today. For all that may have gone wrong yesterday, today makes up for it. Relax and please yourself. By doing so, you make family members happy as well. Avoid competitive activity unless you genuinely do not care who wins. It is a fortunate day for bargain shopping, especially at yard sales or an outdoor flea market. You may be able to add to a collection because you recognize a special hallmark or other identification overlooked by an anxious seller. Bargain over prices even knowing they are low. Half the fun of buying secondhand merchandise is making a special deal. Love makes tonight most memorable.

21. SUNDAY. Rewarding. Helping others is high on your list of priorities today. Lend a hand without waiting to be asked or begged. Give generously of time and effort. What you receive in return will give you more of a lift than any amount of money could buy. There could also be a need to put lifesaving skills to the test. Libras who do not know what to do in case someone starts choking should read standard procedures or take a course. Also be especially alert around water. In fact, be more safety-conscious than usual. Family members are behind you all the way. Harmony reigns at home as well as with in-laws or other distant relatives. A child can be included in all activities.

22. MONDAY. Variable. Do not rock the boat at home or at work. Go along willingly with plans that have already been formulated by your mate or partner. Avoid mentioning possible pitfalls that you envision. Nothing is totally certain; you can only do your best with what is available. Your confidence level is on the rise. Someone whose motives you have been questioning is out to prove that your fears are unfounded. Give them a fair, open chance. It is a favorable day to sign a contract or other binding commitment. You can count on a handshake being as good as a written promise. Negotiations are also promising. State plainly what you will accept, then do not waver from that position.

23. TUESDAY. Good. People are wiling to listen to your views and give them serious consideration, which may come as a surprise. A former teacher is now a student, or anxious to be one. You are the person from whom they know they can learn. A friend of long standing is seeing you in a new light. Romance can blossom on the firm foundation of friendship. Libras interested in a serious relationship need not venture far from their normal operations base. But those of you not quite ready to settle down should be wary of making what sound like promises when you have no intention of keeping them. A dalliance with someone who is a visitor can be fun while it lasts, with no strings attached.

24. WEDNESDAY. Difficult. New projects with unusual requirements tend to throw you off balance. Cooperation is unlikely. There is a pervasive fear of change that can snare you in its grip. While you may be the person delegated to make the changes, you are not comfortable with them and will have trouble convincing others to go along. Check into a new offering that has been proven through a rigorous series of tests. It is not smart to accept any work where payment depends on performance. Gauging the acceptability of your output can be a matter of opinion that leads to a lawsuit or at least hard feelings. Pay what you legitimately owe, and collect debts that are overdue.

25. THURSDAY. Pleasant. Knowing all the ins and outs of a particular situation can affect your attitude and your performance. Find out what is going on behind the scenes. Do not allow yourself to be brushed off easily with a pat answer. Keep asking questions until you are satisfied. It is not so much that people are unwilling to tell you what you want to know. Instead, they probably assume you already have necessary information and may be wondering why you are even asking. Do not get carried away with curiosity, however. Some decisions have not yet been made, and you cannot expect anyone to explain possibilities to you beforehand. Lofty Libra ideals keep you looking onward and upward.

26. FRIDAY. Easygoing. Take it easy today. Many co-workers may be away or getting ready to go on vacation. If you are also planning a getaway, try to finish up everything so that you leave with a clear conscience. Travel plans that have not been finalized will have to be played by ear. It is too late to try to get on a flight except with a standby arrangement. Tickets to a concert or other popular performance may have to be bought secondhand through a high-priced dealer. But if you want to be there in person, you will not mind paying scalpers' rates. Do not expect anyone to do a job that you are unwilling to tackle yourself. There is nothing so important today that it cannot wait.

27. SATURDAY. Manageable. Fun is yours for the taking today, but you may have to encourage your mate or another family member to go along with you. A picnic can be memorable, particularly if you get away with that special person and have a heart-to-heart talk. You could be in for a round of visiting as well as playing host to some drop-by guests. Dress comfortably without concerning yourself about fashion trends. Be sure to wear shoes at all times. There is a danger of getting cut if you go barefoot. Keep spending within reasonable limits. You do not want to stint on having a good time, but neither do you have to spend as though there is no tomorrow. A friend knows when to tell you to stop.

28. SUNDAY. Positive. A new start is starred if you are using your Libra creativity as part of the mix. Do nothing that comes packaged and ready for you in simple-minded steps. You are not going to be satisfied with work that turns out just like everyone else's. Your sense of harmony demands a personal touch to all that you do. A little time spent mulling over recent events can be an eye-opener. Someone you had thought was trying to pull a fast one on you could be the most honest person around. You can imagine motives that do not exist when you are unsure of why certain action is being taken. Trust those around you until they give you good reason not to do so.

29. MONDAY. Demanding. Check out rumors that are making the rounds now. Find out if there is any truth to them and, if so, what can be done. You intend to get to the root of a problem by digging deep. Someone you have known only a short while may be compounding trouble due to lack of insight rather than for malicious reasons. Resist the urge to go on a spending spree. What you buy is not going to make you any happier or more content. After doing some soul-searching, you will come up with a plan that is right for you. There is a better way to handle a situation than that which has been tried so far. Innovative financial planning can be arranged without having to get involved with a bank loan.

30. TUESDAY. Ambitious. Focus on what is most important, then go for it. This is not a day to hold back in any way, shape or form. Libras have a strong urge to belong. A new group is ready to accept you as a full-fledged member if you are willing to pay your dues. Concentrate on obtaining necessary skills for a new job that is likely to be offered to you next month. Get a head start on this work by learning on the job. It is helpful now to prove that you are reliable and dependable without someone having to check on you frequently. Your ambition is taking you to a higher level, and more pay is apt to go along with the responsibility. If a loved one is feeling neglected, plan a special surprise just for him or her.

31. WEDNESDAY. Frustrating. Your heightened ambitions have to be held under tight rein today. Guard against a premature announcement of your intentions. It is not smart to burn any bridges behind you. Someone who has been a staunch ally is beginning to get involved with another person, which may hurt your feelings. But when you look at the situation realistically, you know that you are ready to move on. You should no longer be under anyone's wing. Be wary of taking out your aggressions by picking an argument with someone on the job or at home. What you consider a cleansing disagreement could be viewed as a disagreeable fight by others. Physical exercise helps you release tension in a positive way.

SEPTEMBER

1. THURSDAY. Changeable. A project you have been working on along with other people is rising to an increasing volume of activity. Enlist extra help, even if you have to pay for their services. An expert may be needed to provide advice that helps you past a stumbling block. Drop your resistance to an idea proposed by a person you consider a competitor. Joint effort is necessary for success. You have the will power to cut through red tape by proceeding carefully and cautiously. Avoid making any wild promises or statements that are not quite true. Compromise on some issues, while being assertive on those you know you are unwilling to change. Subtlety comes naturally to Libra.

2. FRIDAY. Unsettling. If you have been tossing and turning at night worrying about a situation, now is the time to face it squarely. Look for alternatives, then choose one and start acting on it. Delay can be costly both personally as well as in a relationship. You should be able to come up with a solution that is so subtle no one will even guess that you had a problem. Libra self-discipline is excellent. You can give up almost anything for a limited time in order to obtain a special objective. A new alliance is foreseen with someone considerably older than you. Your enthusiasm and their connections make a great combination. Avoid giving in to an urge to gossip.

3. SATURDAY. Mixed. Keep your thoughts to yourself if you know they will upset family members or friends. You are still in the indecisive stage. Do not arouse other people to opposition before even you know for certain what you are going to do. Someone you do not know is too unreliable to be counted on when the going gets rough. They may come through for you or they may turn their back. Keep your emotions under control. Those who know you well can see right through you when you become emotionally charged. An outing today may turn into an all-day affair, especially if you run into a person of the opposite sex who is also looking for action. You will enjoy being with that person, but not as a twosome.

4. SUNDAY. Disconcerting. You may have to answer some hard questions posed by a family member. Keep your responses as simple and straightforward as possible. The more you say, the more likely you are to trip yourself up. If you owe anyone an apology, do not hesitate to make it. A loan should also be repaid promptly. Let a friend or frequent date know that you are unwilling to play second fiddle to another person or activity. If you are not important enough to them to deserve special time and attention, you should move on to greener pastures. No one is going to stand up for you; it is up to you to be more aggressive than usual without alienating people on your side.

5. MONDAY. Variable. Consider how a plan that you are contemplating is going to impact on family members. Be sure to consult your mate or partner before reaching a firm, final decision. If you envision having to relocate, broach the subject gingerly. Coming right out and saying what you are thinking can turn off potential allies. Be delicate and gentle. You can persuade even the most adamant person by countering their arguments with valid reasons of your own. Libra shoppers can find special Labor Day values today in a large mall. Compare prices before buying anything. Do not allow yourself to be swayed by a fast-talking salesperson. Those who talk loudest may have the least to say.

6. TUESDAY. Good. New people coming into your sphere are bringing opportunity right to your doorstep. Be ready to try something different and somewhat daring. The cooperative route is best in order to achieve quick results. Put your Libra talents to good use in negotiating terms that are the envy of your competitors. When you give a little you get a lot in return. Your partner or coworker is supportive and inclined to be generous. They will not hold out on you. Good news regarding a contract may be funneled through a former boss or colleague. You are being considered for a higher-paid position. Make it obvious that you can get along with anyone in the context of group endeavor.

7. WEDNESDAY. Sensitive. You are aware of the feelings of a person close to you, but uncertain how to help. Take clues from what they say, and especially from what they do not say. Offer to help without taking over. Be ready to listen for as long as they want to talk. You may provide great relief for them as a sounding board to help them consider all possibilities. It is also a good day to volunteer to work in a nursing home or a shelter for the homeless or as a school aide. You have sufficient energy for all of your activities, plus the help you are providing on the side. A donation of time can be more appreciated than money. Invite a friend to go out for a leisurely lunch or dinner.

8. THURSDAY. Outstanding. Yesterday's complications are beginning to sort themselves out. Give yourself a pat on the back for the help you provided when you recognized a need. Do not look for appreciation from the other person involved, however. Remain behind the scenes today, listening to all that is going on. A snippet of conversation that you happen to overhear can give you a clue as to what lies ahead. You are being considered for an important new position which is apt to involve longer working hours, along with more pay. Decide now if the trade-off is what you want. There is a degree of chaos swirling around you, but you can work through it and not be swept off your feet.

9. FRIDAY. Difficult. Trivial pursuits are not appealing now. Libras are inclined to be serious-minded, and today you will not see much entertainment in all that is going on. A friend's attempt to lighten your load may make you annoyed. Other people are capable of relieving some of your burden, but you may choose to carry on alone. It is an emotionally demanding day. News from someone at a distance could come as a shock, although once you have thought it over you may want to call back and offer congratulations. The boss or another higher-up is turning up the heat to get a project completed ahead of schedule. You may have to work late or take work home with you over the weekend.

10. SATURDAY. Satisfactory. Love is creeping back into your everyday life. Libras have a way of tuning out emotions when the going gets rough. Open up lines of communication with your mate or steady date by making the first move to restore cordial relations. A small gift could be an ice-breaker. Or you may want to suggest going out to a concert or play. Or try for upbeat entertainment. New romance is also possible as the result of a chance encounter. Luck is with you in your love life. This is a most promising day to consider marriage or parenthood. You have ample love to share with an enlarged family circle. Being more demonstrative of your feelings removes any lingering doubts that your mate may be nurturing.

11. SUNDAY. Cautious. Someone who means a lot to you is applying pressure in an attempt to persuade you to change your mind. If reasoning is not enough to quiet them, you may have to resort to putting your foot down and refusing to listen. Find some time alone to think about what they are saying. It is important to stick to a decision if convinced you are right. But do not become so adamant that you leave yourself no options. A long walk can clear your mind. An older relative has worthwhile advice to offer, but you must ask for it. Upsetting news is foreseen from someone at a distance. You may want to plan a visit to help ease their burden. Do not brush off a child's serious question.

12. MONDAY. Fortunate. Luckily you do not have to ask anyone today for a special favor. Independent work and action are sufficient for all that must be done. It will be difficult getting along as part of a group. Your decisions may not be standard enough to be readily accepted by most people. Proceed on your own with confidence; you are definitely on the right track. Results from today's actions should earn you well-deserved recognition. Highlight all that is positive. A resume can help you land a job, but it must stand out from the rest. Break with tradition if you believe you have a better way. Choose words with care so that there is no possibility of double meaning.

13. TUESDAY. Variable. Although an idea may look promising on paper or even in your mind's eye, take time to test its potential. You may discover flaws that are not apparent until you do. A plan you are considering could have negative consequences for a family member, friend or co-worker. Think of them as well as yourself. Pressure is being applied from home and at work. The day's schedule may be changed before lunchtime, and perhaps again in the afternoon. Nothing is certain. Phone calls bring new information that has to be investigated on the sly. By appearing innocent, you can readily learn some inside facts. Check the credentials of a person you are considering hiring.

14. WEDNESDAY. Important. Remain behind the scenes throughout the day. Keep a low profile and let others do the talking. It is not smart to permit the competition to know what you are considering. The day favors becoming better organized. Pay bills before their due dates so that you do not incur late charges. Write that letter; you have been putting it off because you cannot figure out what to say. The fact that you care is more important than how you state your feelings. Some dissension is foreseen due to a third person's prying into your work or love life. A heart-to-heart talk can ease the tension and get you back in tune. Creativity puts you ahead of the crowd. Utilize a talent you have been developing in private.

15. THURSDAY. Fair. Avoid going out on a limb for anyone or anything. You have to abide by the same rules as everyone else. Stick to methods that have been successful in the past. You can waste a lot of time and energy starting from scratch instead of learning from other people. Health may require extra attention. Make an appointment with a doctor if a pain is not responding to home remedies. Be sure to eat nourishing meals on a regular schedule rather than snacking whenever you start to crave some tasty morsel. Buying shoes that are comfortable from the moment you first put them on can make you feel better all over. It is also a good time to purchase a suit for a special occasion.

16. FRIDAY. Changeable. Use your innate resourcefulness to obtain information you need before you make a decision. It should not be necessary to come right out and say what you want. In fact, you may decide to invent a cover-up in order to keep your intentions secret for a while. Conditions are not static. What you have come to expect from a person or an institution is beginning to be obsolete. Keep up with the times. Mold your expectations to the reality of what you see around you. Try to arrange to take some time off today, either by extending your lunch hour or leaving work earlier than usual. You have to shake off the cobwebs and do some deep thinking.

17. SATURDAY. Productive. Do not put off work around the house. Try to stir up some cooperation from family members to make the tasks quicker and more enjoyable. Do not pressure anyone to help, however. You may have to overcome morning inertia by forcing yourself to start; after that you will enjoy physical activity. Keep your mind in low gear. Working with your hands gives you a sense of satisfaction. Make do with supplies already on hand rather than buying anything new. If you want a particular type of equipment, try to borrow it from a friend or a neighbor. Otherwise you may have to rent it for the day. Evening socializing is starred with a group rather than as a twosome.

18. SUNDAY. Fortunate. This smooth-running day favors the Libra in love. Do not hesitate to ask that question you have been pondering. Your mate or date is not going to disappoint you by their response. There is a strong element of good fortune accompanying your actions. It will not take much advance planning to be seen in the right company today. A person who wields power in your community is willing to listen to your ideas. You may also be able to get a special favor based on what you have contributed in the past. Family members are good listeners if you need a sounding board for your ideas. Rely on their experience, but do not count on their financial help.

19. MONDAY. Enjoyable. This should be a relaxing start of the workweek. Come up with a plan for the whole week ahead so that you can pace yourself. Otherwise you may get in a dither worrying about all that you want to do and not accomplish much of anything. Shy away from anyone who acts like a know-it-all. Mutual cooperation can help you get ahead. You will not be comfortable as a follower or a leader exclusively. Protect your good name and reputation by following your own path. There are some conditions beyond your control; worrying about them can be exhausting and useless. Opportunities that surface today should be much to your liking. What you have been trying to arrange clandestinely is apt to occur naturally.

20. TUESDAY. Difficult. You may feel that you have lost touch with a project that you started or helped design. Find out what is going on without trying to take over. People are apt to resent intrusion in their affairs, but you can learn from them. You have not been let in on a secret and could have your feelings hurt. Put up a brave front even if you feel like crying or yelling. Wait to see what develops. It may be that later in the month you will be called upon to come to the rescue. It would be most unwise to threaten to quit or to submit your resignation despite your upset. Trust your own judgment. You know how far you can go and still keep your options open.

21. WEDNESDAY. Mixed. Pay attention to small details that could be overlooked in the rush to finish a project. Double-check facts and figures. Be sure conclusions follow from the information that is presented. Anything put in writing today could cause some problems for you in the future. Be sure that you are not signing a contract or other document because the pressure is on. You must understand all the terms and clauses before affixing your signature. Try to rearrange your schedule to suit yourself better. You may want to take work home to finish tonight when you are not being bothered by constant phone calls and other interruptions. Work when you feel alert even if people are sleeping then.

22. THURSDAY. Outstanding. Favorable influences are affecting all of your decisions today. You can act with less information than you normally require because your instincts tell you to go ahead. Trust your basic Libra judgment; it will not steer you wrong. Find a way to weave around a roadblock instead of charging at it head-on. Friends and family members are ready to lend a hand or a check. There is an aura of excitement as people come and go all day long. Be generous in offering advice when asked. You are seeing the big picture while others focus on small segments. Keep it in focus even while working out the picky details. New investment can reward you with handsome dividends providing you are not seeking a quick profit.

23. FRIDAY. Cautious. Slow down a little and reconsider a decision made earlier in the week. You may not have taken into account a certain option that would make your work easier and possibly improve the results as well. An offer that you rejected is still open. Be alert also to a new opportunity that surfaces today. What seems least likely could become the best choice. Proceed slowly and cautiously. You know what can happen when you rush ahead with blinders on. You should not find it difficult to persuade a co-worker to join forces with you. Do not pay for advice that you want only in order to confirm your own opinion. You can trust your judgment and act on it confidently.

24. SATURDAY. Positive. Catch up with small jobs that you put off during the workweek just past. Do not allow one part of your yard or one area of your neighborhood to become an eyesore. You do not have to make a mess in order to clear one up. Keep activities as simple and straightforward as possible. A family member wants to help, but may not know how. Spend some time teaching a skill that comes as second nature to you. A child deserves undivided attention for part of the day. You may want to go out for lunch or for an afternoon snack to have some quiet time alone. Travel is also favored providing you know the route. Someone at a distance is hoping you will drop by.

25. SUNDAY. Easygoing. A morning argument should be shrugged off without bearing any grudges. Lack of sleep could be making you or your mate sharp-tongued when asked to do a favor. As the day progresses you and those around you begin to mellow. A creative pursuit gives you special pleasure today. Put together your own combinations that appeal to you, whether or not they are currently the rage. A trip to the library could be worthwhile for how-to information on a particular technique that you want to try.

There is unusual opportunity for a breakthrough without even having to wear yourself out. Evening entertainment should be low-keyed. Get together with people who make you laugh.

26. MONDAY. Manageable. Find something good to say about a project or a person lacking support. Your enthusiasm can bring additional attention. The emphasis today is on all that is positive. Staying in the background allows naysayers to be in charge. You can easily manage more than one task at a time. Your mind is clear and your abilities at a peak. Show the boss what you are capable of doing when the pressure is on. A future promotion or pay raise hinges on current effort. An element of secrecy is advised. If you reveal too much too soon, you could be held accountable when plans change. Read about a person whose life is a model of what you would like to be.

27. TUESDAY. Successful. Success continues to follow your footsteps. You are setting the pace once again for others. It is an outstanding day to hire a helper, especially a person with talent but no formal training. Libras interested in a new job can also shine in an interview. Be your natural self; do not blow your horn too loudly or you could come across as unwilling to adapt. Do some research about a possible new business venture. Find out who else is involved or is showing an interest. You do not want to put all of your money into one venture; diversity is an important safeguard. Take a well-calculated chance based on your own prior experience and knowledge. You cannot be fooled if you have been previously involved in a similar situation.

28. WEDNESDAY. Enjoyable. Take a midweek breather today. Relax and let other people carry most of the work load. There is room for some sentimentality in a decision you are pondering. Be guided by feelings as well as facts and figures. You are able now to forgive and forget an event that is long over. Where money is involved, however, you have to be more hard-nosed and realistic. A loan made today will have to be considered a gift; the chances of being repaid are slim to none. Travel is starred. Make plans to stay overnight with a distant friend or relative. You may be able to combine a work-related journey with pleasure. There is no time like the present to buy or lease a new car.

29. THURSDAY. Ambitious. A friend may tell you about an opening that seems made just for you. Be quick to apply or otherwise show that you are interested. Your ambition keeps you from being satisfied with all that you have already achieved. There is more waiting to be learned, more people to be impressed, more money to be made. Someone you know on a social basis may come through with an idea or a recommendation that gives you an edge on the competition. Pay special attention to personal appearance. Look your best throughout the day. Even after work you never know who you may run into while going home or shopping. If you are overdue for a haircut, make an appointment this morning.

30. FRIDAY. Excellent. New starts are not favored this late in the workweek. Try to finish up a project even though it is not due today. Work should proceed smoothly and without a hitch. A minor matter that has been troubling you can be resolved with a few words whispered into the right ears. Higher-ups may not be aware of the problem, but will be quick to find a solution once they are advised. Little is being asked of you now. Your can follow your own inclinations even if you have no particular purpose in mind. Experimenting can lead to a surprising breakthrough when you least expect it. Evening is a time for unwinding instead of seeking emotional stimulation.

OCTOBER

1. SATURDAY. Good. When you show that you care, people will respond in kind to you. Go out of your way to help a family member or friend. Offer what you can afford to give with no strings attached. There is no reason today to make any threats or to issue any ultimatums. Children as well as grown-ups will respond well to reason. Libra singles searching for romance may find happiness with someone considerably older or younger. Do not limit yourself by deciding beforehand what you are looking for in a mate. It is the unexpected that will please you most. If a relationship is not meeting your needs, break it off cleanly with the goal of maintaining a friendship.

2. SUNDAY. Enjoyable. Spending the day in the company of friends is favored. You will enjoy their stimulating ideas and conversation. Take part in a charitable event, or contribute to a political cause that you believe offers a chance for positive change. Romance is on the upswing because of increased trust. A jealous reaction is all but forgotten. Let your heart guide your actions with that special person in your life. There are no hard-and-fast rules to follow. Acting naturally and allowing your Libra feelings to be known is the best way to impress a newcomer. You may be happiest in a group rather than as a twosome. Any work planned for today can be postponed a week without negative results.

3. MONDAY. Disconcerting. Favors are not likely to be granted even by a friend or close working companion. Despite your good reasons for seeking help, no one is willing or able to change their own plans. Whatever is accomplished has to be done almost entirely on your own. A promise is not reliable; nor should Libras make any new commitments. Conditions are changing and you may not be able to fulfill a promise that you make despite your good intentions. There is likely to be pressure exerted from all sides for you to change your mind. A recent decision is causing unrest and upset. You may have agonized before making it, but stick to your guns and have the courage of your convictions.

4. TUESDAY. Unsettling. Conditions remain difficult for the Libra who has any degree of responsibility. An event occurring far from your home base may be having a negative impact on you. What seemed a sure thing only a short time ago is now in a state of flux. Be especially leery of spending money owed to you, but not yet repaid. You could wind up head over heels in debt if the payment is never received. Also look into the status of the bank where you have your money on deposit. If there is any indication of trouble, switch to a safer institution. A delivery is apt to be delayed, forcing you to make do with dwindling supplies on hand. You may have to ration them to avoid doing without.

5. WEDNESDAY. Successful. Work should be going along smoothly, easily within your abilities. There is little being asked of you, so make your own plans and schedule your own deadlines. Do not let up because no one seems to be watching or perhaps even caring. The results of this week's work can have a significant impact on a future promotion or job switch. Do all that you can to impress a higher-up with your potential. If boredom begins to creep in, set short-range goals for yourself. An offer to go out for lunch or dinner should not be refused. Socializing can lead to a breakthrough in getting a higher-paying position. Keep all transactions open and aboveboard. Deals made in the back room can damage your reputation.

6. THURSDAY. Tricky. Decide now if you are willing to pay the price that you know is going to be exacted for what you want.

You may have to neglect family and friends, or even turn your back on them, as you struggle to get ahead. What others are willing to sacrifice may be more than you want to give up. Libras know that there is more to living than making money, but finding the middle ground is not easy. Be wary of a higher-up who paints a rosy picture of the future. It is not a day to sign your name to any document that would be legally binding far into the year ahead. Nor should you hock the future in order to make a major purchase now. Set limits and stay within them.

7. FRIDAY. Satisfactory. Protect yourself by putting in writing only what you would be willing to let anyone else read. Today's thoughts and plans may change abruptly. You do not want to be tied down by promises made now. Keep a fantasy locked away in your heart. Place the needs of a friend above your own agenda for the day. Offer whatever help they seem to need. You can perform a great service by acting as a temporary crutch for a person who is carrying a heavy load. Rumors of a takeover or sale have some truth to them. Decide how you are going to respond if they become reality. You can get along with anyone when you decide to, but it may not be best for your career.

8. SATURDAY. Happy. Friendship and romance dominate the day. Shared activity is likely to work out even better than anticipated. You will be thanked for bringing together two people you feel would be perfectly matched partners. Someone you would like to know better is aware of you and shares your feelings. The direct, bold approach will not be rejected. Variety is the keynote of the entire day. Do not limit yourself in any way. Try at least one new activity that is a challenge. It is an excellent time to refresh cultural knowledge by visiting a museum or tuning in to a concert on the radio. Lack of money should not be a handicap. Juggle your priorities to make some spare cash available.

9. SUNDAY. Pleasant. Romance is taking on a new glow because a jealous reaction has been tempered through better communication. Continue to talk with that special person in your life about the important things. Express feelings and emotions. You should not be restricted because of a love relationship, nor should you be putting any limits on your mate. Your Libra conscience will not steer you wrong. Showing off can attract a new person who has caught your eye. Put your talents and abilities on display. Intellectual compatibility is the first step to new love; looks are secondary. Turn down an invitation from a friend to browse in a shopping mall; temptation to spend money will be too great.

10. MONDAY. Difficult. Someone new on the scene may not be telling the entire truth. Pay attention to what is said; listen for small inconsistencies. You cannot rely on any promises made today, even if put in writing. Do some independent checking of facts with trustworthy sources. You could become involved in a no-win situation and have your feelings hurt as well as your wallet stolen. Be wary of antagonizing people who are on your side, although they appear to be putting roadblocks in your path. The slow, steady approach is best, although your impatience makes it difficult to see the value of careful planning. Be sure to wear protective gear if you are operating any machinery.

11. TUESDAY. Uncertain. A higher-up is monitoring your progress and suggesting changes. Try to be more adaptable than usual. If you are obstinate, you could lose out on good opportunities and also damage your reputation. Decisions are being made behind the scenes that will impact on you. Do not even expect to be consulted about them. You are in no position to demand any favors or concessions. Although it's difficult for you, a wait-and-see attitude is the best option. Keep to a steady schedule. Do not let a co-worker or the boss know that you are having second thoughts about a change agreed to earlier in the year. Libras have to accept the decision of a referee or judge; there is no further court of appeal to which you can apply.

12. WEDNESDAY. Satisfactory. Focus on a particular project that you believe will enhance your reputation once it is finally completed. Strive to move it one step closer to the ending. It is possible for Libras to spend too much time in the planning stages and then begin to panic as a deadline approaches with little to show for their mental effort. Break down work into manageable segments that can be handled easily. Stick with a plan once it has been agreed upon by everyone involved. Do not let your enthusiasm lag. It is much easier to start something than to finish it; prove that you will be there at the end. It may also be useful to brush up on a foreign language so that you will be able to converse with a visitor from abroad.

13. THURSDAY. Disconcerting. Proceed with caution in dealing with higher-ups and others in positions of power. You have to play up to them in order to get attention. Flattery today is going to be useful even though it goes against your grain. What you lack in imagination you can make up for in dogged determination not to give up. If one approach is not working, immediately switch to another. You want to be in harmony with those around you, but cannot do so only on your own terms. A legal problem can interfere with ongoing negotiations. Consult an experienced person for expert advice. You will get what you pay for now. Opt for the best that you or your company can afford.

14. FRIDAY. Frustrating. A loan application may be rejected, or a friend may have a change of heart and refuse to help out. Frustration mounts as you see other people moving ahead while you are standing still. Focus on one project that you can accomplish independently and with materials already on hand. You can make do with equipment designed for another use if you adapt it. Rushing can spoil results. Take your time and enjoy the creative process. A newcomer may be making waves based only on book learning without any practical experience. There is little you can do to change their outlook; time is their only teacher. Romance takes an unexpected turn tonight.

15. SATURDAY. Pleasant. Sports have high priority today, whether you are on the playing field or a spectator in the stands. A small bet with a friend heightens excitement over the outcome. It is important to be a good sport and set an example for others to follow. You will not relish a win if you know it was not fair and square. Children, in particular, have to be shown the way through example and encouragement. Merely telling them how to act is a time-waster; let them see good sportsmanship in action. Libras who are full of energy, but inclined to be studious, can spend worthwhile time in the library. Information that has escaped your attention is waiting to be discovered.

16. SUNDAY. Fortunate. Unexpected income is foreseen, perhaps a check from a relative, or a friend's repayment of money you thought you would never see again. Lady Luck also accompanies the purchase of a raffle or lottery ticket, although you would be foolish to count on winning the grand prize. Coming out a little ahead in a gambling situation is an accomplishment. Romance should be on the upswing. That special person has had a small change of heart that should delight you. Focus on the future; let bygones be forgotten. A friendship may be developing into a more intimate affair. Give it room and air. Too much togetherness can be stifling. Plan on having supper out tonight.

17. MONDAY. Challenging. Travel can put you in the right spot to take advantage of a new opportunity. If you stay by the phone, you are apt to lose out. State your case in person to those who are in decision-making roles. This is a good day to put together a new team or a new proposal. Your ideas have to be made practical so that those in charge can evaluate them. Financial assistance is foreseen from a person rather than an institution. A casual friendship can blossom into a joint endeavor. Trends occurring at a distance should be given extra weight. Your powers of logical analysis are excellent. Figure out what is going to be a lasting trend and what is only passing fancy.

18. TUESDAY. Outstanding. Change your usual routine and you may be pleasantly surprised by what develops. Plan on taking a different route to work, sitting in a different office, having lunch in a restaurant that recently received a favorable review. Business and career affairs are moving forward at a fast clip. A new partnership is starred. Friendship is the first step in putting together a team with whom you can work with well. Do not allow your judgment to be clouded, however, by an emotional interest in someone of the opposite sex. Romance and business can be a bad mix. Use your innate knowledge of human nature to pick out the perfect partner.

19. WEDNESDAY. Good. Extra energy combines with your natural efficiency to help you accomplish all that you want to do today. Do not accept no as an answer; persist until you get what you want. Look into discounts being offered for bulk purchases. You can save money by shopping around and comparing prices as well as quality. An off-brand can perform as satisfactorily as one that is aggressively marketed. Libras involved in any way with selling will be more successful with a low-key approach. Do not downgrade the competition, but highlight your own products or services. What you are being told by a so-called expert may be open to other interpretations.

20. THURSDAY. Sensitive. Try not to show your impatience with people at or from a distance. Listen to all that they want to say even though you have heard most of it before. Your sensitive nature makes you aware of a friend's need before anything is actually said. Step in and help without expecting anything in return. Do not allow a family member to make a decision on your behalf. You know what you want from a relationship and should not have to squelch your needs. It is a good day to hatch a plan for future action. Now, however, is not the time to put the plan in motion. Line up support and check what the competition is doing to thwart you. There is the possibility of deception, so be alert.

21. FRIDAY. Misleading. Believe what you are told and you can wind up in trouble. There is a person or a group putting forth mistruths because they have not been able to have their way. Be more judgmental than usual. Analyze all that is going on based on your own good common sense. What seems too good to be true is probably exactly that. Avoid taking sides in an argument at work or among friends. Let them sort out their own difficulties. If you become involved, you are certain to alienate someone. Be firm with a person who is becoming too dependent on you. Insist that they stand on their own two feet and make a decision and stick with it. There could even be a future lawsuit if you meddle.

22. SATURDAY. Rewarding. Libras who must be at work today should have an easy time. Conditions are favorable for your doing what you want to. People are cooperative, but not pushy. You can get help without having to share credit for what is accomplished. Extra income is foreseen based on current efforts. Do not dwell on what went wrong in the past. You are ready for a new beginning either at work or in your personal life. Someone you meet through a mutual friend could quickly become a steady companion. You have no trouble recognizing a compatible soul even if he or she is in disguise at first. Blending interests is more exciting than being so alike that you grow bored with each other.

23. SUNDAY. Useful. Follow through with a desire to give and share among family members, friends or the community in which you live. A donation of money can be helpful, but giving time is even more valuable. Go out of your way to help a person with lofty ideals, but who is lacking the wherewithal to carry them out. Set your sights high; do not settle for anything less than the best you can do. You can count on a person helping you just as you are willing to do now. An idea that has been brewing can be tried out on a small scale. What is considered unusual by many holds special promise. Phoning or visiting at a distance should put your mind at ease. You may be worrying about what is no longer a problem.

24. MONDAY. Variable. Do not put on any airs pretending to know more than you actually do. In fact, a show of mild ignorance can help you learn what is going on. You may want to enroll for a class, or even to teach one. The time and money you devote to learning will be amply repaid in the future. A property transaction may rob you of a lot of your normal working hours. Negotiations have to be handled delicately. If you are uncertain whether you can remain unemotional, engage a person to act on your behalf. An agent can help you get more than you would be able to negotiate for yourself. Check with the bank about your actual balance on deposit. You may have to take money from one account and put it into another to cover an outstanding check.

25. TUESDAY. Buoyant. Spend some money to please yourself or a family member. An item that caught your eye in a store window can make the difference between enjoying the fruits of your labor and finding work only drudgery. Treat yourself to a piece of jewelry or a new outfit. Your mate or date will light up with pleasure if you offer a surprise gift. Good health is supplying you with ample energy for all that you want to do. Avoid limiting yourself in any direction. You can easily handle more than one major project. It is a good day to volunteer to coach a sports team or arrange a charitable event. Creative pursuits are also starred. Follow your natural Libra inclination and you will not go wrong.

26. WEDNESDAY. Mixed. Keep your personal life free and clear of work commitments. Mingling the two can land you in trouble. It is not smart to become emotionally involved with a coworker. An aura of secretiveness can make you seem more knowledgeable and successful. Avoid blurting out your intentions until you are ready to announce them publicly. What people do not know about you keeps them coming back for more. Your love of harmony is in line with those around you. Minor disagreements can clear the air, but are unlikely to escalate to the argument point. You do not have to give in to keep the peace. There is more power in facts than in physical strength.

27. THURSDAY. Ordinary. A handshake is not enough for you to react confidently. A deal should be formalized with a written commitment outlining who is going to do what and the compensation each will receive. Keep everything on a formal basis. This is not a time to take a chance on secondhand merchandise. You could wind up with a problem that no one is willing to acknowledge or do anything about. Choose your associates with care also. Stay away from a person who tends to make sweeping statements that anger and annoy others. You are known by the company you keep. It is important to protect your good name and reputation. Imagination and enthusiasm are two of your assets.

28. FRIDAY. Pleasant. An unexpected visitor can make this a memorable day. Be open to new ideas, even those that seem a little bizarre. There is excellent opportunity about to open up for the Libra willing to take a chance. Be prepared to drop what you are currently doing and switch to another quite different project.

You may be asked to act as chauffeur and tour guide later in the day. Be sure to make reservations if you plan to go out to a popular restaurant. More can be decided over a five-course meal than at a conference table. A new goal spurs you on to a higher plane. Superiors are willing to bend rules for you, but not to break them. Ask only for what you need, not what you want.

29. SATURDAY. Good. Do not escalate a quarrel at home by taking a firm stand and refusing to budge. Give in on matters that are not very important to you. Then when you are insistent, people know you mean it. Personal relationships are happy. That special person in your life wants to please you in every possible way. Togetherness helps build firm bonds. You will be content staying at home, although a friend's invitation may be irresistible this evening. Get some physical exercise, preferably with a companion. Stretch yourself a little beyond your usual limit. Expressing your feelings in writing can clear up any doubts. A love letter is sure to prompt a favorable response.

30. SUNDAY. Satisfactory. There is no need to rush around today. Relax and enjoy yourself and your companion. Be especially gentle with older family members and with youngsters. Avoid teasing or you could leave them in tears. Your mind is active and thoughts are flowing freely. A new idea is beginning to take root. Find out what has been done in the past as a clue to the future. Some luck is foreseen in affairs of the heart. The Libra looking for love does not have to leave the neighborhood. What you have come to take for granted is very special. An upcoming anniversary is reason enough to plan a party. Be sure to invite a newcomer as well as your current friends.

31. MONDAY. Changeable. Avoid getting caught up in a crowd or in a crowd mentality. You can easily be swept along by a group even if you basically do not agree with what they are doing. Hold your ground and refuse to be budged. Try to avoid stirring up anger by emphasizing all that is positive. You have a definite leadership role to play now. Be sensitive to the desires of other people, but do not base major decisions on how they are likely to react. Look for ways to expand your circle of friends and acquaintances. Joining a club or other group can be mind-expanding. You are ready for change, but should not rush into it. Figure out what you want before you try to get it or you will be in a tough spot.

NOVEMBER

1. TUESDAY. Productive. Do some repair jobs as well as sprucing up so that your work surroundings are more comfortable and you are more productive. It is difficult for Libras to work in chaotic conditions. You have to know that equipment is operating smoothly so that you can concentrate on the essentials. Call a professional for repairs that are beyond your capacity. Do not tinker with machinery, inner workings of which are a mystery to you. File important papers; toss out those you have been planning to read for a month or more. Trying to keep track of everything can wear you to a frazzle. Concentrate instead on what is most vital to your work or hobby. Knowing a lot about a small area of interest is better than having a little general knowledge.

2. WEDNESDAY. Outstanding. Build on what has proven successful in the past. You are right on target with a current project. Seek out one or two more assistants. A family member could be a superb right-hand person for you. It is not necessary to go beyond your own four walls to find the help you need and want. Utilize the creative aspect of your nature to find a new and better way to handle everyday routine. The more you can speed through that, the more time you have for what is most appealing to you. If you put off making changes now, it will be harder to get them accepted later. Libra will power gives you the impetus to do what is necessary in the most efficient manner.

3. THURSDAY. Uncertain. Uncertainty can make you hesitate, giving competitors the edge on you. Trust your basic instincts; they will not lead you astray. What has worked in the past is a clue to future success, but with an updated twist. Any break with routine is apt to disturb you. Ease through the day without fighting matters beyond your control. The boss or another higher-up is taking his or her sweet time making a decision that is going to affect you directly. Trying to rush the process could have a negative effect. You will have to settle for maybe as an answer; push harder and you are apt to be turned down outright. A practical approach is vital. Help a friend or a family member decide about a new job offer.

4. FRIDAY. Sensitive. This last day of the workweek demands getting caught up with outstanding work instead of beginning anything new. Tie up all loose ends that otherwise may unravel the hard work you have done. Have a heart-to-heart talk with a person who has been holding you back. When you know where you agree, you can begin to sort out the disagreements. There is money to be made if you get in on the ground floor of a new opportunity. Today, however, is only a time for planning and reckoning. Juggle figures to make the budget balance. Cutting back in one area gives your more leeway in another. A relationship is slowly emerging from friendship into a new stage. Savor it each step of the way to its climactic moment.

5. SATURDAY. Mixed. Without cooperation you cannot catch up with work around the house and start readying for the holiday ahead. Insist that family members lend a hand; do not take no for an answer despite excuses and promises of future help. Children should be included; assign jobs to them, then be sure they do the work well. It is up to you to set a good example. Prove the old adage that any job worth doing is worth doing well. Avoid offering a bribe in order to get help. You may want to go out for lunch or dinner to celebrate what has been accomplished. Shopping is also favored, especially for household items on sale. Replace kitchen utensils or equipment if needed.

6. SUNDAY. Changeable. Go along with plans that include you even though you were not in on the planning stage. What seems rather uninteresting may take on a special glow when you discover who else is participating. This is a great day to start a friendship or renew one that has lapsed due to separation. Someone who was once an active part of your life is coming back, giving you a great chance for a new beginning. Libras who have been avoiding making a long-term commitment may have a change of heart. The only clear warning is to avoid a romantic triangle. Emotion rules today. The practical approach has no place in the groundwork of love or friendship. Do not choose companions on the basis of what they can do for you.

7. MONDAY. Tricky. Know where you stand, and where you want to go, before entering into any negotiations. You need a firm commitment so that you are not swayed by faulty reasoning that seems to make sense. It might be necessary to consult an attorney or other professional to obtain neutral advice. A friend is likely to say what you want to hear, or at least what they believe you do. And a family member is not able to be objective at all if money or security is at issue. What you have come to take for granted is more important to you than you may think. Do not give up hard-won victories to pursue a new goal. One step forward and two back is not progress. Sidestep an obstacle in order to get around it.

8. TUESDAY. Confusing. Nothing is going according to plan today. From the moment you wake up there is confusion in the air. Just deciding what to wear may take concentration that should be directed to more important matters. Transportation delays can make you late for an appointment, then nervous when you arrive. Or someone could keep you waiting without a word of explanation or apology. A former co-worker is fishing for information; avoid pooling yours with the little they may be offering. Trying hard is not enough today. You have to be on guard and constantly alert for signs of intrigue. You cannot win if you do not play the game the same way as the other players.

9. WEDNESDAY. Cautious. Continue to be cautious in all dealings. Someone you trust is thinking about defecting to a competitor. But you can persuade the person to have a change of heart by proving that you are not going to give up. There is a definite limit to what you can accomplish on your own. Seek help from those around you; if they are too busy, you may have to hire temporary assistance. Working with someone considerably older or younger than you is starred. Their ideas will enhance your own instead of merely mirroring them. A new interest may be taking increasing amounts of your time. It is possible that this will lead to part-time employment. It is not smart now, however, to give up a steady paycheck.

10. THURSDAY. Excellent. Give free rein to your imagination. Breaking with tradition sets you apart in a most positive way. You know what has to be done and how you intend to do it. Get started right away. Dreaming makes the impossible seem within reach. Your easygoing, direct manner inspires people to join your team. Any request you make is apt to be received in the spirit of cooperation. Do not worry now about balancing the scales between giving and taking. All will even out in the long run. What you get from one person can be passed on as a favor to someone else. You do not have to keep ledgers of favors owed and owing. A special request will not be refused. Say what you are thinking.

11. FRIDAY. Harmonious. Your good mood rubs off on all those around you. A meeting today should proceed exceptionally well. Delegate more work than usual as you can count on the results of other people coming up to your high standards. Nor is a lot of nagging or double-checking required. A request that you make is not going to be turned down, even if it was rejected just a short time ago. This is a starred day to apply for a raise or a promotion. Step forward and make your wishes known. No one is able to read your mind. Someone from another country or of a background different from yours can have a significant impact on your affairs. Do not limit yourself based on old prejudices.

12. SATURDAY. Quiet. Generously donate time, money or both to a cause you believe in firmly. Stand up and be counted. A group can make a significant difference, because there is power in numbers. You do not have to participate in a rally or go door-to-door seeking contributions. Libras are often most effective behind the scenes. Preparing for a trip could take most of the afternoon. Be sure to keep a bag packed and ready for short-notice travel. Also check that your passport is current. Do not show up empty-handed if you are going to be an overnight guest. Take along a bottle of wine or some flowers as a gesture of thanks in advance. People around you are sensitive; be gentle with them.

13. SUNDAY. Disconcerting. What you thought had been planned down to the last detail may be unraveling right before your eyes. Try to patch things up so that the basic plan does not evaporate. The goal is more important than the means of achieving it. Demands could be refused, but a plea for help should be better received. It is easier to stick with what is routine and comfortable. Now, however, changing conditions demand different responses. Do not close your eyes to a situation that you regard as unfair or unwholesome. Step right in with ideas as well as actual help. A friend's medical condition is worrisome, but is it up to you to maintain a positive outlook. Provide help without waiting to be asked.

14. MONDAY. Variable. Some travel is foreseen, probably not requiring an overnight stay. A face-to-face meeting should be more effective than phoning or writing. You are especially persuasive when able to counter every argument with good reasons of your own. A current project has the potential of being a money-maker once you make it practical. Look for ways to streamline production. Buy bulk supplies to take advantage of quantity discounts. Working to beat a deadline gives you added impetus. This is a good day to enter a contest; you may not win, but you will learn a lot. Interference from in-laws or relatives makes evening hours tense. Straighten out a misunderstanding before going to bed tonight.

15. TUESDAY. Outstanding. Take credit for what you have accomplished. Get as much mileage as possible from a recent success. Blowing your own horn is necessary while other people toot theirs. Guard against expecting recognition unless you insist on it. An idea that you thought of could be adopted or stolen unless you demand what is your due. Focus on what is most important. Keep the big picture in mind while others worry over petty details. Libras never relish a fight, but they are tough when there is no choice. Respect is an important part of the harmony you want in all relationships. Do not hesitate to offer opinions and express your own views. People listen, which may surprise you.

16. WEDNESDAY. Unsettling. Money matters could take up a lot of time. Pay bills before late charges become due or a threatening letter is sent to you. There may be problems with a joint bank account. The balance may be lower than what you have recorded because your mate or partner made a withdrawal and forgot to enter it. Maintaining separate accounts could be the best cure. Someone you have known for a long time is making demands that you cannot meet or do not even want to consider. There could soon be a parting of the ways. Romance may be rocky, especially for the Libra preoccupied with work or with outside interests. It is up to you to make some adjustments without demanding anything in return.

17. THURSDAY. Stressful. Yesterday's upsets are not going to be cured overnight. Work at maintaining good relations with people you see daily. Talk less and listen more. If your expectations are too high, you are bound to be disappointed. Branching out in new directions helps take the pressure off. It is important to reconcile contrary information received from various people and decide what is the truth. An unbiased opinion could help. Do not believe a rumor currently making the rounds. If travel is on your agenda today, allow ample time to reach your destination. Delays are foreseen, especially with public transportation. Keep your money stashed away with only a minimum amount in your wallet.

18. FRIDAY. Good. Matters are beginning to fall into place quite nicely. A disagreement with a co-worker or family member has cleared the air and offered an opportunity for a new start. Joint effort is favored in all areas. Teaming up with someone who complements your Libra talents and skills can be advantageous to all involved. Opportunity to advance is more important now than earnings. An idea is beginning to attract favorable attention. Continue to refine it as you go. Do not settle for the first terms offered to you. If you hold out, you will get a better deal. Romance is happy, especially for those who have already tied the knot. Your mate wants to please you in every way.

19. SATURDAY. Pleasant. Come to know your neighbors on a personal basis by stopping to chat or inviting them over for informal entertaining. There may be a community issue that you can resolve without having to resort to officials or bureaucrats for help. Libra parents should be keeping close tabs on their children's activities. Do not allow them to infringe on a neighbor's property or rights. It is a good day to make a major purchase for your home. Furniture that is on sale could spruce up your living quarters and even lead to a new color scheme that is more to your liking. Be sure to have ample lighting; buy a new lamp that is designed to help you avoid eyestrain.

20. SUNDAY. Confusing. Stay in bed late, or plan on taking an afternoon nap to restore your energy. Matters are not well defined. What seemed to be settled only a few days ago is now open once again for debate and discussion. A friend who has always been on your side may be taking the opposite view; consider the possible reasons and be open to a different viewpoint. Avoid saying too much or making any threats. You will be held accountable for whatever you say, and could come to regret it later. Also do not make any new commitments for yourself or on behalf of a family member. You do not want anyone putting words in your mouth; and they do not want you interfering in their plans any more than would you.

21. MONDAY. Mixed. Casual conversation may lead to plans for a more formal get-together with those in positions to make decisions. Do not let an idea die on the vine. Follow through to see where it may take you. Someone at the top is willing to listen; the trick is to get in to see the person. A letter to the newspaper editor could serve a useful purpose in notifying people in your community of a problem or its solution. Impulsiveness can land you in hot water. Consider what you are going to say or send before taking any action. Allow at least an hour between writing an angry note and delivering it. You may have a change of heart meanwhile. You have the wrong idea about a family member's motivation; allow for the benefit of doubt.

22. TUESDAY. Sensitive. Avoid making any changes because you are bored or restless. This sensitive day calls for restraint in all activities. You are likely to overlook certain facts because you are blinded to them. A politician, especially one whose views are not similar to your own, has good ideas and a plan of action. If you can look at it with an open mind, you may find its merit. There is more than one way to arrive at the same result. Health must be protected. Be sure to wear clothing suitable for the weather even if it's not stylish; staying warm and dry makes sense. If a medical problem has been worrying you, make an appointment for a checkup. Do not neglect a dental checkup, either.

23. WEDNESDAY. Buoyant. A project that has suffered through some bad times and lean moments is now taking wing, much to your satisfaction. Sit back and enjoy the compliments coming your way; you deserve them. Be gracious but not humble about accepting thanks. This is an auspicious day to come to know a Leo better, or to join forces at the start of a new task. You will be more in the role of follower than leader, but you can contribute significantly. Confer with your mate or partner before making a decision that involves both of you. Working behind the scenes gives you better insight into what is going on and who is wielding the real power. The person out front may be only a mouthpiece.

24. THURSDAY. Happy Thanksgiving. Take advantage of the peaceful aspects today to review all that has been going on and to make some plans for the remainder of the year. A relative may come to you for advice. Be willing to share your own similar experience; but do not make any specific suggestions regarding what they should do. Knowing you care may be all it takes for the person to do what is necessary to find their own solution. Luck is with you when it comes to love. New beginnings are favored for the Libra looking for a long-term commitment. You could discover that there is such a thing as love at first sight. Let your heart rule now. Jealously has no part in a Libra life; you have enough love.

25. FRIDAY. Quiet. Working in solitude is favored today. You should be contemplating a plan rather than taking action. Consider the impact it is likely to have on other people as well as on you. Make some revisions so that fewer changes are required initially. Gradually build up to what you hope to accomplish over a period of time. It is best to leave some things unsaid. A promise or a threat uttered now could come back to haunt you later. Get to the bottom of a situation involving someone who is inexperienced. Do not allow them to be taken advantage of, even if they are not voicing any objections yet. Get in touch with a friend at a distance and make plans to rendezvous before the end of the year.

26. SATURDAY. Variable. You are more likely to be on the outside looking in today rather than the center of attention. Bide your time; your turn is coming. Take part in all that is going on at home. Be especially attentive to an older family member who enjoys telling stories of the old days. You may have heard them before, but prove yourself an attentive audience once again. Drop by a friend or relative's home to see if they need any special help. Someone recovering from an illness would welcome an offer to run a few errands. Libras shopping today may be disappointed. An advertised sale is unlikely to live up to its promises. The best bargains may be unexpected markdowns.

27. SUNDAY. Pleasant. Look your best even if you have no special plans to go out today. An unexpected invitation is too promising to resist. Be ready on short notice or you could miss out. A sports event or musical presentation is sure to be enjoyable. Friends make the best company. A relative is beginning to get on your nerves. Stay away from this person for a short time and your patience should return along with your good humor. You will also enjoy meeting new people and expanding your circle of friends. Let your views be known about an upcoming ceremony that involves you directly or indirectly. If you leave all the planning to others, you have no grounds for complaining if their arrangements upset you.

28. MONDAY. Difficult. Getting back into the swing of work does not come easily. Avoid overloading your schedule, and concentrate only on essentials. It will be difficult to handle more than one task at a time. News in the morning paper or on television may be upsetting, especially to your humanitarian desires. You may want to send a contribution for emergency relief. A local charity would doubtless welcome you as a volunteer. Keep in mind that you cannot mend the world; do a small share and encourage others to do their part as well. Someone high up in the chain of command may blame you for an error that was not really your fault. Make it clear you did your best, but were not instructed properly.

29. TUESDAY. Favorable. Follow your plans for today unless something is suggested that you find irresistible. Changing gears can be difficult. What you drop in favor of another project may go unnoticed and unfinished until the New Year. If a friend calls to gossip, make it clear that you are not going to listen to negative rumors. You may want to start a positive one of your own to counteract what is being said. You are more emotional than usual today and ready to take up the cause of the underdog. Do not expect an exception to be made for you by a government official. You have to follow the same rules and regulations as everyone else; why would you expect special treatment?

30. WEDNESDAY. Stressful. There is a lot to be done, but you may not feel up to it. Be sure to take any medicine that has been prescribed for you, but nothing else. Keep your goals for the day within reasonable hope of achievement. If you are going in ten directions at once, you may wind up stretched past your limit. Handling a problem will take longer than expected. Bear in mind that there are at least two sides to every story; you may discover even more. This is not a good day to sign a contract or any other legally binding document. Ask for more time to consider alternatives. Financing can be arranged, but at a price. You may have to give up some vacation plans in order to arrange for a loan.

DECEMBER

1. THURSDAY. Good. People at and from a distance are busy opening doors for you, and so it is up to you to knock and walk right in. Do not wait for a formal invitation before getting on with your own agenda. Developments at a distance are impacting on your work and your personal life. Stay in close contact with former colleagues who are employed overseas. There may be special opportunity for travel or relocation through them. New beginnings are favored now. Family members are not going to stand in your way, although they may show less enthusiasm than you would like. In all transactions with other people, show your independence. Tonight you can advance business while having a good time.

2. FRIDAY. Fortunate. An open mind allows you to absorb new ideas without making a commitment regarding them. Listen more than you talk. Guard against becoming surrounded by people who parrot your views and feed them back to you. There is a strong element of good fortune affecting personal or work finances. A prior investment can be sold for a handsome profit. If you hold out much longer, you could wind up losing money. Set goals and be glad when you are able to meet them. Exceeding them only means you are taking a risk or you did not set high enough goals. Buying into a start-up company can prove especially profitable. Consider loaning money to a relative just opening a service-providing business.

3. SATURDAY. Happy. Few demands are being made now. Plan your own schedule and stick to it. Libras involved in any way with crafts have a good opportunity to make money selling them directly or through a middleman. You may also want to concentrate on a gift you are crafting for a special person. Put more of your creativity into everything that you touch. Even if you are working from a kit, add a few extras to produce a unique product. Your creative approach combines well with the practical nature of your spouse or another family member. Together you could begin a part-time business with future potential. Getting together with friends is favored before the holiday season goes into full swing.

4. SUNDAY. Uncertain. Reassess a situation that has defied your best efforts to resolve. You may have to try a new approach. Personal relationships at home benefit from less nagging and more encouragement. Decisions that you make today are likely to work out well if you give them time. You cannot afford to alienate an older family member or to turn off a member of the younger generation. Someone new on the scene is trying to make a good impression on you, but having trouble getting through. Look for ways to expand your circle of friends and acquaintances rather than limit it. There is some opportunity now involving real estate. Buying is favored over selling, at least until later in the month.

5. MONDAY. Variable. Travel is favored, although you may not be able to get away this week. Begin now to make plans, especially if you will be visiting during the Christmas period. Purchasing tickets in advance can save you a lot of money. Be sure to read the fine print first to be certain you can abide by the restrictions imposed on such travel arrangements. Stay in the background today. Play a wait-and-see game with those who are pushing you to make up your mind. There is nothing so important on your agenda that it cannot wait until midweek. The conservative side of your Libra nature is in full control now. Anything out of the ordinary is likely to make you nervous and irritable.

6. TUESDAY. Disconcerting. A frank discussion with a person who has been talking about you behind your back can clear the air. You may be able to work out a compromise solution satisfactory to both of you. If this is not possible, at least come to an understanding about where you differ. Agreeing to disagree can be useful. A family member who has been offering unsolicited advice regarding your work or personal life must be satisfied, but without making any promises. They have your best interests at heart, though do not understand the pressures with which you are coping. There is no use trying to buy attention or affection. Your Libra love of harmony must not make you give up on a matter of principle.

7. WEDNESDAY. Mixed. You should be more effective as part of a team rather than as an independent operator today. Pair up with a person whose skills supplement your own. Someone considerably older or younger can make the best teammate. Who you know is as important as what you can do. Develop contacts among government officials, especially elected representatives. Consider getting more involved in politics at the local level. You can influence a decision affecting your family and your neighbors if you attend open meetings and read all that is being written about a new regulation or other proposal. If you stay out of the fray and let others decide, you have no right to complain at the outcome.

8. THURSDAY. Harmonious. A relationship that seemed to be breaking up can be restored with a heart-to-heart talk. Libras have an excellent opportunity today to act the part of negotiator or counselor. Because you care, you can help a marital partnership or a parent-child relationship that is under stress. If you want to get on better terms with someone you see regularly, make the first move. Apologize even if you were only partly to blame. Give extra attention and affection to family members. Nostalgia can be a good cure if you have been drifting apart. Get out old yearbooks or love letters and enjoy reading them together. Do not neglect exercise. Take a walk, go jogging or dance to a favorite tape.

9. FRIDAY. Changeable. Be careful what you say and how you phrase your thoughts. People are paying more attention to your words and may misinterpret them. Be sure your actions reflect how you really feel. Before signing anything, read it carefully. Be sure a legally binding document spells out all the promises that were made to you. An aggressive salesperson could say almost anything in an effort to get you to buy; making good on the promises is another matter. A partnership has to be strengthened if it is to endure. It is up to you to make some changes and compromises before expecting the other person to do so. Someone you want to know better avoids you; be aggressive in pursuing your goal.

10. SATURDAY. Easygoing. Libras who must work today can look forward to a relaxing time without much pressure. Careful preplanning allows you to put a plan into motion exactly as you outlined it. Those of you in sales may be the exception, however. Business is likely to be brisk. Take time with each customer and provide as much service as possible. Avoid the hard-sell approach; it is unnatural for you and unlikely to be successful. Turn a deaf ear to negative comments. You cannot possibly please everyone. Do what seems right and you cannot be faulted. A gathering of people you see all too infrequently should be memorable. Dress to stand out from the crowd; you want someone special to notice you.

11. SUNDAY. Frustrating. Despite your best intentions nothing is going to go quite as planned. Family members have their own agenda for the day, and you may be excluded. Togetherness is difficult now. If you want companionship, call a friend. Money can be the source of frustration. A gift that you know would be perfect for your mate or a relative may be too expensive for you. If it goes on sale, you may be too late and only able to get a rain check for an after-holiday purchase. You may find more to buy for yourself than for anyone else; resist the temptation. No one is going to listen to your complaints, so you might as well put a smile on your face and be cheerful.

12. MONDAY. Outstanding. Good ideas are floating all around. Pluck one out of the air that seems most promising and begin working on it without delay. You can waste precious time in overplanning. Use materials already on hand. Accept whatever help is offered, especially from a person you have never worked with before. You have high energy now and can take a project from start to finish. Self-confidence is also soaring. You should be able to convince a higher-up to grant you special privileges, which may include more time off to pursue your own interests. Romance is a highlight of the day. Your mate or steady date will welcome a surprise dinner and some affection afterward.

13. TUESDAY. Variable. Pitch in with helpful advice or more useful assistance wherever you see the need. Do not wait to be asked or cajoled. Minor repairs made now can save the cost of calling a professional for a major job later. You are especially good at reading and following directions. Writing also comes naturally. Prepare the first draft of a report or other written document that will be the result of combined effort in the end. Advertising and public relations efforts can reward you with new customers and more recognition. There are strong indications of a new partnership designed around a special project. You can get along with anyone on a short-term basis.

14. WEDNESDAY. Ordinary. Nothing out of the ordinary is foreseen for Libras. Stick to what you know best and are comfortable doing even if other people are watching. Decisions affecting you are being made in a back room. When the announcement is finally publicized, you may recognize its basis in today's work. A future promotion or pay raise depends on doing what you are told, but adding a little extra to make your work noticeable. Be wary of anyone selling over the phone or door-to-door. Do not fall prey to a salesperson who has a hard-luck story. Nor should you contribute to a charity you have never heard of before without investigating it. A friend's good news is the perfect excuse for celebrating.

15. THURSDAY. Lackadaisical. If someone wants to take over a job you have been working on, step aside and let them. Pare down your responsibilities as much as possible; do only what is essential today. Your stamina is lower than usual. What usually comes easily may be a chore. A remark intended to be helpful could be misinterpreted as criticism. Your moods are not synchronized with those of colleagues or family members. Any effort at teamwork is likely to be disappointing for everyone today, although you can make plans for future joint effort. Make as few demands as possible; keep a low profile standing on the sidelines. A hobby you can enjoy offers promise, as creativity helps you.

16. FRIDAY. Sensitive. Personal relationships remain sensitive. You can be swayed by what you think is happening, but your view could be distorted. Avoid offering unsolicited advice. If someone wants to borrow money or anything of value, say no in the most pleasant way possible. You could also be expecting too much of a family member. They cannot make a decision for you and should not be asked to do so. Stick to a budget even though a new purchase could make you happy for a short time. You will come to regret going into debt more than you relish what you bought. Do all that you can to maintain property values. It is not smart to put up holiday decorations if they will leave marks.

17. SATURDAY. Pleasant. Put your talents on display decorating around the house or at a community building. Neighbors and friends make excellent companions, particularly someone you have not seen in a while. Include children in today's projects. Gear activities to what they will enjoy and take pride in. Be sure to take along a camera to record the hard work being done. Someone you know on a casual basis is being drawn to you through shared interests. New friendship or a possible romance is foreseen. You could also be playing Cupid in bringing together two lonely people. Home entertaining should be as enjoyable this evening as a night on the town. Keep expenses low while having a good time.

18. SUNDAY. Fair. There is significant potential in a new idea just beginning to formulate, but do not proceed too fast. Slow, methodical planning can ensure eventual success. A family member is the prime candidate to work alongside you in this new endeavor. Initial lack of interest should not be taken as the last word. Continue to promote what you want to do; you will win more and more converts. Enjoy some mild flirting without becoming too involved. You have a number of admirers and can pick and choose. Be sure to respond to a recent note or invitation, again without making any added promises. Do not be too nosy or you could stumble on something not meant to be seen quite yet.

19. MONDAY. Lucky. The spotlight turns in your direction today. Personal relationships are on an even keel and make you content. You know all that you have to be thankful for, and you are more aware of the feelings of those you care about most. A love affair that has withstood a difficult period is stronger now. A compliment you receive should be cherished more than any gift. Lock it away in your heart for a time when you long to recall it. Lady Luck is beaming on you. There may be a fortunate coincidence allowing you to meet with a person who can push the right buttons on your behalf. Take quick advantage of whatever breaks come your way; you have worked hard for them and deserve them.

20. TUESDAY. Excellent. Modify a plan to incorporate a new idea or a burst of insight. Future goals are important, but the here and now deserves even greater attention. Pass out compliments freely, particularly to a person who has been trying hard, but not making the progress desired. You can do a lot to keep them from giving up. People are turning to you for leadership; do not let them down. Being in at the start of a project can produce special rewards. You have highly regarded talents at launching time, while those born under other Signs are more adept at tying up loose ends. It is not too late in the year to interview for a new job or to let the boss know you are interested in relocating.

21. WEDNESDAY. Useful. Do not hold back when presented with new opportunity. The less you know, the more you have to learn. Carefully observe a master at work, then ask for help in getting started. There are so many interesting activities that you may have trouble deciding which ones appeal most. Specializing attracts your Libra need to know. It is difficult to be satisfied with a superficial smattering of knowledge of many matters. Instead you feel more content when you start being acknowledged as an expert. Devour all the books in the library about this new interest, but do not stop there. Tell friends and family that you are onto something exciting and hope to mingle with others in the field.

22. THURSDAY. Pleasant. Family and friends dominate your attention today. Check once again to be sure you have presents for all those on your gift list, plus a few extra for any surprises that come along. An upscale boutique can offer a few unusual items to use as fill-ins. Take a long lunch break to do some shopping, or go to the stores immediately after work before they become crowded. Later you may want to walk around looking at window displays and recapturing some of the magic of the season remembered from your younger days. It is a great time for nostalgia. Give generously to a charity that is soliciting funds, after ascertaining that it is legitimate. If you have never heard of it, ask a friend.

23. FRIDAY. Exciting. Very little actual work is going to be accomplished today. If you have a project that must be finished before the long weekend, get an early start. Do not anticipate much cooperation from co-workers. Strive for completion rather than perfection now. The good feelings of the season naturally lead to partying. Share refreshments or something more substantial with people you see daily in your work environment. An old grudge can be smoothed over and a relationship put back on track. There is no room today for jealousy. The boss or another higher-up wants to socialize without worrying about work. Avoid serious subjects or a personal appeal such as a raise or promotion.

24. SATURDAY. Productive. It should come as a pleasant surprise that your preplanning allows you to enjoy today without a long list of chores. Spend time with younger family members who are already bubbling with anticipation. Divert their attention, if only for a short time by going to the movies or an ice-skating rink. You and your mate or date will enjoy a drive to view decorated homes and the town. Do not overdo in any area. Ration your energy so that it is not at a low ebb this evening. A get-together then promises fun and entertainment. Look your best and turn on the charm. Someone new on the scene may capture your attention, but probably not in a romantic vein. There is a gem of an idea waiting to be plucked from conversation.

25. SUNDAY. MERRY CHRISTMAS! It is traditionally thought better to give than to receive, but today you will enjoy being at both ends of that saying. Open your gifts slowly so that you can savor the anticipation. Be sure to show special appreciation for a present that was handcrafted especially for you. Wear it or display it proudly throughout the day. A child's offering should be praised most extravagantly. You may have to spend some time putting together a toy that requires some assembly, making do with your own skills. There may be a most welcome announcement by a family member that immediately puts you in a planning mood. Today's news is the basis for a family get-together.

26. MONDAY. Satisfactory. There could be a little letdown from yesterday's peak of excitement. Sleep late and loll around the house this morning. Make no specific plans. Go along with what your mate or another family member proposes. If you must exchange a gift that you received, be sure to tell the giver why you are doing so. Write those necessary thank-you notes while you are in the mood. There should be few difficulties at home. Everyone is preoccupied and will leave you in peace by evening time. Welcome unexpected visitors without going out of your way to entertain them. If there is company for dinner, order food to be sent in rather than trying to come up with an impromptu meal.

27. TUESDAY. Harmonious. Good feelings continue to spill over from the holidays. Getting along with co-workers should be a snap. Even the boss is in an easygoing mood, not inclined to give orders or expect much production. You have time now to get better organized and do some cleaning up so that you are not always searching for supplies. When everything has a place of its own, you can put your hands on what you need quickly. There could be a great sale that is too good to miss. Buy more than one, but not so much that you then have a storage problem. Hold down personal expenditures to necessities only. The temptation of a jewelry sale should be strongly resisted. Love gives you a special glow tonight.

28. WEDNESDAY. Quiet. Stay in low gear without putting pressure on yourself to begin anything new. Finishing up work is the most that you should do. Spend some time considering what is most important to you personally and also what is necessary for the good of your family and your work. Aim for a compromise where no needs are overlooked and none are overemphasized. Balance is vital to your own happiness and good performance. Avoid making any new commitments. This is not a good day to wander far from your usual base of operations. If someone at a distance wants to get together in person, let them do the traveling. You are most comfortable and effective in your own surroundings.

29. THURSDAY. Productive. For the first time since the holiday break you are interested in a new project. Do not allow this inclination to go to waste. A new offering or opening is too good to resist, even at this late date in 1994. Sign on now. Let the boss know that you are willing to put in some overtime in order to meet a deadline. A government official may be willing to bend rules or regulations for you. Teamwork is especially favored in all affairs. You or a co-worker or family member can form an unbeatable partnership. Do not hesitate to ask that all-important question. The answer you receive is sure to please you.

30. FRIDAY. Rewarding. Whatever help you need is available, although you may have to make some future commitments in exchange. Financial action now is starred. Consider buying or selling based on current market prices. You are quick to spot a trend and take advantage of it. Changes are occurring even though you prefer the old ways. You cannot hold back the tide of progress. Consider signing up to learn how to operate new machinery or run an updated computer program. There could be new job opportunities once you have mastered these skills. Be discreet when looking or talking about a job change. If the boss learns that you are dissatisfied, you could lose out on a promotion.

31. SATURDAY. Enjoyable. Share an idea for the New Year with a family member or a friend. Get their input as well as a clue about whether they would like to join you in the new venture. Let others do the talking, even if you do not like what they are saying. There are two sides to every thought, and you may not have considered negative aspects in your enthusiasm for the new idea. Be patient with an older relative; figure out how to include them in your evening plans. A last-minute invitation can be as much fun as a carefully planned New Year's Eve gala. Whichever it is, welcome 1995 at midnight, wherever you are.

October–December 1993

OCTOBER

1. FRIDAY. Exciting. Your competitive urges are on the rise. Take on a new challenge and prove that you are able to lick it. Team sports or any sort of teamwork can be exciting providing you are on a par with the ability of your teammates. You will enjoy being the star but also need strong backing. A feeling of restlessness makes you quick to accept the opportunity for travel, especially if you do not have to pay for it out of your own pocket. Find out what is happening at a distance. Be quick to adapt new information to your own situation. If staying out of town overnight, opt for the most luxurious accommodations you can afford.

2. SATURDAY. Easygoing. Devote yourself to improving a personal relationship that has been rocky lately. Go out of your way to be friendly, or at least to speak civilly if you have been avoiding a certain person. There is no time like the present to bury the hatchet and return to your former friendliness. Libras can excel at manual work, including putting together anything requiring a diagram to understand the parts. Do not allow yourself to feel so confident of your abilities that you ignore instructions. It is also a starred time for a get-together planned on the spur of the moment. Invite a few friends to watch TV and have a potluck dinner. Or you may want to go out to whatever movie happens to be playing at a neighborhood theater.

3. SUNDAY. Optimistic. Things are definitely looking up. Continue to do all that you can to make a relationship that you value even stronger than it has been. Shared experiences can be the best bond. Include that special person in your life in whatever you plan to do today. If it will be a new experience for them, be sure to stay close by their side so they feel comfortable. A kiss and a hug make it obvious how you feel. You will enjoy the company of friends, whether you are the host or a guest. Go out of your way to be attentive to children, too. Take an interest in their pastimes as well as their schooling. Stifle an urge to tell them about your own childhood experiences.

4. MONDAY. Difficult. You may be under a lot of pressure as you weigh options and come to a decision. Listen to advice but do not feel that you must heed it. You are the one on the hot seat;

whatever you decide must be on the basis of your own choice. Be wary of a person who claims to have knowledge that could be useful but wants a promise before revealing it to you. There may also be an unexpected challenge from someone you thought was firmly on your side. Just because you are not very competitive does not mean that others are equally chivalrous. Libra can wriggle out of a difficult spot without hurting anyone's feelings.

5. TUESDAY. Quiet. Persistence pays off for you. Do not allow a troubling situation to drag on. Take steps to clarify what the problem is and then to resolve it. Find the person who is in charge and deal exclusively with him or her. Try to lend encouragement to a co-worker who is fearful of taking a stand. It might help if you play devil's advocate with them, thinking of all that could go wrong. Show that you have confidence in their abilities to handle their own problems. A new offer received today should be given careful consideration. You may be able to extract what is particularly favorable and pawn off the rest on someone else.

6. WEDNESDAY. Variable. Do not take on any additional work until you have finished up all that is currently on your schedule. Say no firmly or you will be pestered to death by a person hoping you will change your mind. Working in solitude is favored. You can speed through routine tasks if you are free to work as you choose instead of under direct and constant supervision. Get household priorities out of the way early in the day. Call a repairman if necessary, or phone the doctor for an appointment. You may have to go to the post office to pick up a package or to buy stamps. It is important to make a good impression on higher-ups by doing a little more than is actually expected of you.

7. THURSDAY. Positive. Be wary of making so many plans that you never actually accomplish all of them. Focus on one or two projects that are most important. Include some special time for yourself. Develop your skills by working on a hobby; at a later time you may be able to turn them into a money-making proposition. Money, or the lack of it, will not stand in your way if you devote some effort to seeking a grant or other financial assistance. A relative who has a healthy bank account may be willing to stake you to a down payment on a major purchase. This is a most positive time for buying a car, house or other high-cost item. A contract signed now offers good terms; do not pass it up.

8. FRIDAY. Happy. There is a strong element of luck accompanying all of your actions today. Happiness is yours for the asking, but you must be the one to make the first move. Do not sit back and wait for the phone to ring or for a knock at the door. Be more aggressive than usual. Go after what you want with full confidence that you will get it. A chance meeting could bring someone new and exciting into your life. Accept an invitation to a party or other gathering that will include people from all walks of life. The grocery store or the library could also be the setting for a memorable meeting. It is important to give everyone you encounter today the benefit of the doubt. Trust what they say.

9. SATURDAY. Mixed. Money that is owed to you may not be repaid, forcing you to decide whether to pester the person who owes you or write it off as a bad debt. If you know they cannot come up with the cash now, suggest other ways of repaying. You may be able to use their services around the house in lieu of collecting the money. Or they may own something that you would be willing to accept as payment in full. The day is starred for serious shopping in pursuit of bargains. It is not too early to begin stocking up on holiday presents while stores are still uncrowded and salespeople available. Do not beat around the bush with a family member who is getting on your nerves. Come right out and say what is annoying to you.

10. SUNDAY. Confusing. An argument at home is a looming possibility. Be careful of what you say in the heat of anger; you could blurt out a secret that you never intend to reveal. There is an element of confusion in home relationships. A person who is usually reliable may let you down, while someone who flits from one thing to the next becomes absorbed in a joint venture with you. A child can be the best companion now. People are relying on you, especially a relative going through a tough time. Do not let them down, or force them to ask twice for a favor. Knowing that they have your support can make a significant difference. Freely pass out compliments to everyone you meet.

11. MONDAY. Changeable. Break away from your normal Monday routine. Take a different route to work, or get up a little earlier than usual and enjoy a leisurely breakfast at home or near your office. Be especially pleasant to a secretary or clerk who you know would like to get to know you better. This is a difficult day for organizational matters. People do not want to be regimented and will resist your attempts at getting them to line up in a straight row and do as they are told. Dealing with one person at a time is apt to be most successful. In front of a group you might as well be talking a foreign language. There is no reason to accept more than your fair share of less desirable chores.

12. TUESDAY. Profitable. The reward you have worked long and hard to obtain is almost within reach. Do not let up now. Give that final push and you will cross the finish line a winner. Unexpected profit is possible, but you are more likely to get what you have earned fair and square. Be sure that you are not underselling yourself or your efforts. Find out what competitors are charging for services or products similar to those you offer. Do not reveal what you know because of inside information. Act surprised if you are pumped for information about that particular matter. There are conflicting stories. Go directly to the top for the answer.

13. WEDNESDAY. Buoyant. Your energy level is soaring off the charts today. Use it to your best advantage. Concentrate on work requiring both mental and physical stamina. You will not find your energy lagging. Working as part of a team is starred providing you are not held back by a slower partner. You should have no trouble handling more than one thing at a time. Hop from project to project, doing what you can and then waiting for other people to catch up with you. Travel can be worthwhile even if you have not made an appointment or other arrangements in advance. You could learn a lot by dropping in unannounced. Your enthusiasm sparks confidence and cooperation.

14. THURSDAY. Easygoing. If you are experiencing any health problems, make an appointment for a physical checkup. You could waste a lot of time and worry needlessly. Find out what is going on and your mind will be more at ease. The health of a friend may be what is troubling you. Urge them to see a doctor; you may even want to offer to go along to provide support. Focus on what lies ahead in the future, not on the past. Let bygones be quickly forgotten. It is not wise to hold a grudge; doing so saps your own strength. You can score a few points with higher-ups by doing more than is expected of you. Afternoon is a prime time to make that important phone call.

15. FRIDAY. Misleading. Do not allow a rumor to throw you off track. You know where the truth lies. Be guided by your conscience even if others seem to be following another path. It is important to listen more than you talk. Let others make the first moves; then you can jump in. Something you have long believed to be true could be challenged or proved false. You will have to do some soul-searching about a basic value. Refusing to adapt can keep you from reaching the top. Something you said during the week without really thinking about it could come back to haunt you. If it turns out you were wrong, be sure to make a public apology to anyone you hurt by your remarks.

16. SATURDAY. Fortunate. Chance, or what others think is pure luck, can put you in the right place at the right time. Take quick advantage of a fortuitous meeting. Stand up and be heard. This is not a day to take a backseat to anyone. Do not hesitate to accept a responsible position even if it involves campaigning to get elected. It is probable that other people recognize talents that you have not consciously been developing but come by naturally. Your Libra personality is a strong drawing card. You will not fail to live up to their expectations of you. This is an ideal day to begin looking for new living accommodations that will offer you more intimate privacy.

17. SUNDAY. Satisfactory. Be charitable today. Give either your time or your money to a cause you believe in strongly. Have the courage of your convictions. You are in a leadership role, with people looking to you to be the first to take action. You may be puzzled about the recent actions of a friend or family member. It is best now not to ask too many questions. What they have in mind is probably intended as a surprise for you. Do not allow yourself to be swayed by a person who is ultraconservative. Nothing ventured, nothing gained is your motto now. Tie up the loose ends of a project started by someone else and then left unfinished.

18. MONDAY. Positive. Wear an outfit today that makes you feel comfortable even if it is not in the height of fashion. When you are in a relaxed state you tend to do your best work. Intuition should guide all of your actions now. Spend time at the start of the day going over what needs to be accomplished in the workweek ahead. When you have a plan in mind you are most productive. Avoid flitting from one thing to the next with no preconceived idea of what the following step will be. Conditions are in a state of flux, but you must be especially constant. Make your views known both to colleagues and to the boss. If you recognize a problem situation, do all that you can to rectify it.

19. TUESDAY. Easygoing. A casual approach is again the best way to handle all that is going on. People are likely to be pleasantly amazed at all you are able to accomplish without becoming ruffled. A strong drive for additional education could lead you to sign up to take a course offered by correspondence or through televised classroom lessons. It is important to upgrade your skills to keep abreast of technological change. Concern for the welfare of others is also uppermost in your mind. Find out more about a volunteer job that is currently going begging. You will be welcomed as a helper even if you have no prior experience. Romance is highlighted when you least expect it.

20. WEDNESDAY. Mixed. Travel can be eye-opening. Get away from your usual environment. People at a distance have different viewpoints that can help you settle on a future course of action. Nothing is set in stone. Be ready to adapt to conditions as they alter. Something you thought had been settled may have to be renegotiated. And someone who was formerly on your side may be going over to the opposition. It is vital now to put together a new team to back up your personal efforts. Find people you can trust; a family member will not let you down. This is an unfavorable day to seek approval; you have to give yourself a pat on the back and wait for others to recognize your achievements.

21. THURSDAY. Rewarding. Reorganize your priorities based on who is available to help. Most can be accomplished by working as part of a group. If someone is out sick or too busy to lend a hand, find another project while you are waiting for them. There is no time to waste if you are to meet a deadline. Look for ways to improve the efficiency of what you do on an everyday basis. You can cut corners without diminishing quality. Get your desk in order and also your checkbook. What is currently going on behind the scenes is not going to affect you adversely. Stay out of it. If you ask a lot of questions, you will have to come up with some of the answers. Love brightens the dark tonight.

22. FRIDAY. Variable. A casual remark could make you angry even though no harm was intended. Try to let it roll off your back without becoming obsessed by it. Be careful, too, that you do not make a joke at the expense of a colleague or family member. Keep conversation as neutral as possible. Look for the positive attributes of those you come into contact with every day. There is more than one way to achieve what you want. If a current strategy is not panning out, change course now. Be very wary to protect your good reputation. If you go back on your word in any way, you could lose support as well as a friend. Who you choose to associate with reflects your basic values and judgment.

23. SATURDAY. Pleasant. This day is yours to do what you like. Get household chores out of the way early. You will enjoy competition on the playing field, either as a participant or a spectator. If going to a game, get tickets for the best seats you can afford. News from a family member is likely to lift your spirits even higher. Have confidence that the changes they are contemplating will be positive for you as well. Libra shoppers can expect good bargains even if a sale is not advertised. Shop around away from the crowd. Digging through a bin of merchandise can help you unearth a real treasure. Evening is a time to relax at home.

24. SUNDAY. Sensitive. Deep thoughts will keep you focusing on what could be instead of what is. Concentrate on ways that you can improve conditions for those less fortunate than you. Do some philosophizing about why and what if. When you understand what is going on, you get needed insight for improvements. This is a starred day to adopt a pet, especially one that is unwanted and currently unloved. Be aware of the views of a family member who seems to be sulking. Find out what they want you to do. Oblige them if possible, or at least explain why you cannot do so. Be wary of allowing passion to interfere with your usually good judgment.

25. MONDAY. Lackadaisical. Ease into the workweek without worrying about all that lies ahead. Let co-workers carry the ball today. There should be no major decisions for you to make. Once you have delegated certain responsibility, do not attempt to micromanage how it is handled. This is a favorable period to get to know someone of the opposite sex on a more personal level. Drop the kidding around and be a little more serious. A trip early in the day should produce desired results without obligating you in any way. What you see with your own two eyes and hear with your own two ears is real to you; secondhand reports have little direct impact. By evening you take time to put your feet up and rest.

26. TUESDAY. Excellent. Pretending to know more than you actually do can delight your friends and confound your enemies. Put on a good show. Keep a mysterious smile on your lips. You are able to change people to your point of view through the power of your persuasion. Have facts and figures at your fingertips to back up your statements. Try to obtain a recommendation or endorsement from a person everyone trusts. Libras looking for a new job may have special success riding the coattails of a family friend or a former colleague. Who you know is as important today as what you have shown yourself capable of doing. Reputation hinges on positively using all of your abilities in tandem.

27. WEDNESDAY. Sensitive. Today you may be the person searching for some security and reassurance. Turn to a family member, not a colleague. You do not want to reveal any special weakness to someone who might turn around and use it against you at a later date. Gather information from sources at a distance. You may want to visit them in person, but a phone call should suffice. Guard against allowing a feeling of power to go to your head. You still have a lot to learn even if you are the teacher. It is all too easy now to delude yourself. Be careful not to confuse a dream with reality. Plant your feet firmly on the ground and keep them there. Support is available if you seek it out.

28. THURSDAY. Mixed. The outdoors calls on this workday. Try to spend as much time as possible away from an office environment. Walk at least partway to work or school. Someone could be leading you up the garden path. Be wary of believing even half of what you are told. Even a so-called reliable expert may not know all that is going on. A matter of principle could be put to the test. Stand up for your basic beliefs no matter who is opposing you. Dealing with an elected official requires special patience. You can find a way to speak the truth without ruffling anyone's feathers. Choose words with extra care. Know what you are going to say before even opening your mouth to speak.

29. FRIDAY. Unsettling. If one timeworn approach is not working, switch to a new one. There is more than one way to reach your objective. Taking the long way around may actually prove to be more expeditious than a direct course. A shortcut that seems promising has hidden pitfalls, but you will not recognize them until sucked into the trap that has snared many others before you. If you can laugh off the mistake you will win new friends and influence many others. It is difficult now to get changes accepted by higher-ups. Bide your time making small inroads while waiting for a major breakthrough. Enjoy a friendly rivalry, but do not allow it to become an all-out free-for-all where the winner takes all.

30. SATURDAY. Variable. Today's Full Moon warns Libras to concentrate on what is already in the hopper instead of initiating anything new. There are many loose ends that need to be firmly knotted before you venture farther afield. Stick to what you know and do best. There is no time like the present to collect a past-due debt. You may have only to issue a gentle reminder; or a more serious approach, such as the threat of a lawsuit, could be necessary. Consult an attorney if in doubt about your legal rights. Do something to make your home more livable and comfortable. Rearrange furniture to suit yourself. Adding more lighting can be important. Plan on having dinner out tonight.

31. SUNDAY. Positive. If you believe you can accomplish something that others have tried and failed at, you have an edge right away. Do not back off from a challenge. Give it your all and you may surprise even yourself. Family members are more than willing to lend a hand or offer financial backing. Turn to an older relative for reassurance. What has worked in the past is a clue to the future, with a new twist that you can supply. Do not limit yourself in any way. Set your sights high. The grass may well be greener at a distance, but you do not require lush surroundings in order to be happy and productive. Stay close to home.

NOVEMBER

1. MONDAY. Difficult. Fighting over money antagonizes your friends and angers family members. Pay your own fair share and no more or less. Be certain bills are paid in full if possible. You do not want to fritter away your hard-earned cash on penalties and interest charges. If you do not have sufficient funds to pay for something in full, put off buying until you have the money on deposit. Look into current investments and bank accounts. Be certain you are not flirting with the danger of a bankruptcy that could tie up your available resources. If a company is not showing a healthy balance sheet, switch to one that seems in better shape.

2. TUESDAY. Routine. There is no need for anything out of the ordinary today. Concentrate on those activities you have been doing for a long time and on which you have built a certain reputation. Returning to school may appeal, but you do not have the time now to give to homework on top of your regular work. Studying on your own is the next best alternative. Stick to an original offer and do not lower your sights. You have the perseverance to outlast those in competition with you. You can get what you want right now at a high price, or wait a while and get it cheaper. Your partner has some objections that have to be met.

3. WEDNESDAY. Good. News from someone at a distance should lift your spirits. There may be good reason to rush out and buy a present or send a bouquet of flowers. Pass along the good word to mutual friends. You have ample energy today for all that you want to do as well as all that must be accomplished. Do not waste a minute on self-doubt. Plunge ahead confidently. People are going to react positively to your can-do approach. Ideas are flowing at a steady clip. Jot down those that you cannot use immediately so that you can refer to them in a leaner period.

4. THURSDAY. Outstanding. You have precious things that money alone cannot buy. Recognize the friendship and love that is the basis for all you are able to do. Even the richest person in the world has reason to envy you. Let your creative urges have free flight. Do something that is considered daring by those who lack your confidence. There may be a perfectly good reason for breaking a rule that you find inhibiting. Be ready to pay the price for doing so while accepting the accolades that accompany a breakthrough. Work on cultivating a better relationship with people who wield power and influence.

5. FRIDAY. Satisfactory. Do not walk out your front door in a huff this morning. Settle a disagreement before leaving, even if doing so means you will be a little late for work. You need a clear head to make an important decision affecting your job. Consult a respected older colleague for advice regarding your career. It may be time to make a change; you are ready for additional responsibility and can use the added pay that accompanies it. If there are limited opportunities in your present company, look around for another employer. Self-employment is also an option that should be explored. Your Libra self-discipline makes you a prime candidate for being successful as your own boss.

6. SATURDAY. Useful. Concentrate on improving the physical appearance of your home. Spend some time shopping for new wallpaper or carpeting. Slipcovers can give new life to furniture that has seen a lot of wear but is so comfortable you do not want to replace it. Cast an eye around the house as a stranger might do. Brighter colors will give you a lift as well as make visitors feel more at ease. Freely use a mix of patterns and textures. The kitchen, too, should be spruced up. Clean off counter surfaces so that they do not seem cluttered. Sparkling windows are worth the effort, although you may want to pay someone to wash them for you. A decision made with your mate can be a turning point in your life. Consider it carefully from all angles.

7. SUNDAY. Ordinary. Back off from a stand that you have taken with a certain family member. Find a way to gracefully change your mind without seeming to give in totally. An invitation that you recently turned down is still an option; call to say that you would like to come to the event. Be sure to include your mate or steady date in today's outing. You will be happiest in the company of those you know well. Keeping up a false front for a stranger can be tiring as well as stressful. Act naturally and you will attract favorable attention. Put your manual skills to good use. Fix a broken toy or piece of sports equipment. Children depend on you, so do your best not to disappoint them.

8. MONDAY. Disconcerting. Nothing is going to proceed according to your well-laid plans. Be ready to change direction on a moment's notice when you encounter a roadblock. Higher-ups are apt to distrust your first suggestions, but at a later time they may come around to your point of view. Try to avoid an I-told-you-so attitude when this happens. The past is a good guide to the future. Find out what has worked for others who were in a situation similar to that in which you currently find yourself. There is a way out that will keep everyone mollified if not happy. The art of compromise can be learned even by strong-willed Libras. An influential person is keeping a watchful eye on you.

9. TUESDAY. Fortunate. A stroke of good fortune makes this a day to remember. You tend to be in the right place at the right time. Let intuition be your guide. There is special opportunity in a plan that involves close cooperation with someone at a distance. Money can be made the old-fashioned way: through hard work. Be willing to do more than the next person and you are almost guaranteed success. Raise your hand when the call goes out for volunteers. Do not be shy about showing that you are eager to get ahead. In romance, too, Libra singles will be most successful by taking the direct approach. Let that person know your mind.

10. WEDNESDAY. Exciting. Events are moving at a faster rate than you ever imagined. Cling to the bandwagon as it rushes forward. Do not settle for anything less than the best. It is important today to dress the role that you are playing. Someone you meet for the first time will be influenced by your appearance before even getting to say a word to you. There is positive pressure to take action before plans are completely finalized. Do not fear acting on impulse in a crucial situation. You have the background to make the right moves when under the gun. A professional is apt to turn in a good report after meeting with you.

11. THURSDAY. Changeable. Morning hours are likely to be more hectic than later in the day. Be sure to eat a good breakfast so that you are alert and energized. You may be called upon to arbitrate a dispute involving people who work for or with you. Be guided by the facts of the situation, not emotions. You may not be too happy about current arrangements but must nevertheless be true to your word. Go out of your way to placate a person who feels they have not gotten a square deal. Point out the obvious opportunity that exists. Being able to speak a foreign language has special advantages now. If your skills are rusty, know where to find a translator. The Moon in your sign now unlocks hidden talents.

12. FRIDAY. Tranquil. Be nice to everyone you meet and you will be rewarded with their friendship. Your Libra personality is a strong drawing card. Emphasize all that is positive and overlook negative implications. It is important today to concentrate on things you can manage from behind the scenes. No one wants to feel that they are being manipulated like a puppet on a string. That special person in your life also needs extra attention. Make plans early in the day for an evening on the town. You will not have to spend a lot in order to have an enjoyable time. Check the newspaper listing of shows and performances. Buy tickets in advance.

13. SATURDAY. Mixed. A sense of frustration could be heightened by today's eclipse of the sun, even if it is not visible in your part of the world. Focus on what can be done, not what needs doing. Give added confidence to a family member who is facing a tough decision in the week to come. Let them know that you will stand behind whatever they decide is best. If you have some strong feelings about the matter, express them as your views only. It is your role today to guide and not to mandate. Share without holding back any love or other emotion. The New Moon also makes this a starred period for new love. Even Libras who have suffered heartbreak can now find happiness with a new partner.

14. SUNDAY. Demanding. Do not let anyone walk all over you. Stand up for what is rightfully yours, but do so in a dignified manner. Be firm in saying no and sticking to it. The problems affecting a family member or a close friend could be haunting you. Try not to take their burdens on your own shoulders or you will not be of much assistance to them. Instead, offer to listen as they talk out loud about the possibilities as they see them. By this evening you should realize that you have been more help by remaining silent than you would have been in taking an active role. A plan is being formulated, and you will be directly involved in it.

15. MONDAY. Slow. Sloppy work will have to be redone at a later date. Try to be extra thorough. Check and check again totals as well as spelling for accuracy. Try to beat a deadline so that you are not pressured to produce. The day is slow when it comes to obtaining help and cooperation. People who are normally eager to join with you are preoccupied now. You may be rebuffed if you seek a favor from them. A phone conversation is apt to be cut short when they are summoned by another person. You have not yet been given the green light to proceed with a new project. Only planning is possible until this permission is put in writing for you.

16. TUESDAY. Challenging. Negotiations currently under way hold great promise. Be ready to give in on minor matters that are not really important to you in order to get concessions in areas that you care about. Hold out for a little more than you might actually be willing to accept. People are unusually cooperative if you give them a chance. Presenting your demands, however, can make them angry. A property deal should be closed before the end of the day. This is a propitious time to consider moving to larger accommodations for home or work. You need space to expand before you become so crowded that you feel penned in. Do not allow a dream of foreign adventure to remain a fantasy.

17. WEDNESDAY. Rewarding. Your views and advice are being sought by family members and colleagues. Freely give any opinion that you have, but do not insist that your way is the only way. Look for opportunity close to home. You can earn extra money by taking over a project being abandoned by someone with less determination and experience than you possess. There may also be an important opportunity to do a favor or, more likely, to accept one being done for you. Make a few phone calls to find out what is going on at a distance. Rumors will probably be only half-truths. You have the cooperation of people in power; use it wisely.

18. THURSDAY. Manageable. Do as much work as possible from the confines of your own home or office. Let others come to see you instead of doing the traveling yourself. You will be most at ease on your home territory. Be careful not to become overly concerned about petty details. Look at the big picture and delegate minor responsibilities to others. You may be uncertain about a person who is new on the scene. Put them to the test today. If a situation is puzzling you, find out what others think. Build on what has been done in the past. It would be most unwise to risk getting a ticket. Do everything according to the letter of the law.

19. FRIDAY. Tricky. Be cautious about signing on to a new project or accepting a new idea. Allow yourself extra time to think through all the implications. Someone is applying pressure to make you decide in a hurry. Resist them strongly. There is an element of unintentional deceit that could trap you in a situation where you would be working with people on the fringes of corruption. You need to protect your good reputation by carefully choosing your associates. A last-minute agreement should be postponed until next week even though you could lose out on good terms. Find out from your mate or date what their preference is for weekend entertainment, then comply with their wishes.

20. SATURDAY. Variable. Avoid discussing subjects that you know are apt to lead to an argument. With people you do not know well, stick to the weather and shun political topics. A difference of opinion with a family member may make homelife tense. In-laws could get into the act as well. Insist that children follow your guidance even though they moan about their friends being allowed to do whatever they want. You have nothing to lose by being firm. This is a good day for home entertaining along informal lines. Do not try to put on a grand show when a potluck dinner is more your style. If health is worrying you, cut out a habit you know is medically unsound. You have the necessary willpower.

21. SUNDAY. Good. Go out of your way to help those in need. Your humanitarian impulses are particularly strong today. Offer whatever assistance is requested and is within your capabilities. If money is most needed, figure out a fund-raiser that will be profitable as well as enjoyable. Something you consider a favorite hobby could be in demand at a raffle or auction. A crowded place is the ideal spot to express yourself. There will be opportunities to talk with many people you ordinarily would not meet. Social gatherings are also appealing, although you might be cornered by someone who will not leave you alone.

22. MONDAY. Mixed. Personal plans should proceed without a hitch, but work may have its ups and downs. Getting along with those who are paid to do a certain job is not always easy. You are probably more conscientious or at least care more about producing the very best under less than ideal circumstances. Try to convey your enthusiasm to co-workers. Joining a new group can bring additional people into your sphere. Get out and socialize with those who are not considered the in-crowd. You are apt to find that they are just your type. Your Libra nature makes it difficult to settle down to a specific task and see it through to the end.

23. TUESDAY. Outstanding. Display your talents for all to see. Do not hide behind the scenes and let other people get credit for what you have done. Publicize yourself and your abilities. This is a starred day to begin a cooperative venture. New partnership is particularly promising, either as a money-making venture or in the realm of romance. A legal decision offers you the chance for a new start. Aggressively seek an elective office in a club or other organization in which you have been a member for some time. Friends are more than willing to go to bat for you. You could be the lucky winner of a prize, but be wary of gyp artists.

24. WEDNESDAY. Buoyant. Libras can look forward to another day of opportunity. Events at a distance have a very positive effect on your chances for success. Find out as much as possible about current happenings in a country where you once lived or where you plan to live in the future. Teaming up with a foreigner will be lucky for both of you. Give free rein to your creative urges. Experiment with a new technique that you have only read about. Your mind is aggressive and competitive, making you ready for new challenges. An unusual idea is apt to capture your imagination. Bypass working through an agent if you know what you want.

25. THURSDAY. Positive. Working in harness with your mate or partner should be especially effective. It is worthwhile to team up with someone who is your exact opposite in many ways. You can serve to spark one another and keep the ball rolling. By mealtime you should be ready for some easygoing socializing. Linger over coffee and dessert. What is discussed in a social setting can be the start of an exciting new idea. You are almost finished with one project and ready to take on another. Pick and choose with care. Know who you are dealing with before making a commitment of time, money, or emotion.

26. FRIDAY. Variable. There is not sufficient vitality today for anything new or out of the ordinary. Stick with routine work that you can handle almost with your eyes shut. Ongoing work may suffer from lack of enthusiasm. Handling the paperwork is not your favorite part of a project, but there is no one else as capable as you now. One public appearance could be required. Practice beforehand so that you do not become tongue-tied. Know what you want to say, and say only that. A false start is possible, but you can quickly make necessary adjustments. Do not underestimate the will of a person who has the money to buy almost anything.

27. SATURDAY. Changeable. Worry can be a waste of your effort and a drain on your reserve of energy. Concentrate instead on changes that can be made now to improve a situation. This is a sociable day to spend with friends or neighbors. Keep topics of conversation as neutral as possible. If you have a request to make, be sure it is termed in that way and not as a direct order. Actions definitely speak louder than words. Guard against impatience, especially when dealing with someone who is young in years or outlook. You will get along best with an older person. Some friends are dependable, others are less so.

28. SUNDAY. Frustrating. Plans for the day may have to be changed due to conditions beyond your control. Reschedule an outing if the weather does not cooperate. When in doubt, it is usually best to hold back. Today you must do so to avoid getting involved in a messy situation. Do not come between a husband and wife or a parent and child. Resist all pressure to deal with business affairs even though you know you have a lot to do in the coming week. You need to clear your mind through physical activity. Go out for a long walk, or engage in competitive sports for the fun of it. You will be thankful for a kind word tonight.

29. MONDAY. Difficult. Getting back into the swing of everyday routine will not be easy. Your mind is active and fast-moving, but events are just the opposite. You are in no position to dictate terms now. Having to wait for other people to make up their minds is sure to be upsetting. Try to hide your impatience by becoming actively involved in a project not requiring cooperation. An influential person wants to be told what he already believes is true. Current surroundings may not be to your liking, but for the present you will have to make do. Carve out a special spot for yourself. Libra communication abilities are peaking now.

30. TUESDAY. Important. Strive to exceed what is expected of you and what you expect of yourself. Reach farther and higher. There is no time like the present to learn something new. Sign up to take a course, or to teach one. Either way, you are going to expand your horizons. Someone considerably older or younger than you has specialized information that can make a decision more obvious. But you have to ask the right questions to get them to reveal what they know. You have nothing to hide; avoid being secretive or mysterious. Do not assume too much at this stage. Accept terms that you believe are as good as you are going to get.

DECEMBER

1. WEDNESDAY. Rewarding. Something beyond your immediate control is exerting a strong influence on all of your affairs. This may be a person, but it is more likely to be a chain of events working in your favor. Money is going to be the least of your rewards; satisfaction stemming from knowing you have done your best and achieved all that you desired is the real prize. Matters that have been simmering on the back burner are now ready for action. Do not delay even a moment once you are given the green light to proceed. Acting with your mate or partner can be particularly rewarding. Anything you are able to accomplish on your own can be done more easily and more enjoyably with a companion.

2. THURSDAY. Happy. It is another day when you can get special pleasure from teamwork. Freely share your talents while leaning on people who possess attributes you have not developed. Love life should be sublime. That special person wants only to please you in every way possible. Spend as much time together as work and other outside commitments will allow. There is no time like the present to make an announcement to parents and friends concerning your future plans. Let everyone see how it feels to be on top of the world. A relative is apt to be in a very generous mood. If you need a loan, now is the time to ask.

3. FRIDAY. Sensitive. Try to control your innermost feelings. Do not let family members, friends or work associates become aware of what you are thinking about doing before the end of the year. Plans should be kept secret until you are prepared to reveal them. Even hinting at a surprise could ruin it for you and for them. You need to keep all of your options open now. More information is turning up and deserves to be considered. Libras may not be given the benefit of the doubt when it comes to parceling out blame for a botched job. You will have to prove your innocence.

4. SATURDAY. Enjoyable. Being surrounded by people can lift your spirits and keep them high. Throw yourself into an activity planned by someone else. Take responsibility for one aspect of it even if you are not totally in charge. A local volunteer group would welcome more help; you have only to offer. Someone new is coming into your life as the result of a joint effort with a common goal. An interest in antiques could be the stimulus for romance or friendship. Try to find out more about your own family's heritage. Listen to a tale related by an older relative. Evening is the best time for quiet conversation. You do not need loud noise and blaring music to cover up feelings.

5. SUNDAY. Mixed. Do not allow an argument to escalate any further. Look for humor in the situation and you should be able to reach an amicable agreement. There is nothing so important today that you will even remember it a year from now. Take a long-range view of all that is going on. It is likely you are responding too emotionally to a disagreement. Hold yourself back from blurting out a secret you vowed to keep. Children will brighten the day. Share an outdoor activity with them. Advice from an older person could be biased, but a child's-eye view is right on target.

6. MONDAY. Productive. Apply reason to whatever you choose to do today. Let logic guide your actions. Do not allow yourself to be stampeded into action that goes against your better judgment. Just because other people are responding in a certain way does not mean that you must follow their footsteps. Make your own path. There are special rewards for those brave enough to buck current trends. Your Libra backbone gives you strength and courage. Be ready to make evasive moves to avoid confrontation. Offer an alternative to those who cannot see any options. Much can be accomplished working on your own.

7. TUESDAY. Variable. Your mate or partner may be seeing things that you have overlooked. Ask for their opinion, although you do not have to accept it. Become more involved in methods and procedures going on behind the scenes. You need to know how something works in order to put it to best use. Changes should come from within. Details appeal to Libras, and you want to understand the inner workings of both people and machinery. Use imagination to alter a plan so that end results correspond to your vision. Get rid of excess extras and you will be left with the essence. Laugh off a remark intended to make you angry.

8. WEDNESDAY. Good. Set up a meeting with those who are pulling the strings. Find out what they are intending to do in the future, and how their plans affect you. Then you will be in a position to make important choices. The time has come to help a family member by offering more than advice. Go along on an interview or to assist them in applying for benefits. You may also decide to provide some financial support to help them over the current hump. New romance is foreseen for Libras wishing for a long-term commitment. A friend is waiting for you to indicate an interest beyond mere friendship.

9. THURSDAY. Satisfactory. Reason prevails and logic wins out. Act unemotionally and without looking back. Concentrate on the job at hand without worrying about what is yet to come. An older person has a special message for you. Listen without presenting any arguments. An open mind helps you absorb what is being said and also what is actually meant. It may pay to keep out of the way of your boss or other supervisor. A low-key approach helps make you seem all the more knowledgeable. Open your mouth one time too many and people will begin to recognize your shortcomings. Anything underhanded will come back to haunt you and could even result in a messy lawsuit.

10. FRIDAY. Excellent. Use your powers of persuasion to the fullest extent. Start with those at the bottom and work your way up, convincing people that you are on to something important. Overcoming opposition to change is your biggest obstacle now. Separate business affairs from your personal life. Do not make any judgments about a co-worker's living arrangements. Make full use of expertise that you must pay to obtain. Consult a lawyer, doctor or other professional for their considered advice. You can avoid a lot of trouble by getting their help before a situation escalates. Be a true friend to someone in need.

11. SATURDAY. Ordinary. Stick to your usual weekend routine. If there is work to be done around the house, finish it up as soon as possible. Share tasks with other family members. Do not pay a professional for repair work that you can do yourself with the help of a how-to book. If planning a trip soon, check your car to be certain no repairs are needed. Also be sure the tires are not worn beyond safety limits. Preventive maintenance can save you a lot in the long run. Love should be relaxed and comfortable. Do not make any demands of that special person in your life.

12. SUNDAY. Buoyant. Get in touch with a relative at a distance. Find out their plans for the end of the month so that you can adjust yours accordingly. Travel arrangements should be finalized now. Do not wait for the last minute or you may be disappointed. It is a great day for a buying spree at a local mall offering special sales and discounts. Stock up on some extra presents to have on hand if you are given a surprise gift. News from a family member may be good reason to begin making something special for them. Go out of your way to socialize. Attend a meeting or other gathering where you will be welcome but not expected.

13. MONDAY. Manageable. The New Moon ushers in a new phase where opportunity exists at every turn. Jump at a chance to branch out in a different direction. Pair up with a person who has ideas running contrary to your own. Having to justify what you want to do can make your ideas stronger. Some travel could be on today's agenda. You will be unusually successful dealing with people face-to-face instead of by phone or letter. Do not worry about venturing far from your home territory. You should be comfortable and at ease wherever you go.

14. TUESDAY. Outstanding. Libras are being given the benefit of the doubt. Do not hesitate to make a decision based on information now available. The longer you put off acting, the more muddled the situation is apt to become. Higher-ups are open to new ideas, including a request for a raise or promotion. Make it clear that you are eager to get ahead but will pay your dues along the way. You cannot leap right to the top, but should be able to make a steady progression up the ladder of success. You know there is a lot to learn and you are prepared to make some sacrifices in order to beat the competition.

15. WEDNESDAY. Excellent. This is another day when your vim and vigor can conquer the status quo approach others are taking. Charge ahead confidently. Your mind is stimulated by originality and imagination. You can find an easier way to handle routine tasks, saving both time and money. Your vision is clear. What needs to be done is not a mystery to you. Expansion plans can be pushed forward. A merger or new partnership is especially promising. You may be asked to take on additional responsibility while a permanent replacement is sought; you could get the job full-time by proving your abilities. Do not rely on luck.

16. THURSDAY. Mixed. Travel can be a special opportunity. Matters at a distance are having a direct impact on you. Find out firsthand what is going on outside your normal sphere of operations. Begin now to discuss the possibility of a transfer with your mate or partner. A foreign connection can be profitable. Do not allow arrangements to remain private. Something you are trying to shelter from public view could become a rumor that spreads like wildfire. Be open and aboveboard, although you do not have to say too much. Take care to treat your marriage or business partner as a full and total equal in all dealings.

17. FRIDAY. Rewarding. Look for a way to accomplish what someone keeps telling you is a pie-in-the-sky dream. Your practical outlook should not keep you from dreaming. There is a way to get what you want without risking all that you have worked so hard to obtain. A silent partner could provide the necessary financing. Or a relative may be willing to back you. Start small and build on each success. Libra creativity helps you overcome what could be pitfalls for other people. A journey can be fortunate for you if you get to see the person at the top. Do not settle for a meeting with someone not able to make independent decisions.

18. SATURDAY. Fortunate. Just when you are ready to give in, someone with whom you have been feuding may come up with an offer that seems fair and equitable. Take your time before accepting it. Read all the fine print of any document you are asked to sign. Pretending to know a secret could give you added leverage. A sports event can help you shake off problems and relax. Play hard or root hard; whatever the final outcome, you will be the winner. A party with a purpose should not be passed up. You may meet a person who soon becomes an important part of your life.

19. SUNDAY. Easygoing. Take things one at a time today and you will not feel so rushed. Invite family members to share in the work you have lined up. Brush aside any doubts that have been keeping you from proceeding. You can make things work out with the force of your own will. Getting better organized gives you a sense of security. That special person in your life is ready and willing to go along with an idea that you have for significant change. Together you should be able to convince a reluctant parent or in-law. Try your best to please everyone, although you know this is not actually possible.

20. MONDAY. Useful. Set limits for yourself so that you do not try to do too much. Weed out what is important from what would be nice but can be put off till a later date. Make the most of partnership cooperation. You cannot handle everything personally. There is no point stirring up matters that have been swept under the carpet. Time can be a surprising cure-all. Work routine is going to be interrupted by numerous phone calls. Treat each one as though it were extremely vital to you. Do not let a person hang up believing you are preoccupied and do not care about the subject they wish to discuss.

21. TUESDAY. Slow. With no one looking over your shoulder and egging you on, you may be tempted to sit back and relax. But one important project needs to be finished up for your own satisfaction. Pleasing yourself is most important. Nothing new is likely to come up. Plan on getting together for a long, leisurely lunch or after-work get-together. Catch up with the latest happenings in a friend's life. They may be puffed with pride about the accomplishment of a child or their mate. Share their exultation without trying to brag about your own affairs. This is also a starred night for romance with that special person who knows all your secrets.

22. WEDNESDAY. Quiet. Do not allow an aggressive person to spoil your day. Hide out so that you are not made to feel guilty for preferring to do next to nothing. If you keep a high profile, the boss or another important person may nab you for a rush project. Issue a quiet reminder to a friend or family member who owes you money. Offer to arrange installment payments or to forgo interest. Give to a charity without seeking thanks. You have a lot to be thankful for and can express your gratitude by helping someone less fortunate than you. Physical exercise can have a soothing effect. Spend some time in a dance routine or other activity that can be done to music. Encourage artistic talent in your child.

23. THURSDAY. Manageable. Everything is looking up. An announcement that you have been awaiting anxiously should at last be made. You are apt to receive well-deserved congratulations. There could also be word of a bonus or other extra payment that eases financial constraints you have been imposing on yourself. If buying anything today, charge the purchase if possible. You need to keep cash on hand for the hectic days ahead. Honesty is certainly the best policy in dealing with a family member who is asking serious questions. Offer advice only if it is specially requested. Otherwise keep your opinions private. Postpone all but the most necessary travel until the new year.

24. FRIDAY. Easygoing. Before beginning any celebrating, be sure to drop by a friend who is sick or homebound to see if there are any last-minute errands you can do for them. Be as generous in doing favors as you would hope people to be if your positions were reversed. Now is a starred time to put aside any grudges or hard feelings. Let bygones fade away without even trying to sort them out analytically. It is harder on you to stay angry than to let go of that feeling. Any personal worry seems less burdensome if you broaden your outlook. The love that surrounds you makes you realize how very well off you are to have such a relationship.

25. SATURDAY. MERRY CHRISTMAS! Do not allow one person's criticism or negative reaction to put a damper on this day for you. Offer to return a gift that is not exactly what they wanted. Libras should stay out of a family disagreement. Attempting to play the role of arbitrator can only intensify the situation. Your good humor is going to be infectious as the day progresses. Organize a songfest or other group activity. You may also have to spend some time putting together a toy or other gift that comes in pieces. Be sure to read directions before beginning. Include friends in your activities. You may want to make some long-distance calls.

26. SUNDAY. Relaxed. With no one expecting you to be happy, you should be more relaxed and at ease. Take another look at presents received yesterday. Figure out how to exchange one or two that are the wrong size or color. If doing so would hurt someone's feelings, you may choose to store the item in your closet to give away to someone else at a later date. Share in activities planned by a relative or close friend. You will be comfortable as a guest but may not have the stamina to host a party. Check in with a person who is negative about holiday celebrations. You may discover that they are quite content just hearing about your fun. Someone older than you is craving attention.

27. MONDAY. Uncertain. False starts are indicated as you try to get back into the swing of normal activity. Allow plenty of time for activities that usually take only a few minutes. If doing any traveling, do not exceed the speed limit or plan on making connections that are timed to the second. Your restlessness makes a trip especially appealing, but where to go could be the big question. A travel agent could come up with good suggestions. A change may be forced on you by someone in a superior position. When you know you have to go along with it, be as agreeable as possible. Complaining every step of the way will not do anything to enhance your reputation. A wave of nostalgia late tonight confuses you.

28. TUESDAY. Mixed. Write that letter you have been putting off since early in the month. Be sure to include questions that are nagging at you. If you hint about what you want, you are apt to be disappointed. Come right out and ask directly. A friend who lives some distance from you is eager to hear your news. This is a good day for proposing a new idea without getting into the specifics. See what reaction you get in general. If it is favorable, you can begin to concentrate on details. It is possible you are a little ahead of the times and must wait for others to adjust to your way of thinking on their own. The secret is to operate in the background so that you are ready when they are.

29. WEDNESDAY. Disconcerting. There is a lot to be said, but you must select your words with special care to avoid ruffling the feathers of an important person. If you come on too strong you could wind up on the losing side. Everyone wants praise, including the boss. Find something good to say before you press for change. Adjustments are necessary on your part as well as by others. Plans may have to be altered or put on hold because cash is in short supply. Scale down a project if possible so that you do not have to shelve it. Guard against jumping to the wrong conclusion on the basis of incomplete information. You may be overly suspicious.

30. THURSDAY. Variable. Although you feel like hiding away and avoiding human contact you must mask your feelings. Plaster a smile on your face and pretend everything is all right. You may even wind up fooling yourself, at least for a while. Someone close to you is having trouble understanding your intentions. Be wary of giving them any false hope. Changes need to be made close to home before you can turn your attention to distant affairs. Pay bills before taking a break for the New Year holiday. Make more than the minimum payment due to cut your interest charges. When making a list of resolutions, consider ways to save more by spending less. Your willpower melts at a hot sale.

31. FRIDAY. Enjoyable. As 1993 draws to a close, spend time making plans for the future rather than lamenting anything about the past year. Be willing to forgive yourself for oversights and carelessness that may have gotten you into some trouble. Aiming for perfection is a Libra trait, but you must not expect it of yourself or of anyone else on a regular basis. If you must travel, leave early in the day to avoid some of the holiday crowd. Driving requires special care and concentration. Allow ample time to arrive at your destination. Your mate or date is looking forward to a rollicking evening of fun and laughter. Avoid bringing up anything that could put a damper on partying this New Year's Eve.